I0810631

IMAGES
of Rail

Copper Country Streetcars

On the Cover: A westbound Houghton County Traction Company streetcar operates in downtown Houghton, near the intersection of Shelden Avenue and Huron Street, in 1926. (Michigan Technological University Archives/Copper Country Historical Collection.)

IMAGES
of Rail

Copper Country Streetcars

William J. Sproule

ARCADIA
PUBLISHING

Copyright © 2013 by William J. Sproule
ISBN 978-0-7385-9986-1

Published by Arcadia Publishing
Charleston, South Carolina

Printed in the United States of America

Library of Congress Control Number: 2013931052

For all general information, please contact Arcadia Publishing:
Telephone 843-853-2070
Fax 843-853-0044
E-mail sales@arcadiapublishing.com
For customer service and orders:
Toll-Free 1-888-313-2665

Visit us on the Internet at www.arcadiapublishing.com

This book is dedicated to Jim Alain,
whose collection was the spark to start this book project.

Contents

Acknowledgments

It is amazing to look back on how a book project starts. Almost 10 years ago, I was fascinated by the story that professional hockey started in Houghton, Michigan, and I began digging in the Michigan Tech Archives to find out more. Along the way, I discovered the enjoyment of historical research. At about the same time, I was fortunate to be asked by the Keweenaw National Historical Park to undertake a research assignment to explore alternative transportation systems for the park, and the project included a review of the railroads and streetcars that served the area during the copper mining boom. Last year, a local railroad and streetcar enthusiast named Jim Alain passed away. Although I had never met Jim, I was fortunate to end up with boxes of materials and notes from his streetcar collection. This got me thinking that maybe I could add some additional photographs and share them with others.

I would like to extend my gratitude to several people, without whom this project would never have happened. Frank Fiala, former superintendent of the Keweenaw National Historical Park, helped in guiding the original research assignment. Florence Bashaw, Gloria Walli, and Gerry Perrault at the Houghton County Museum Archives welcomed me and were so helpful in finding stories and photographs. Jeremiah Mason at the Keweenaw National Historical Park Archives was excited to assist in locating photographs in its collection. Kurt Smith and Bob Gilreath thought of me when they were helping Jim Alain's family following his passing. My special thanks to Erik Nordberg, Michigan Technological University Library archivist and good friend, for his advice, enthusiasm, and encouragement for this project and my other historical pursuits.

Several others contributed, and I specifically wish to thank Chad Hewitt, Larry Lankton, Larry Molloy, and Ralph Raffelli for sharing their passion for Copper Country history. I must also thank Jason Gray and P.J. Sproule for their computer skills and helping me organize photographs and images and Sandy Shalton, Katie Toussaint, and Jacel Egan of Arcadia Publishing for their patience and understanding in guiding me through the publishing process.

I am especially grateful to my wife, Hilary, and our two sons, Davy and P.J., for their inspiration to take on fun projects and be kind enough not to ask why.

INTRODUCTION

When the Michigan Territory was established in 1805, it included only the Lower Peninsula and the eastern portion of the Upper Peninsula. As Michigan was preparing for statehood in the 1830s, several proposals for boundaries left out the Upper Peninsula, and there was a border dispute with the state of Ohio. In 1837, a compromise was reached in which the coveted Toledo Strip would be part of Ohio, while the Upper Peninsula would become part of the state of Michigan. At the time, Michiganders felt that they had been cheated in the trade, but this opinion soon changed when rich mineral deposits were discovered. Douglass Houghton, the official geologist of the newly formed state of Michigan, reported on the prospects for copper mining in the Keweenaw Peninsula to the state legislature in 1841. His report sparked a rush of adventurers and investors hoping to become rich, and it marked the first US mining boom, preceding the California Gold Rush by five years. While many of the early mines failed, a few were successful, and eventually several major mining companies formed. From the Civil War to the turn of the 20th century, the Upper Peninsula alone produced more copper, iron ore, and lumber than any other state in the union. The center of copper mining was the Keweenaw Peninsula, a strip of land jutting into Lake Superior. During this boom era, over 70 percent of the nation's copper was produced, and the region became known as the "Copper Country." Thousands of Americans and immigrants moved to the area during the mining boom. The first wave was the Cornish from England, with centuries of mining experience, followed by Irish, Germans, and French Canadians. Then, in the 1890s, Finnish immigrants began settling in large numbers.

Travel has always been a particular problem for people living in the region. From the arrival of the first settlers until the last of the copper mines closed, travel was challenging in spite of continual development of transportation technologies. It was not until the first railroads were laid through the region in the mid-1800s that a reasonably dependable mode of transportation served the area and provided a means to haul freight and people in and out. The demand for transportation continued to grow in the late 1800s as the area's population increased to serve a growing copper-mining industry.

It was during this time that streetcars, or trolleys, made an appearance in many cities throughout the United States and electrically powered interurbans replaced intercity steam trains for short-distance travel between towns and cities. On August 4, 1899, the Houghton County Street Railway Company was incorporated, with the vision of building a streetcar and interurban system to serve Houghton and Keweenaw Counties and to provide a quick, affordable, and dependable means for area residents to travel year-round. The Peninsula Electric Light & Power Company was the parent company, with additional financial backing from the Stone and Webster Company of Boston. Stone and Webster was an industrial engineering and design firm for urban power companies, which would often establish streetcar and interurban companies. It became one of the leading design firms for these systems across the country. Construction of the system began on June 20, 1900, and service started a few months later, on October 27, 1900. For over 30 years, the Houghton County system provided an invaluable transportation service to the Copper Country.

One

The Copper Country

In 1864, Edwin J. Hulbert discovered a copper-bearing section in Calumet Township and immediately recruited Boston investors and formed two companies: the Calumet Mining Company and the Hecla Mining Company. Hulbert was a major shareholder in both companies and was in charge of mining operations, but his inexperience resulted in low yields, frustrating his financial backers. In 1867, investors replaced Hubert with Alexander Agassiz, a Harvard-educated engineer and scientist. Under Agassiz's management, the mines rapidly increased production, and within three years they were producing over half of the copper in the United States. In 1871, the two companies merged to become the Calumet & Hecla Mining Company (C&H), and the village of Red Jacket formed next to the mines. A few years later, the Laurium Mining Company incorporated a town just south of the C&H mine workings, calling it the village of Calumet. Although visitors to the area referred to the whole region as Calumet, it was not until 1895 that the town south of the mine was reincorporated as Laurium. It took several decades for Red Jacket to formally change its name to the village of Calumet in 1929. As other mines opened along the Keweenaw Peninsula, several small mining towns and communities—such as Ahmeek, Boston, Frenchtown, Mohawk, and Wolverine—developed.

Calumet & Hecla built itself into a copper-mining giant, and it became the leading copper producer in the world. By the early 1900s, the company had 16 shafts and operated large ore-treatment facilities in Lake Linden, Hubbell, and Hancock. The annual copper production peaked in 1906, and a debilitating strike in 1913–1914 reduced the company's fortunes. The combination of the Great Depression and declines in the price of copper forced the company to cease mining operations in the 1930s. Although C&H was the largest company, the Quincy Mine (north of Hancock) and mines owned by the Copper Range Company (south of Houghton) were major copper producers during this era. During the peak of the copper boom, the population of the area approached 100,000 people.

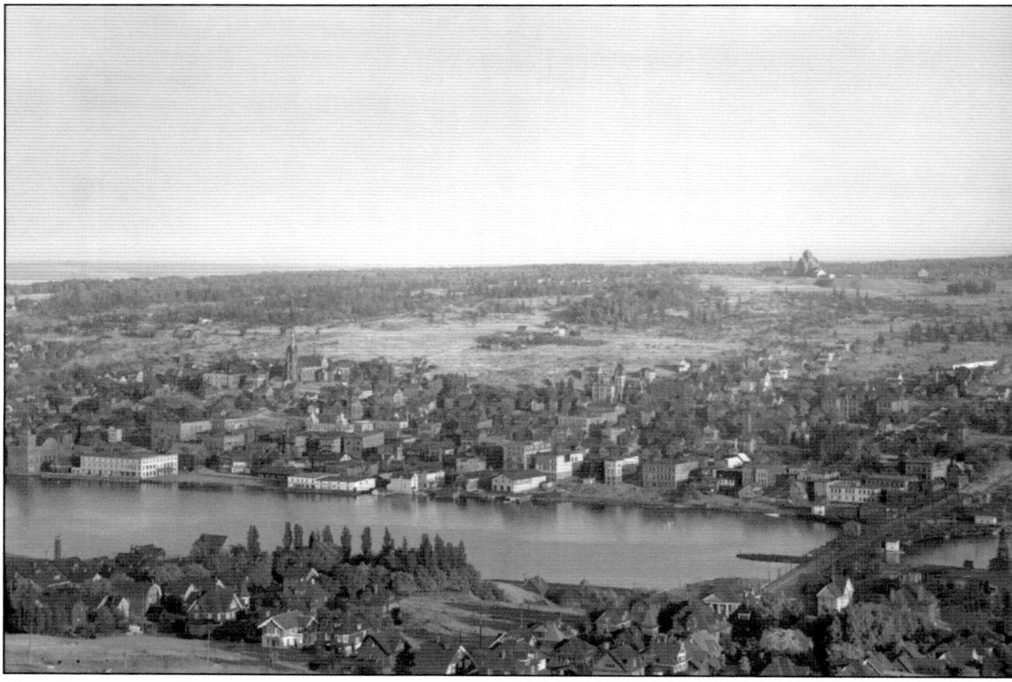

Houghton was the transportation gateway to the Copper Country, with rail connections and shipping docks. This is a view of Houghton in the early 1900s from Hancock looking south. The waterway is Portage Lake, and Hancock is located in the foreground. A bridge connecting Houghton and Hancock is in the right foreground. (Michigan Technological University Archives/ Copper Country Historical Collection.)

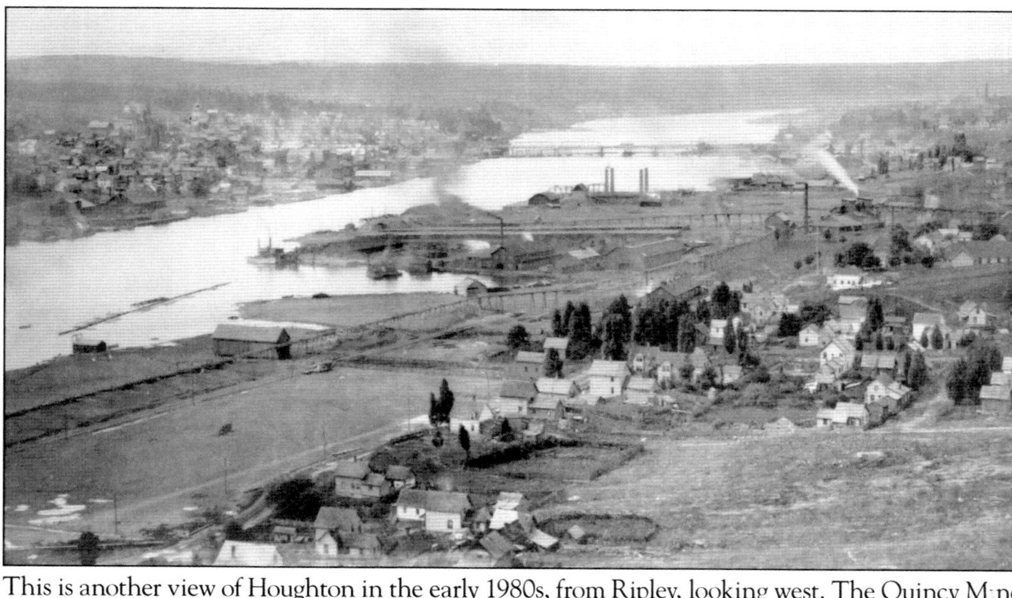

This is another view of Houghton in the early 1980s, from Ripley, looking west. The Quincy Mine smelter operations in Ripley are located in the center of the photograph, and Hancock is located on the right in the distance. In 1910, the population of Houghton was about 5,000 and Hancock's was 9,000. (Michigan Technological University Archives/Copper Country Historical Collection.)

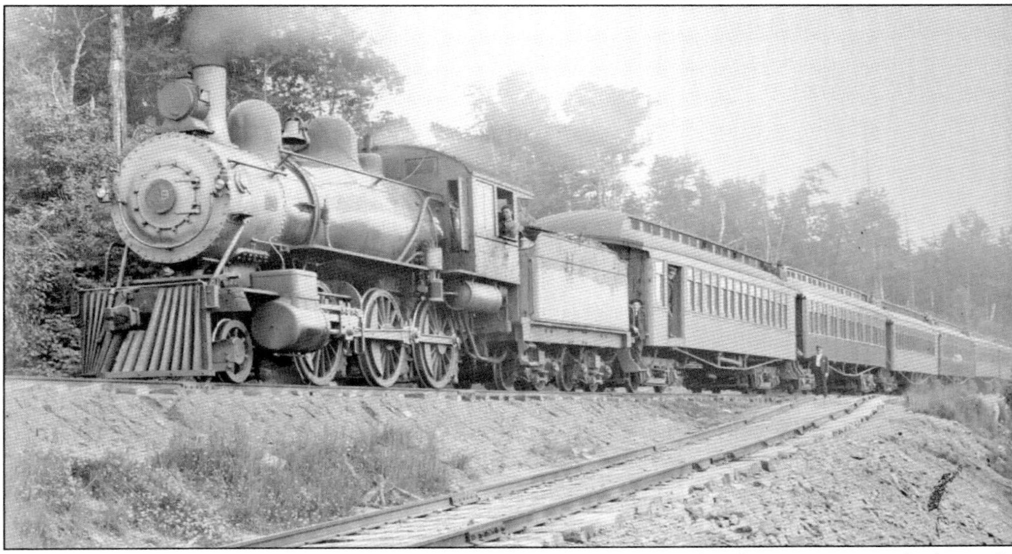

In the late 1800s and early 1900s, the railroad was the primary mode of transportation linking the region with areas to the south. The Copper Country is over 400 miles north of Chicago. The Copper Range Railroad; the Duluth, South Shore, and Atlantic Railroad (DSS&A); and the Mineral Range Railroad (a subsidiary of DSS&A) provided daily passenger and freight service on several trains. (Michigan Technological University Archives/Copper Country Historical Collection.)

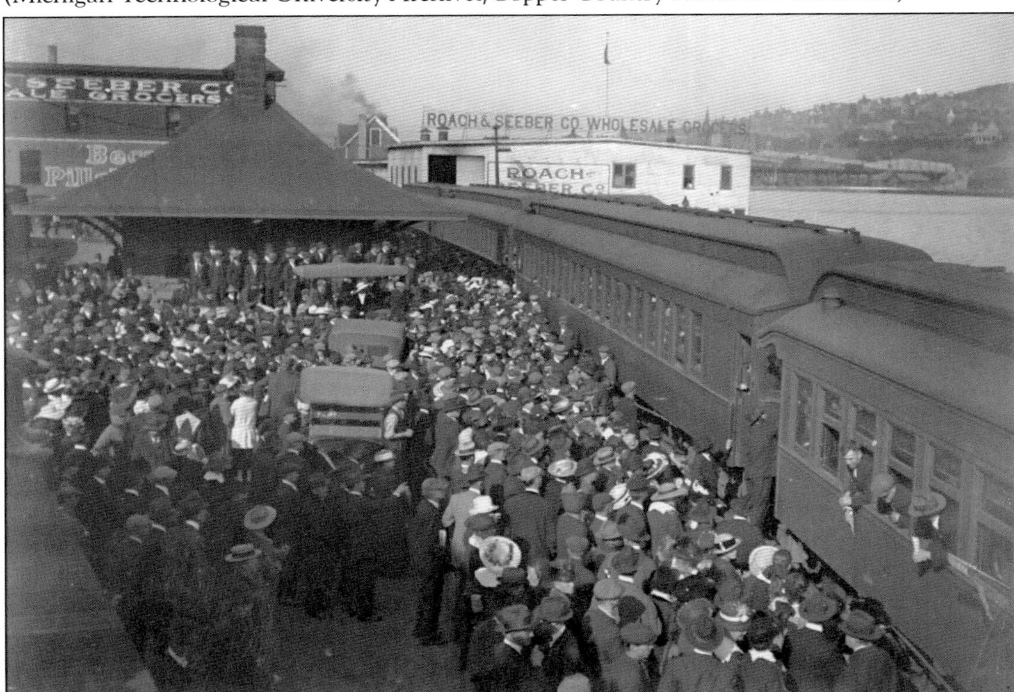

The main Houghton station was operated by the Mineral Range Railroad and located on the waterfront in downtown Houghton. A second Houghton station, operated by the Copper Range Railroad, was immediately west of the Portage Lake Bridge. (Michigan Technological University Archives/Copper Country Historical Collection.)

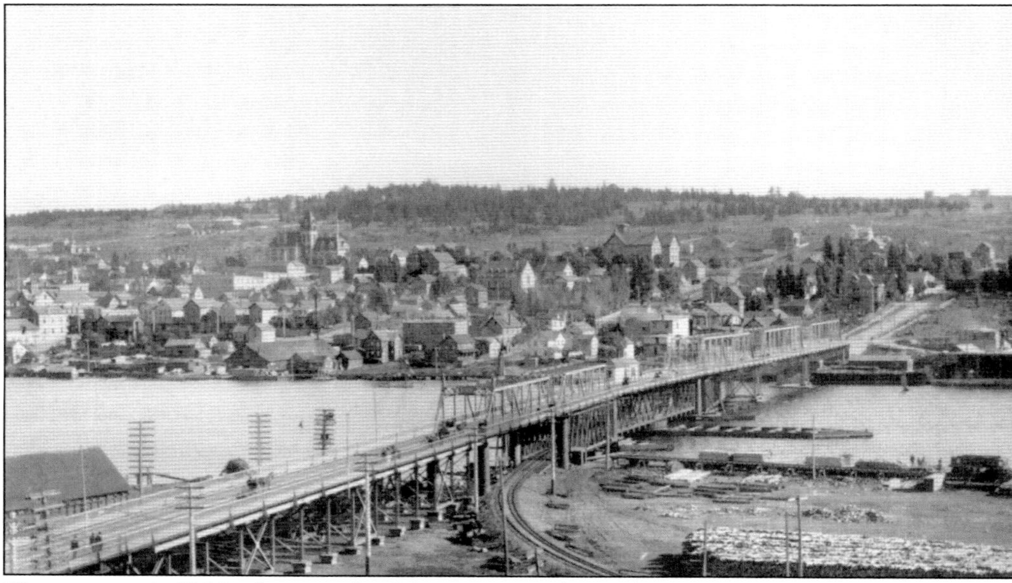

This is an early-1900s photograph of the Portage Lake Bridge linking Houghton and Hancock. The bridge, which opened in 1895, had a top level for vehicles, pedestrians, and horse-drawn carriages and a lower level for railroad operations. (Michigan Technological University Archives/Copper Country Historical Collection.)

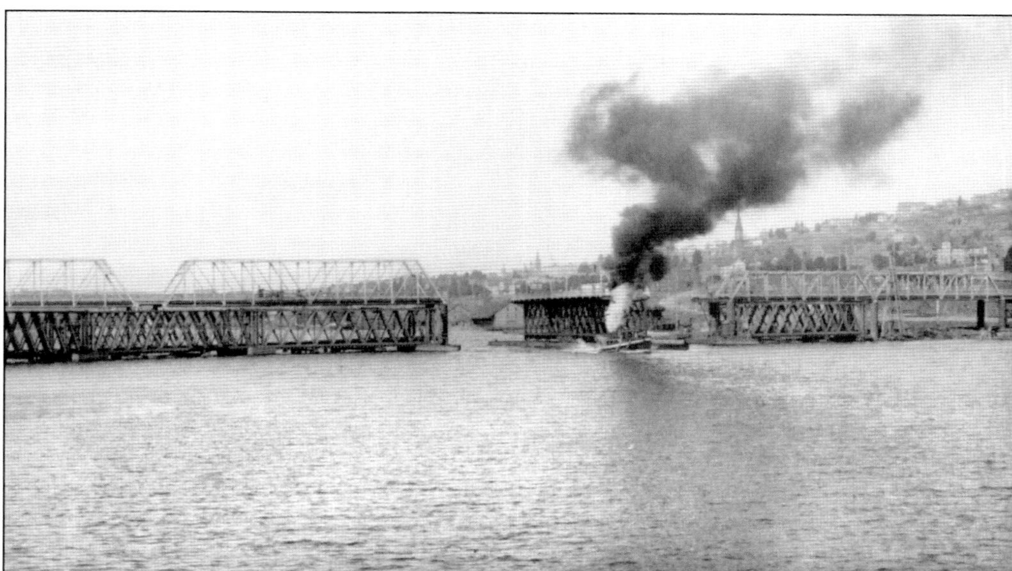

The Portage Lake Bridge was a swing bridge; its middle section rotated to allow ships to pass. In 1959, this bridge was replaced by a two-level lift bridge, which still operates today. (Michigan Technological University Archives/Copper Country Historical Collection.)

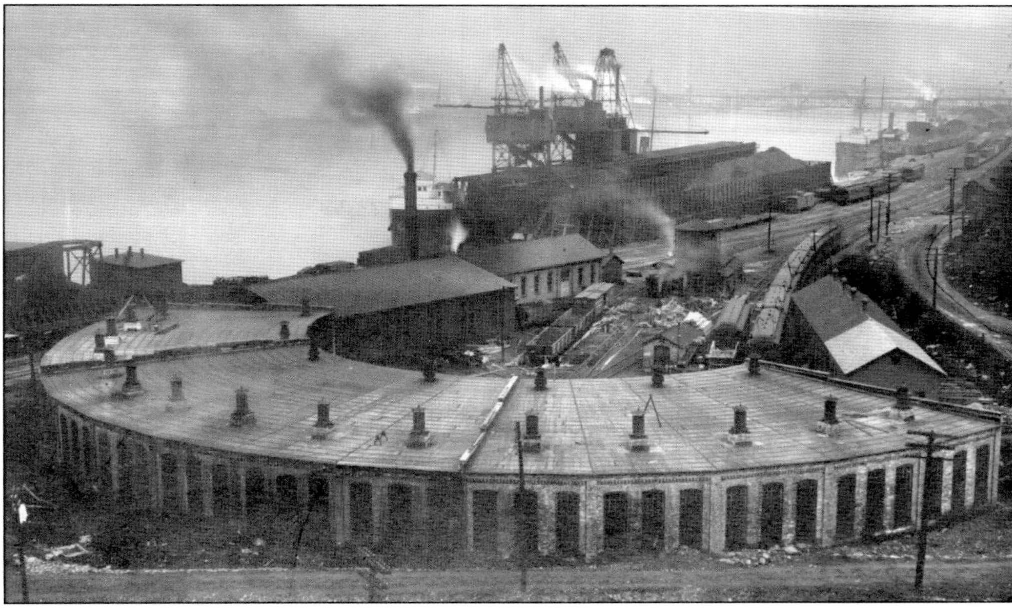

The Copper Range Railroad yard was located on the Houghton waterfront, west of the bridge. It included a roundhouse and freight yard for unloading supplies and loading copper ingots. Today, this area is a waterfront park. (Michigan Technological University Archives/Copper Country Historical Collection.)

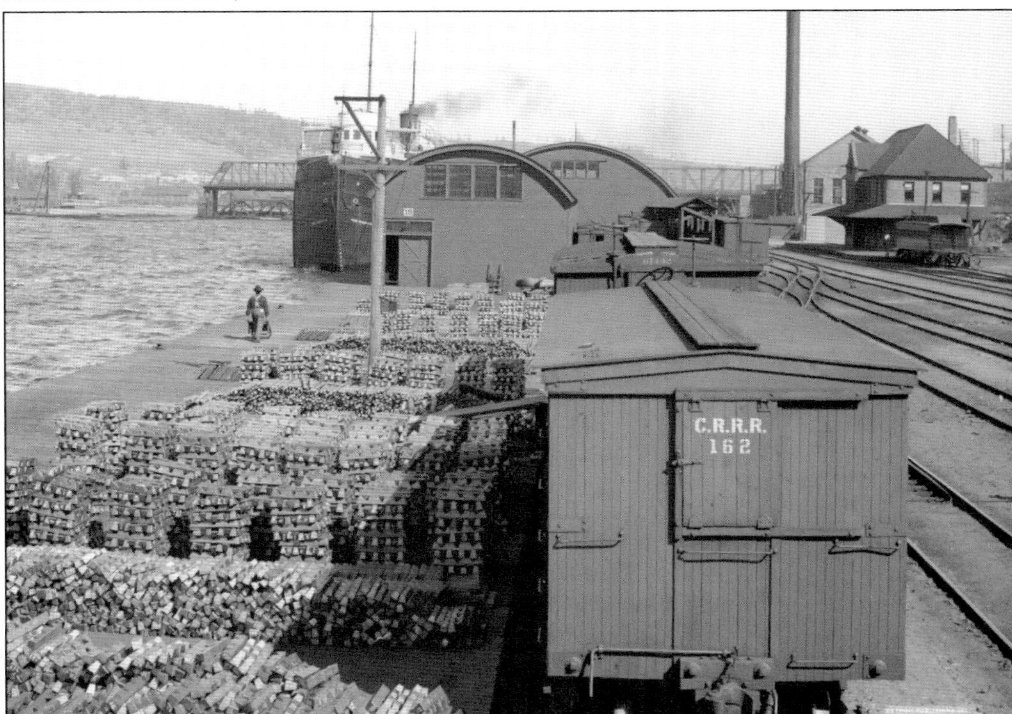

This is another view of the Copper Range Railroad yard looking east. Copper ingots are gathered, ready for shipping. The Copper Range Houghton station is seen on the right. (Library of Congress.)

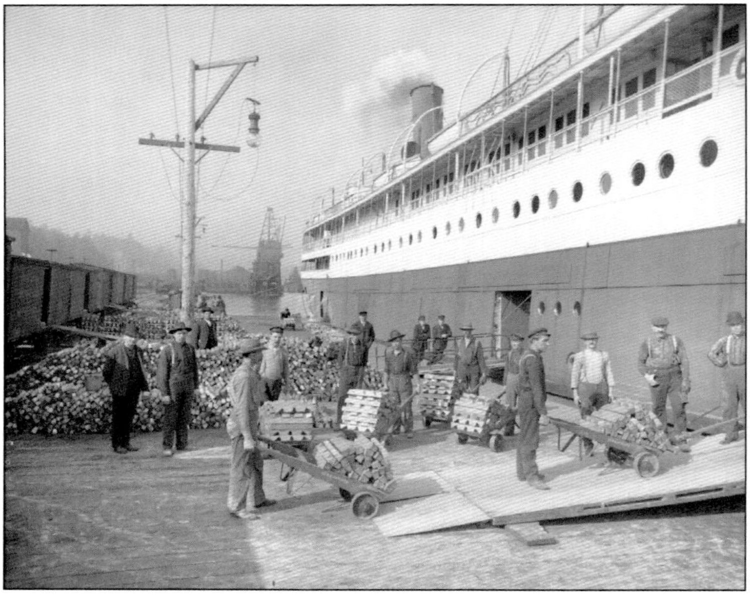

Copper ingots are being loaded by handcarts into a ship for transportation to Chicago, Detroit, and other ports on the Great Lakes. (Library of Congress.)

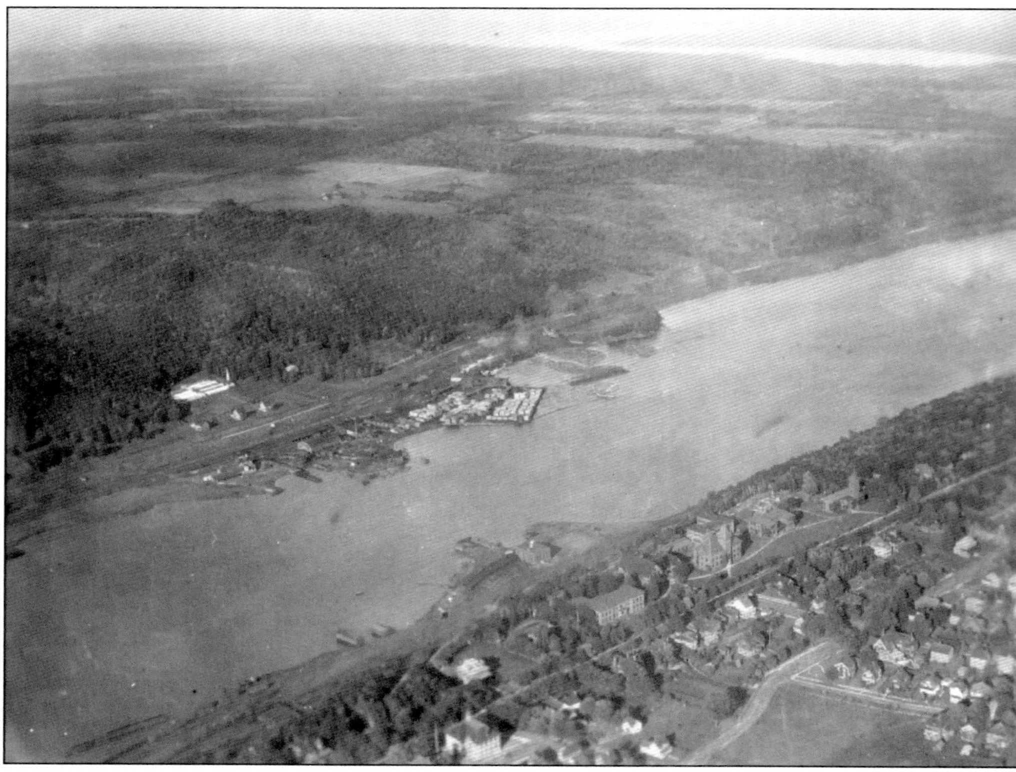

The Michigan Mining School was founded in 1885, and its first classes were held on the upper floor of a downtown Houghton fire station. A few years later, development of a campus east of downtown Houghton began, and in 1897 it became the Michigan College of Mines (MCM). This is a 1923 aerial view of the MCM campus. (Michigan Technological University Archives/Copper Country Historical Collection.)

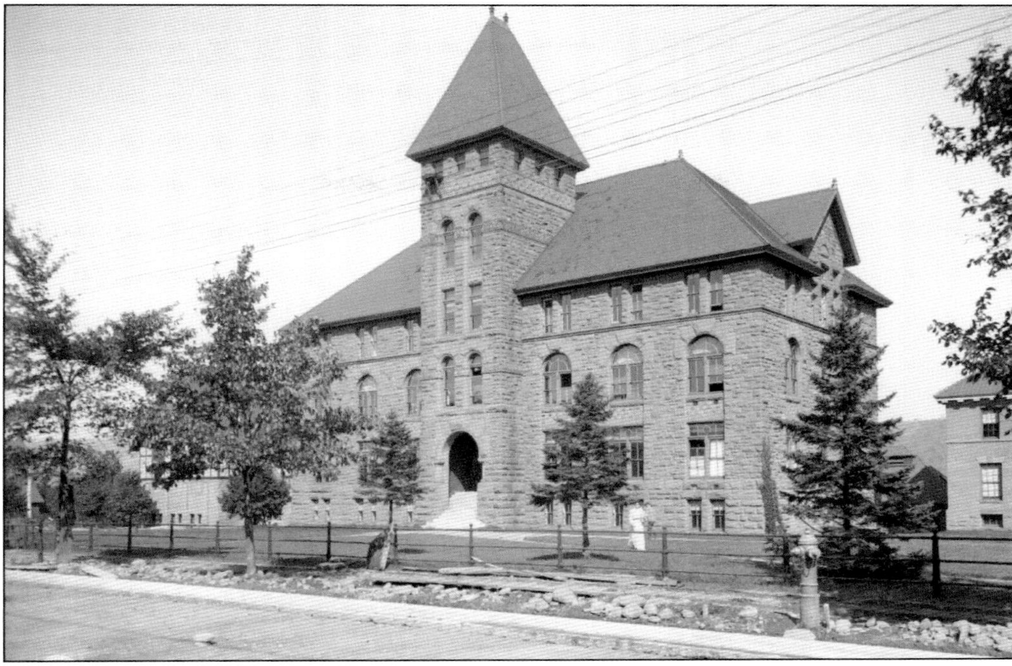

Hubbell Hall was one of the original buildings on the Michigan College of Mines (MCM) campus. Jay Abel Hubbell, a lawyer and state senator, initiated the legislative act that resulted in the establishment of the MCM. (Library of Congress.)

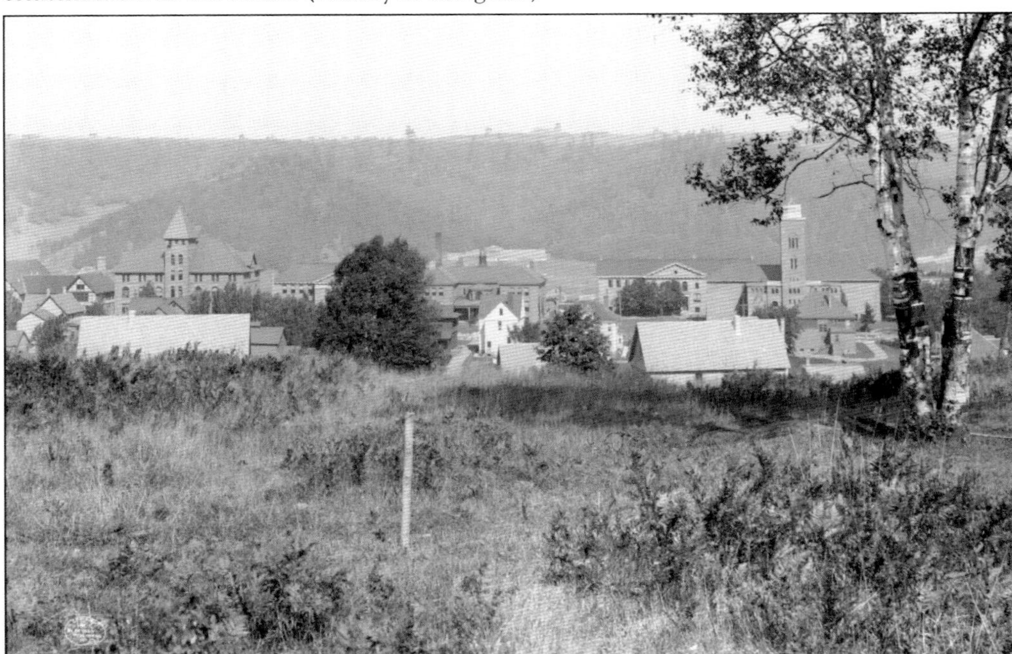

This 1920s photograph of the MCM campus was taken from south of the campus. Hubbell Hall can be seen on the left. In the background, across Portage Lake, is Quincy Hill. (Library of Congress.)

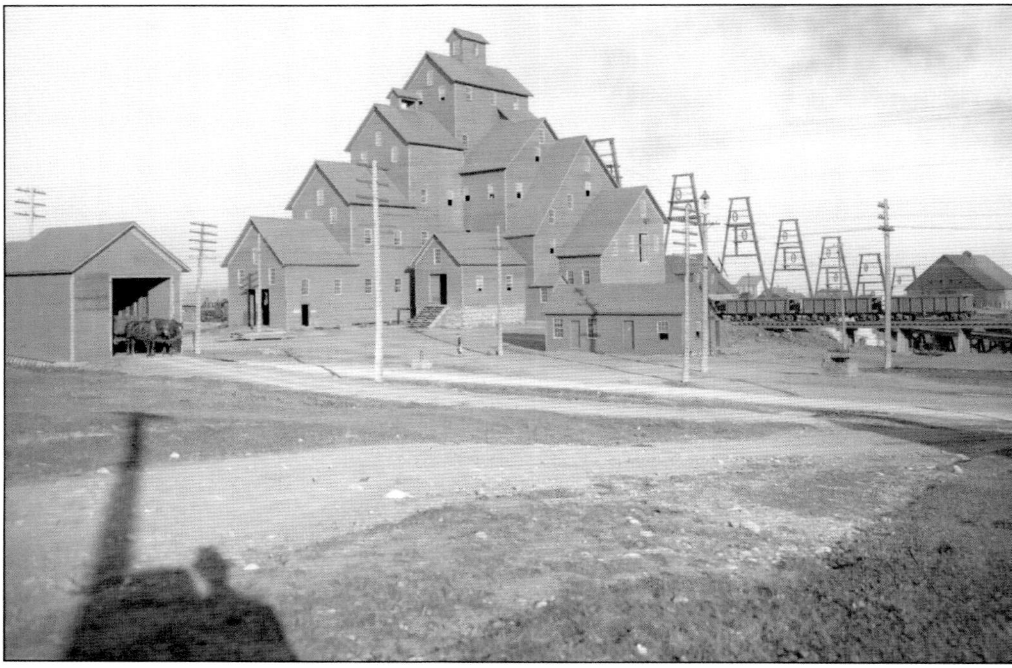

Copper mines were developed throughout the Keweenaw Peninsula as the region became known as the Copper Country. Quincy Mining Company's No. 6 shaft and rock house on Quincy Hill, shown here, was the most photographed shaft house in the area. It burned down in 1956. (Library of Congress.)

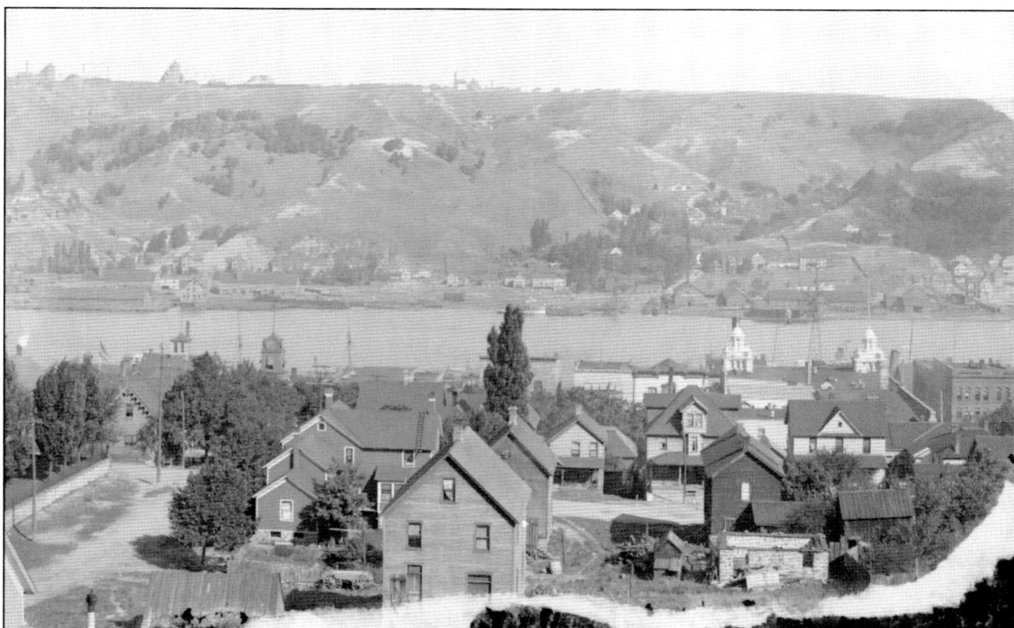

This photograph was taken from south of downtown Houghton. In the background, Portage Lake and Quincy Hill can be seen. Quincy was the home of the Quincy Mining Company, one of the major copper-mining companies of the region. (Library of Congress.)

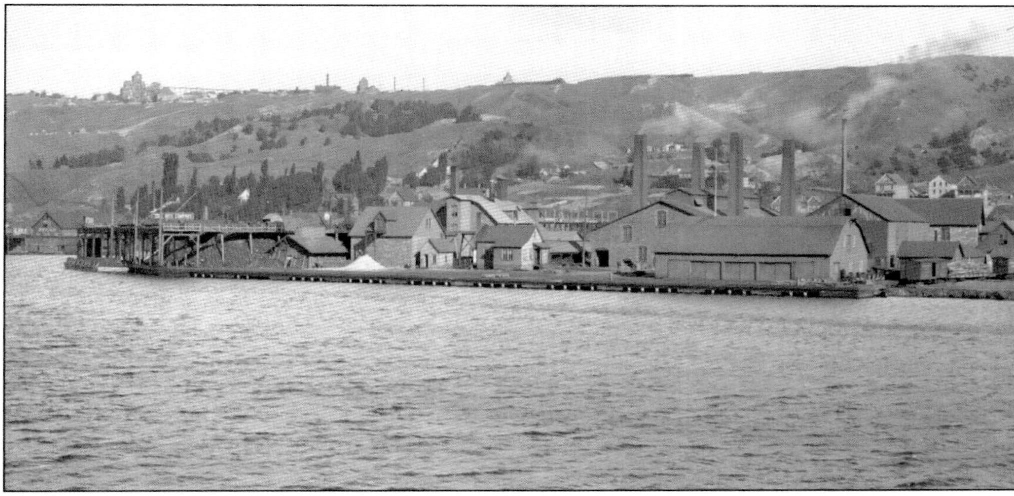

After copper-bearing ore was taken from the ground, it was hauled by rail to stamp mills, where crushing operations separated copper from the ore. The copper was then taken to a nearby smelter to produce copper ingots or plates for shipping. As part of the Quincy Mining Company operations, the Quincy Smelter was located in Ripley on the Portage Lake waterfront and stamp mills were located in Mason on Torch Lake. (Library of Congress.)

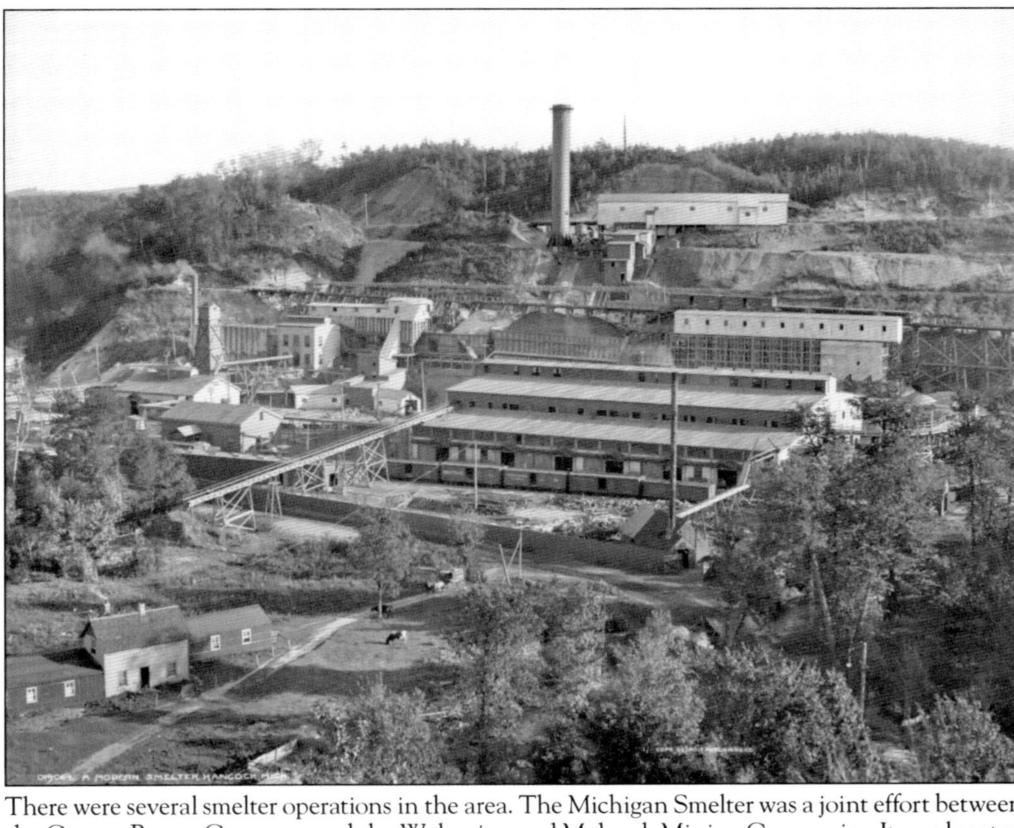

There were several smelter operations in the area. The Michigan Smelter was a joint effort between the Copper Range Company and the Wolverine and Mohawk Mining Companies. It was located west of Houghton on Portage Lake. (Library of Congress.)

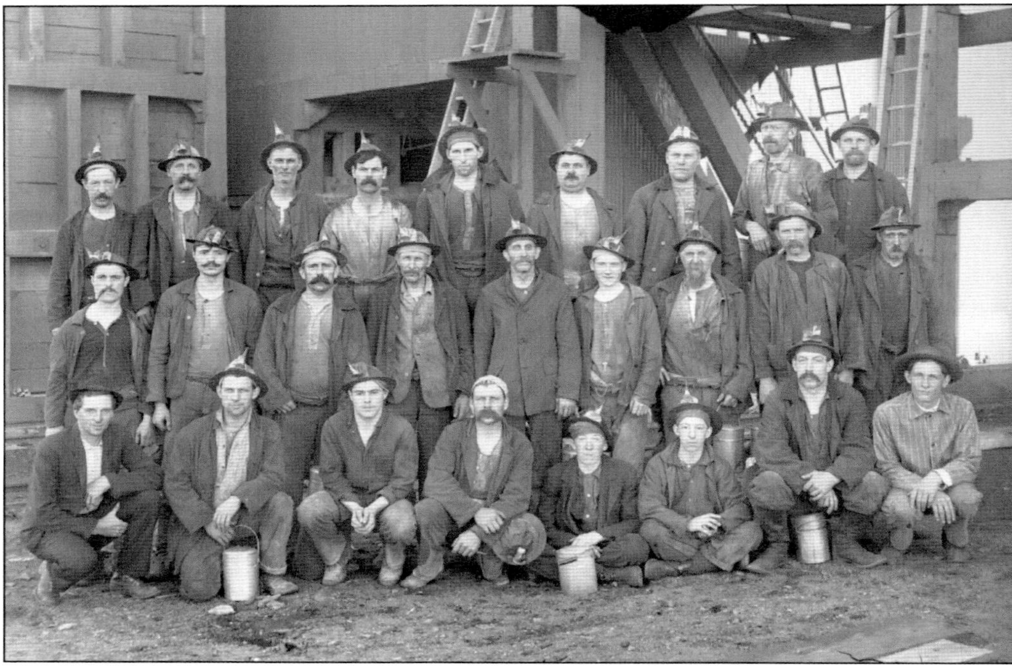

The copper mines provided employment for thousands of workers from around the world who came to seek their fortune. In the early years, Cornish, Irish, German, and French Canadians were the largest immigrant groups. In the late 1890s, Finns became as the largest group arriving in the Copper Country. (Michigan Technological University Archives/Copper Country Historical Collection.)

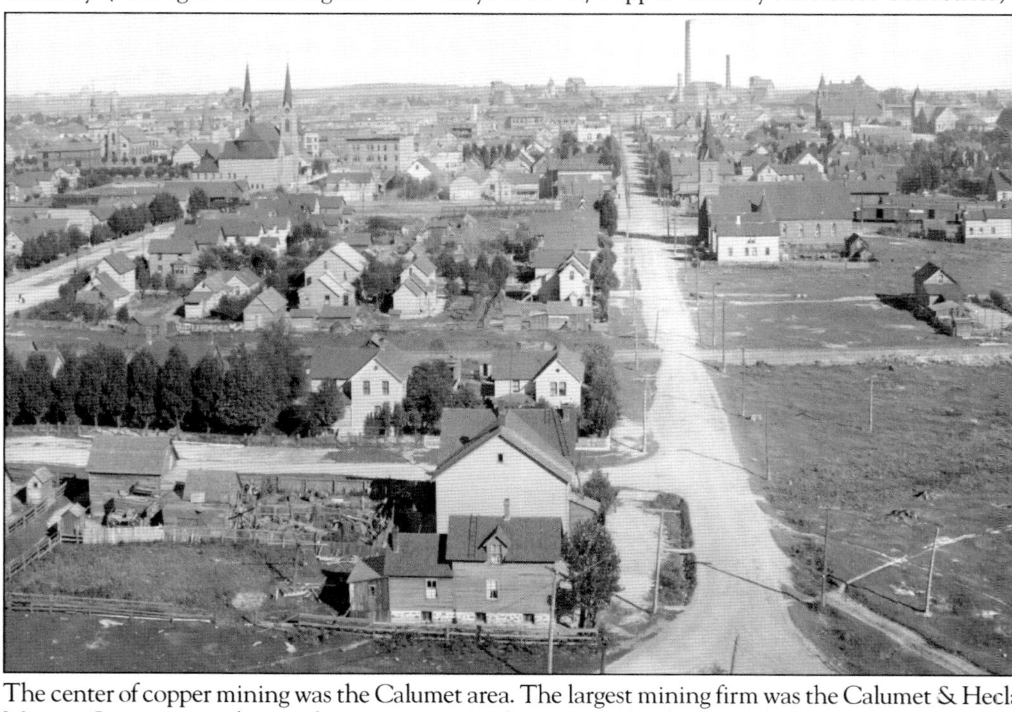

The center of copper mining was the Calumet area. The largest mining firm was the Calumet & Hecla Mining Company, and part of its operation can be seen in the distance. (Library of Congress.)

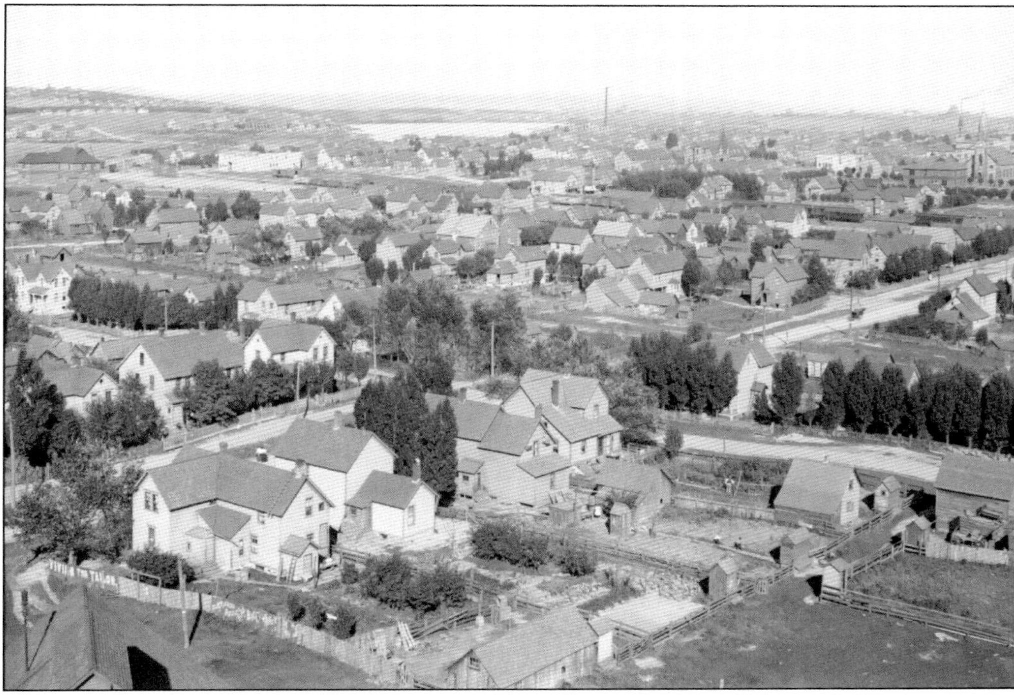

This is another view of the Calumet area in the early 1900s. Here, Calumet & Hecla provided housing and numerous services to its employees. (Library of Congress.)

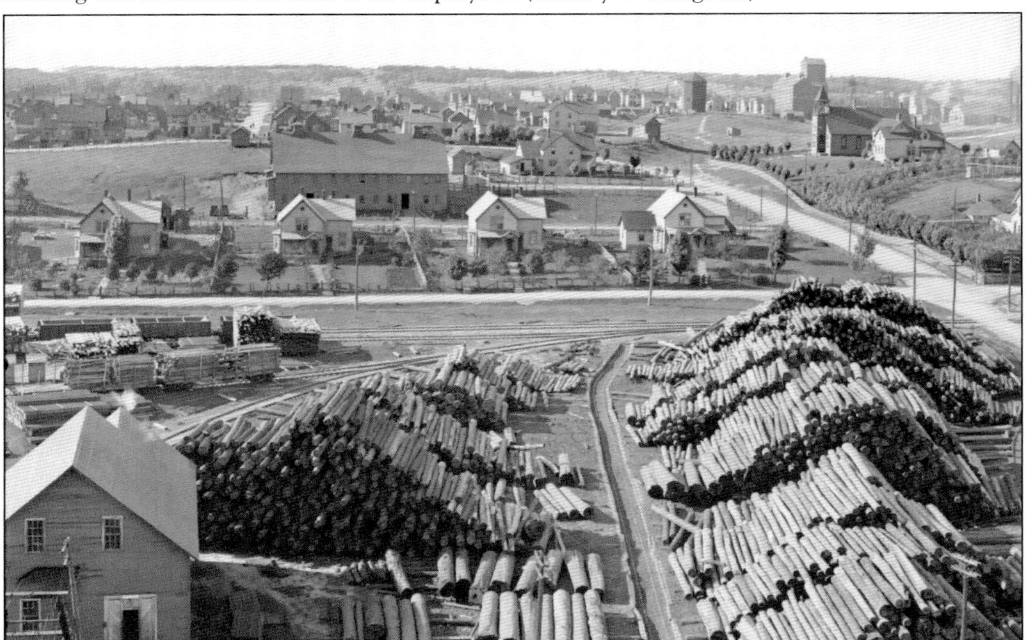

Lumbering also played an important part in the development of the Copper Country. Lumber was used extensively in the mines and was a major export from the area. This photograph shows a lumber operation near Calumet. (Library of Congress.)

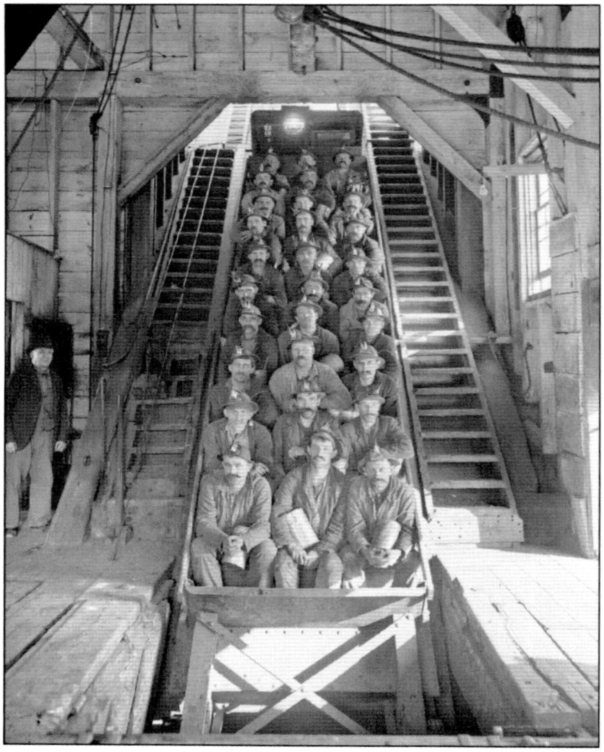

The type of copper mining undertaken in the region was deep-shaft mining. This photograph shows workers descending on a man car into a Calumet-area mine. (Library of Congress.)

This is a view of one of the Calumet & Hecla smelter operations. It was located in the Calumet area. (Michigan Technological University Archives/Copper Country Historical Collection.)

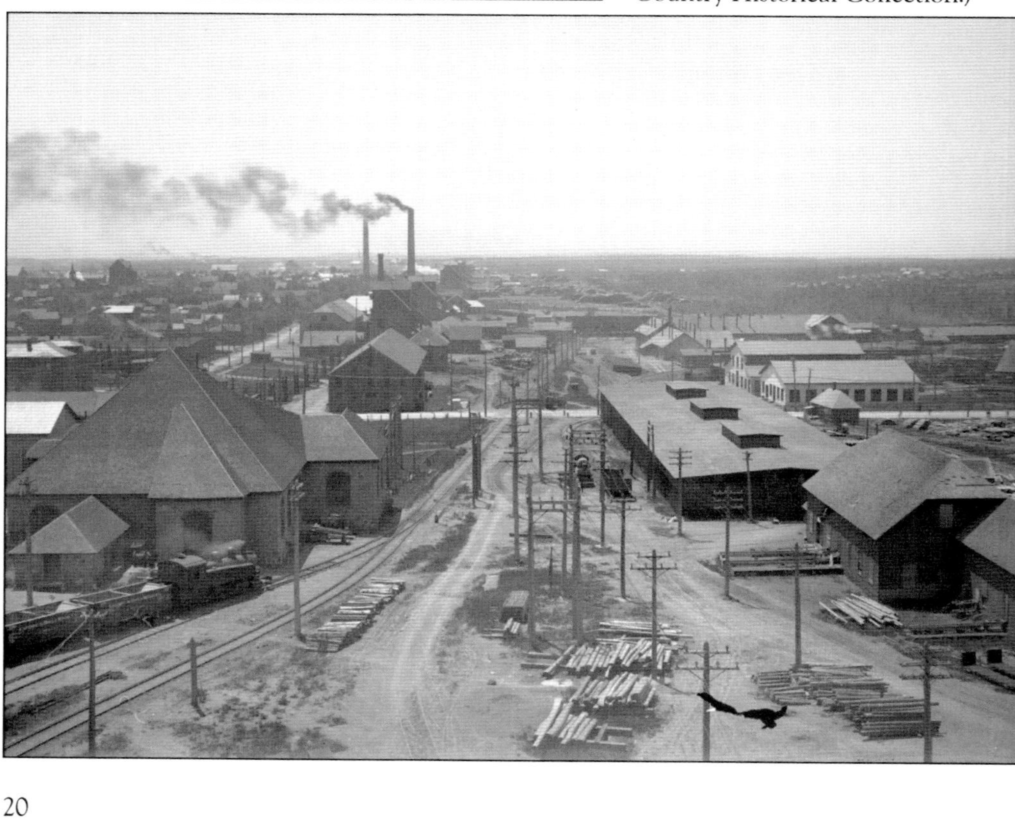

Red Jacket (now known as the village of Calumet) was developed next to the Calumet & Hecla mining operations. Featuring numerous stores and office buildings, Fifth Street was the main commercial thoroughfare in Red Jacket. This photograph was taken from the corner of Fifth and Pine Streets. In 1910, the population of the village and the neighboring community of Laurium approached 35,000. (Michigan Technological University Archives/Copper Country Historical Collection.)

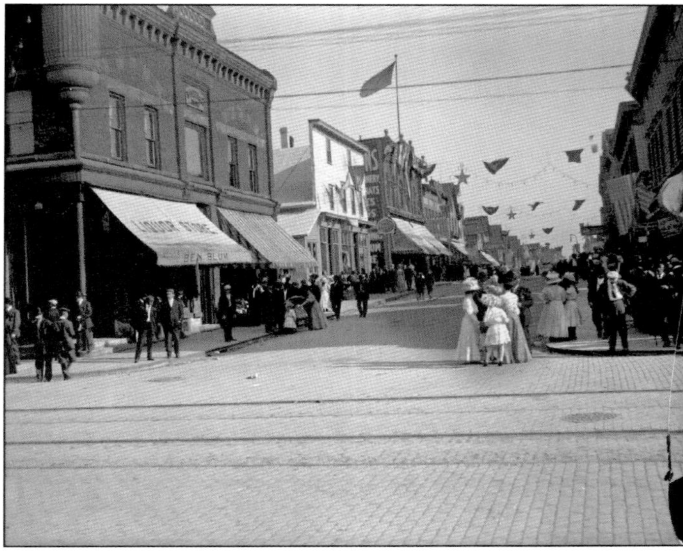

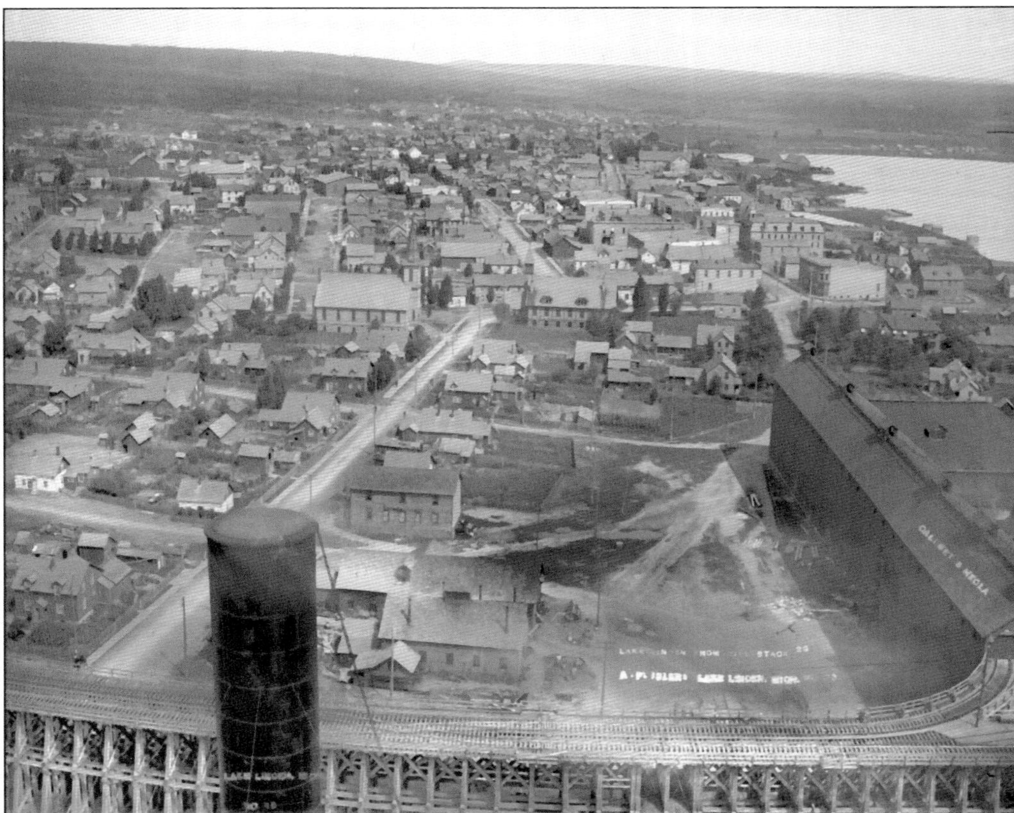

The village of Lake Linden, east of the Calumet area, grew around Calumet & Hecla Mining Company's surface operations. (Michigan Technological University Archives/Copper Country Historical Collection.)

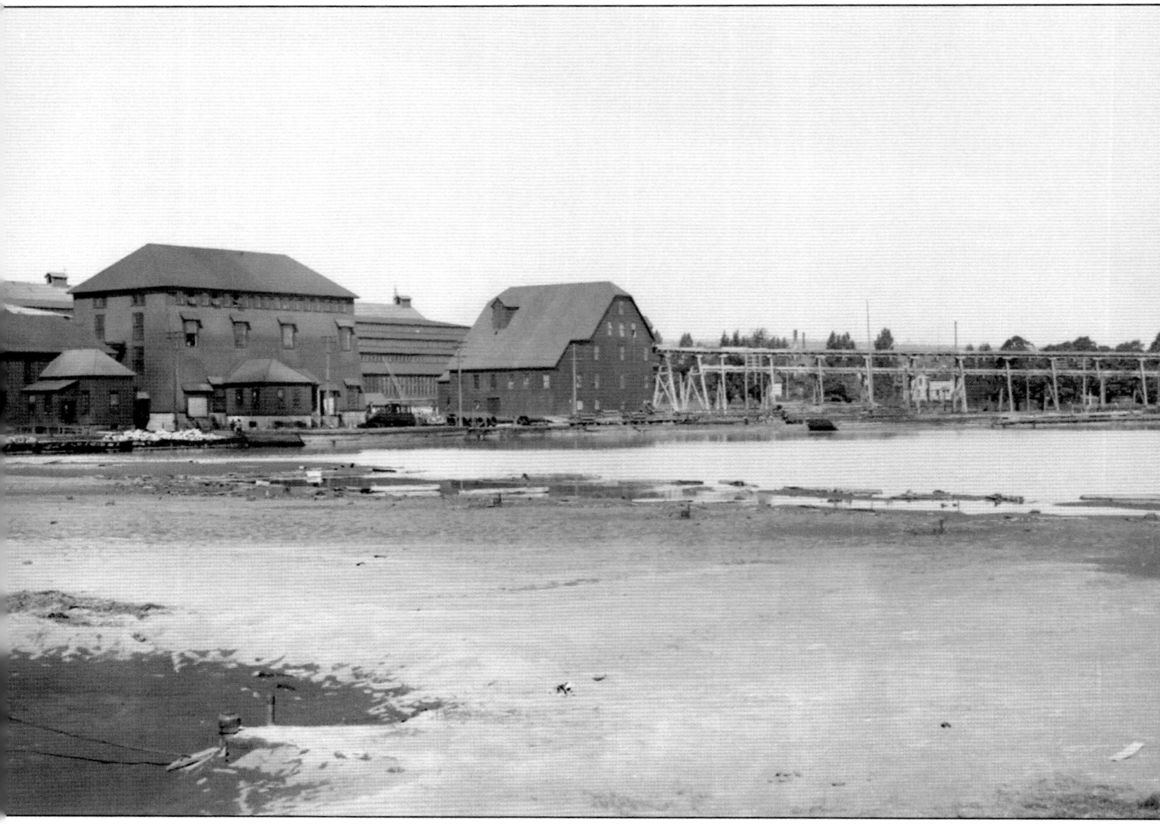

As part of the copper extraction process, copper ore was crushed or stamped. Shown here is a Calumet & Helca stamping mill in Lake Linden. After copper was extracted, the waste ore material was disposed into the lake or other holding areas. (Michigan Technological University Archives/Copper Country Historical Collection.)

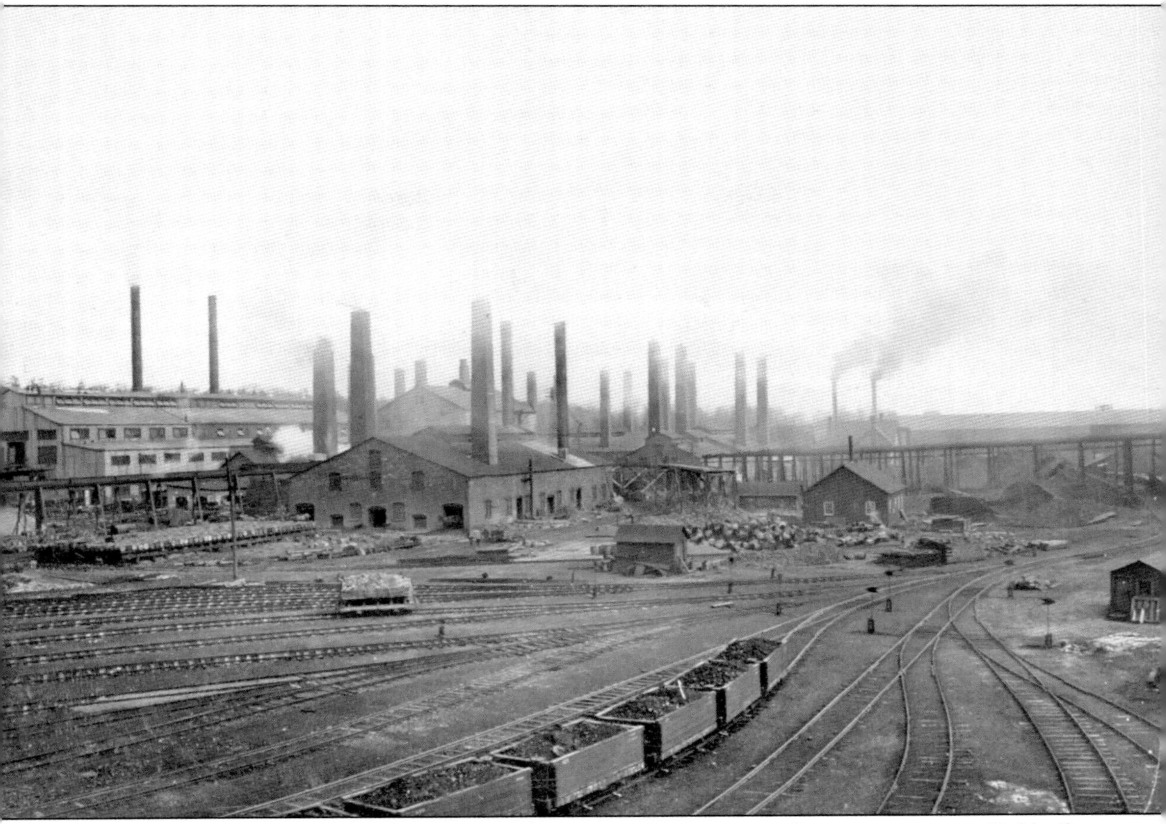

This is a view of one of the Calumet & Hecla Mining Company smelter operations in Hubbell. Hubbell and Lake Linden are located on Torch Lake, east of Calumet. (Michigan Technological University Archives/Copper Country Historical Collection.)

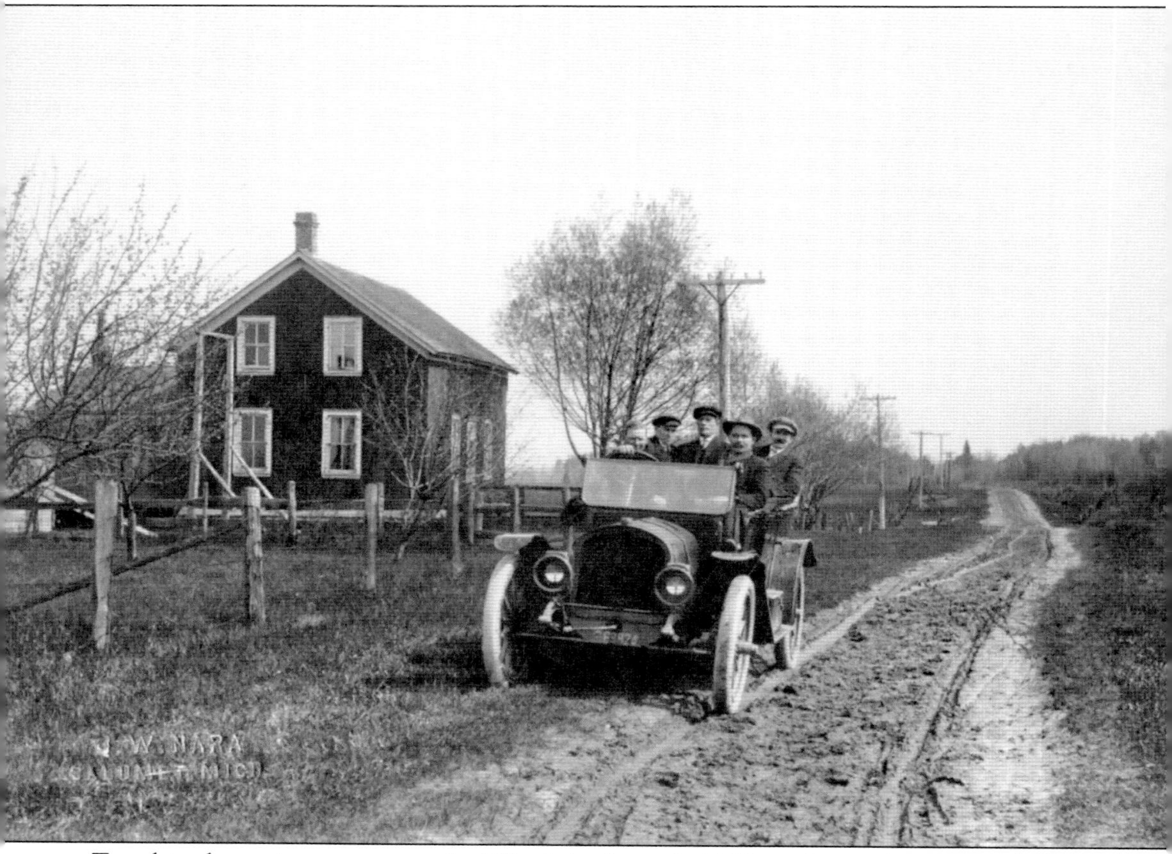

Travel in the region was extremely difficult in the early 1900s, as few roads were available and not many people owned automobiles. (Michigan Technological University Archives/Copper Country Historical Collection.)

Two

Houghton County Traction Company

Operations on the initial streetcar line between Houghton and Boston began on October 27, 1900, and it was reported in the local newspapers that on the first weekend of operations well over 5,000 people rode the system in standing-room-only conditions. With the success of the line in Houghton and Hancock during the first months of operations, the push to extend the line farther north was heightened. In the summer of 1901, the line was extended north from Boston to Laurium and Red Jacket. Entry into Red Jacket was accomplished by an indirect route to the Mineral Range railroad station. The presence of a large railroad yard to the east of town could have been the reason for the route, but some have suggested that the Calumet & Hecla Mining Company pressured leaders not to place the line on Red Jacket's main road (Fifth Street). Alexander Agassiz, the president of Calumet & Hecla, was known to be opposed to the streetcar line because he felt that it would serve as a gathering place for workers, whereby they might discuss and complain about working conditions, resulting in negative impacts to his company. Although the line was built on an indirect route in Red Jacket, the ridership was still high, as the service was a great way of traveling to Houghton, Hancock, and other areas. Building continued north on the line, and service to Wolverine began in September 1901. A branch line to Lake Linden and Hubbell opened in the summer of 1903. The construction of this extension was delayed due to a dispute over snow-removal costs. In 1908, the main line was extended farther north from Wolverine to the mining town of Mohawk. With this final extension, the total system trackage was 27 miles. There was talk about extensions east of Hancock to Ripley and Dollar Bay, and south of Houghton to Hurontown and Dodgeville, but they never materialized. In 1908, the name of the company was changed to the Houghton County Traction Company.

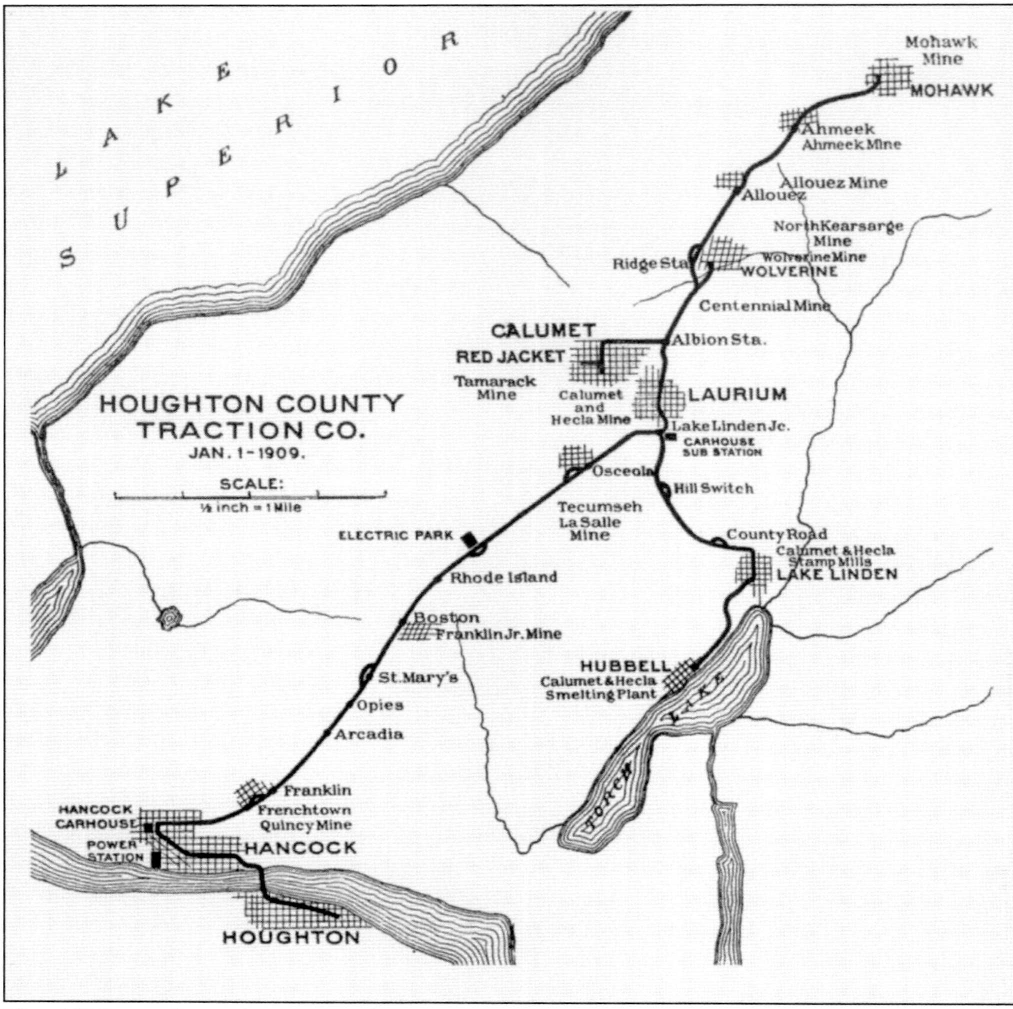

This 1909 map shows the route and stations on the Houghton County Traction Company system. Service began between Houghton and Boston on October 27, 1900. In 1901, the line was extended farther north to serve Laurium, Red Jacket, and Wolverine, and in 1903 a branch line opened to Lake Linden and Hubbell. The system was completed when the section between Wolverine and Mohawk opened in 1908. (Michigan Technological University Archives/Copper Country Historical Collection.)

James R. Dee was the general manger of the Peninsula Electric Light & Power Company, the parent company of the Houghton County Street Railway Company. He was a community leader and, as president of the James R. Dee Real Estate Company, was responsible for the construction of many buildings in Houghton. Dee was involved in numerous undertakings, including telephone service, the Douglass House, the Portage Lake Golf Club, the Onigaming Yacht Club, and professional hockey and baseball. (Michigan Technological University Archives/ Copper Country Historical Collection.)

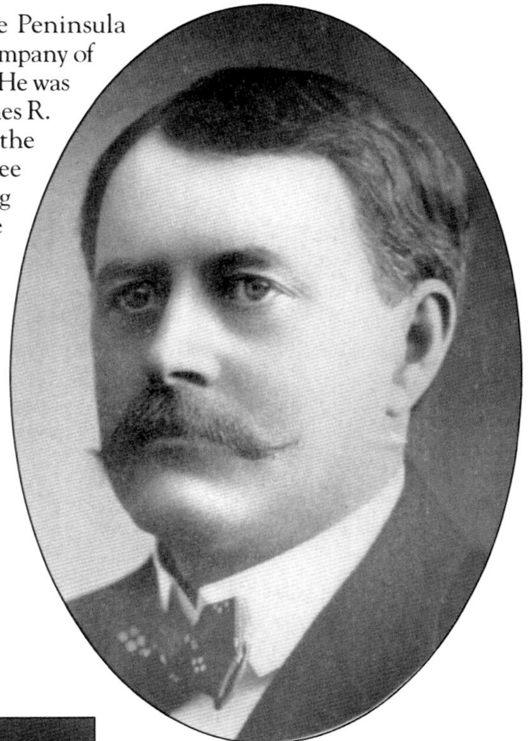

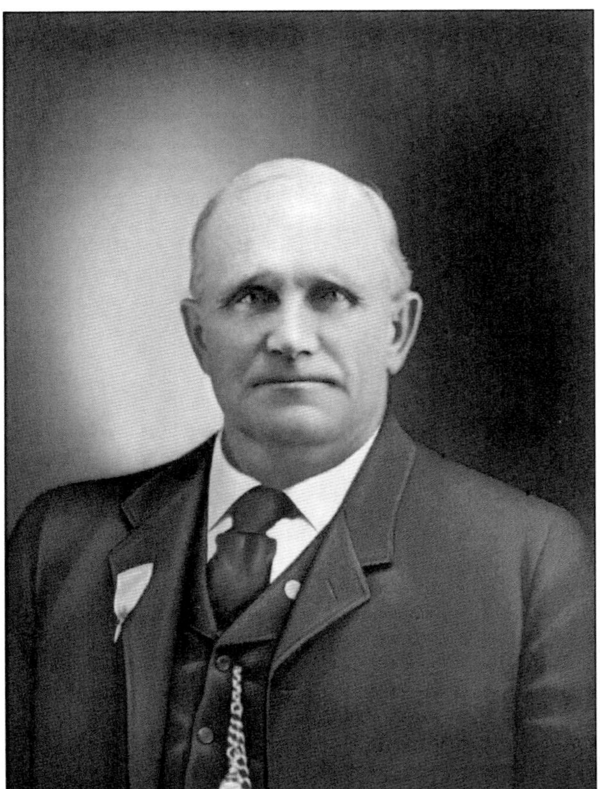

Andrew Johnson, a successful Hancock businessman, directed construction work on the initial streetcar line between Hancock and Boston. He was active in numerous local affairs, including the founding of Suomi College. (Michigan Technological University Archives/Copper Country Historical Collection.)

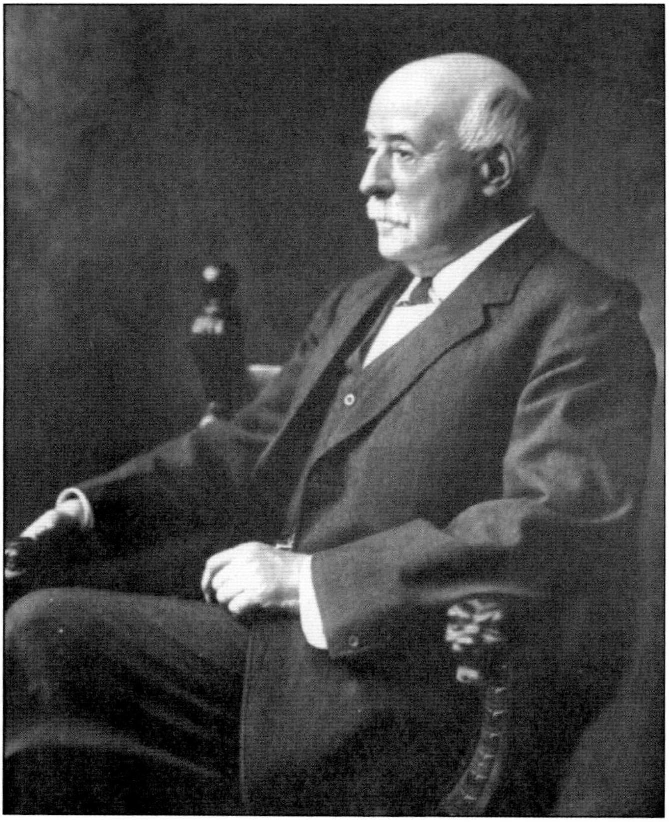

Alexander Agassiz was the powerful president of the Calumet & Hecla Mining Company from 1871 until his death in 1910. Agassiz and C&H were initially opposed to a streetcar line in Red Jacket, but relented. Agassiz was a fascinating man. When he discovered that the mining company did not require his full-time, year-round attention, he returned to Boston, Massachusetts, to pursue research interests in natural history at Harvard and lead world expeditions. (Michigan Technological University Archives/Copper Country Historical Collection.)

HOUGHTON COUNTY TRACTION CO.

TIME TABLE.

	A. M.		P. M.
East Houghton for Hancock and Calumet, half hourly	5:35	to	11:05
Calumet for Hancock and East Houghton, half hourly	6:00	to	11:30
Calumet for Lake Linden and Hubbell, hourly	6:45	to	10:45
Hubbell to Lake Linden and Calumet, hourly	6:50	to	10.50
Calumet to Mohawk, hourly	5:50	to	10.50
Mohawk to Calumet, hourly	6:30	to	11:30
Calumet for Wolverine, hourly	6:10	to	11:10
Wolverine for Calumet, hourly	6:30	to	11:30
Laurium Carhouse for Red Jacket, quarter hourly	6:05	to	10:35
Douglass House, Houghton to Hancock, quarter hourly	7:12	to	10:30
Sullivan's Curve, Hancock for Houghton, quarter hourly	7:00	to	10:30

Sundays the same, starting one hour later.

Saturdays, Mohawk and Wolverine routes—40 minute service, starting at 12:30 P. M.

Sundays, Mohawk and Wolverine routes—40 minute service, starting at 7:10 A. M.

Subject to change without notice.

Streetcars ran every day on published schedules, with service beginning as early as 5:30 a.m. and continuing until midnight. This timetable was published in the *Houghton Daily Mining Gazette* on December 17, 1913. Frequent service was available for local passengers every 15 minutes, and interurban service ran every half hour or hour depending on the destination. (Houghton County Historical Society.)

IN EFFECT JANUARY 1, 1910.

HOUGHTON TO CALUMET / CALUMET TO HOUGHTON

M	P M	P M	P M	P M	P M		A M	A M	A M	A M	A M	A M	Miles	Stations	A M	A M	A M	A M	A M	A M		P M	P M	P M	P M	P M
28	11 58	11 28	10 58	10 28	9 58	And every half hour until	9 28	8 58	8 28	7 58	7 28	6 58	.0	Ar.......Red Jacket......Lv.	6 00	6 30	7 00	7 30	8 00	8 30	And every half hour until	9 00	9 30	10 00	10 30	11 00
18	11 48	11 18	10 48	10 18	9 48		9 18	8 48	8 18	7 48	7 18	6 48	1.2	........Albion Station........	6 10	6 40	7 10	7 40	8 10	8 40		9 10	9 40	10 10	10 40	11 10
10	11 40	11 10	10 40	10 10	9 40		9 10	8 40	8 10	7 40	7 10	6 40	2.5	.....Laurium, Third St.....	6 20	6 50	7 20	7 50	8 20	8 50		9 20	9 50	10 20	10 50	11 20
05	11 35	11 05	10 35	10 05	9 35		9 05	8 35	8 05	7 35	7 05	6 35	3.1	...Lake Linden Junction..	6 25	6 55	7 25	7 55	8 25	8 55		9 25	9 55	10 25	10 55	11 25
52	11 22	10 52	10 22	9 52	9 22		8 52	8 22	7 52	7 22	6 52	6 22	6.5	.........Electric Park.........	6 37	7 07	7 37	8 07	8 37	9 07		9 37	10 07	10 37	11 07	11 37
47	11 17	10 47	10 17	9 47	9 17		8 47	8 17	7 47	7 17	6 47	6 17	9.1	..............Boston..............	6 43	7 13	7 43	8 13	8 43	9 13		9 43	10 13	10 43	11 13	11 43
38	11 08	10 38	10 08	9 38	9 08		8 38	8 08	7 38	7 08	6 38	6 08	11.7	..............Franklin.............	6 52	7 22	7 52	8 22	8 52	9 22		9 52	10 22	10 52	11 22	11 52
30	11 00	10 30	10 00	9 30	9 00		8 30	8 00	7 30	7 00	6 30	6 00	12.3	.....Hancock Carhouse.....	7 00	7 30	8 00	8 30	9 00	9 30		10 00	10 30	11 00	11 30	12 00
20	11 50	10 20	9 50	9 20	8 50		8 20	7 50	7 20	6 50	6 20	5 50	14.6	Hancock Bank Cor.	7 10	7 40	8 10	8 40	9 10	9 40		10 10	10 40	11 10	11 40	12 10
12	10 42	10 12	9 42	9 12	8 42		8 12	7 42	7 12	6 42	6 12	5 42	15.5	.......Douglass House.......	7 18	7 48	8 18	8 48	9 18	9 48		10 18	10 48	11 18	11 48	12 18
05	10 35	10 05	9 35	9 05	8 35		8 05	7 35	7 05	6 35	6 05	5 35	16.5	Lv...East Houghton..Ar.	7 25	7 55	8 25	8 55	9 25	9 55		10 25	10 55	11 25	11 55	12 25

LAKE LINDEN TO CALUMET / CALUMET TO LAKE LINDEN

M	P M	P M	P M	P M	P M		A M	A M	A M	A M	A M	A M	Miles	Stations	A M	A M	A M	A M	A M	A M		P M	P M	P M	P M	P M
43	10 43	9 43	8 43	7 43	6 53	And every hour until	12 43	11 43	10 43	9 43	8 43	7 43	.0	Ar.......Red Jacket......Lv.	6 45	7 45	8 45	9 45	10 45	11 45	And every hour until	5 45	6 45	7 45	8 45	9 45
33	10 33	9 33	8 33	7 33	6 33		12 33	11 33	10 33	9 33	5 33	7 33	1.2	........Albion Station........	6 55	7 55	8 55	9 55	10 55	11 55		5 55	6 55	7 55	8 55	9 55
25	10 25	9 25	8 25	7 25	6 25		12 25	11 25	10 25	9 25	8 25	7 25	2.5	....Laurium, Third St.....	7 05	8 05	9 05	10 05	11 05	12 05		6 05	7 05	8 05	9 05	10 05
20	10 20	9 20	8 20	7 20	6 20		12 20	11 20	10 20	9 20	8 20	7 20	3.1	...Lake Linden Junction..	7 10	8 10	9 10	10 10	11 10	12 10		6 10	7 10	8 10	9 10	10 10
59	9 59	8 59	7 59	6 59	5 59		11 59	10 59	9 59	8 59	7 59	6 59	7.0	..Lake Linden, First St...	7 28	8 28	9 28	10 28	11 28	12 28		6 28	7 28	8 28	9 28	10 28
50	9 50	8 50	7 50	6 50	5 50		11 50	10 50	9 50	8 50	7 50	6 50	8.3	Lv......... Hubbell ....Ar.	7 37	8 37	9 37	10 37	11 37	12 37		6 37	7 37	8 37	9 37	10 37

WOLVERINE TO RED JACKET / RED JACKET TO WOLVERINE

M	P M	P M	P M	P M	P M		A M	A M	A M	A M	A M	A M	Miles	Stations	A M	A M	A M	A M	A M	A M		P M	P M	P M	P M	P M
	10 50	9 50	8 50	7 50	6 50	And every hour until	10 50	9 50	8 50	7 50	6 50	6 10	.0	Ar.......Red Jacket......Lv.		6 10	7 10	8 10	9 10	10 10	And every hour until	6 10	7 10	8 10	9 10	10 10
40	10 40	9 40	8 40	7 40	6 40		10 40	9 40	8 40	7 40	6 40	6 00	1.2	........Albion Station........	5 40	6 20	7 20	8 20	9 20	10 20		6 20	7 20	8 20	9 20	10 20
30	10 30	9 30	8 30	7 30	6 30		10 30	9 30	8 30	7 30	6 30	5 50	2.7	Lv....... Wolverine.......Ar.	5 50	6 30	7 30	8 30	9 30	10 30		6 30	7 30	8 30	9 30	10 30

MOHAWK TO RED JACKET / RED JACKET TO MOHAWK

M	P M	P M	P M	P M	P M		A M	A M	A M	A M	A M	A M	Miles	Stations	A M	A M	A M	A M	A M	A M		P M	P M	P M	P M	P M
10	11 10	10 10	9 10	8 10	7 10	And every hour until	12 10	11 10	10 10	9 10	8 10	7 10	.0	Ar.......Red Jacket......Lv.	5 50	6 50	7 50	8 50	9 50	10 50	And every hour until	5 50	6 50	7 50	8 50	9 5
00	11 00	10 00	9 00	8 00	7 00		12 00	11 00	10 00	9 00	8 00	7 00	1.2	........Albion Station........	6 00	7 00	8 00	9 00	10 00	11 00		6 00	7 00	8 00	9 00	10 0
50	10 50	9 50	8 50	7 50	6 50		11 50	10 50	9 50	8 50	7 50	6 50	2.7	........Ridge Station........	6 10	7 10	8 10	9 10	10 10	11 10		6 10	7 10	8 10	9 10	10 1
45	10 45	9 45	8 45	7 45	6 45		11 45	10 45	9 45	8 45	7 45	6 45	3.8	.......Allouez Station.......	6 15	7 15	8 15	9 15	10 15	11 15		6 15	7 15	8 15	9 15	10 1
40	10 40	9 40	8 40	7 40	6 40		11 40	10 40	9 40	8 40	7 40	6 40	4.9	.......Ahmeek Station.......	6 20	7 20	8 20	9 20	10 20	11 20		6 20	7 20	8 20	9 20	10 2
30	10 30	9 30	8 30	7 30	6 30		11 30	10 30	9 30	8 30	7 30	6 30	7.0	Lv.Mohawk Station..Ar.	6 30	7 30	8 30	9 30	10 30	11 30		6 30	7 30	8 30	9 30	10 3

SUNDAY SCHEDULE the same, starting one hour later. Transfer Points:-Albion Station and Lake Linden Junction.

Local cars in addition to the above, give 15 minutes service between Houghton and Hancock, and between Red Jacket and Laurium from 7:15 A to 10:45 P. M. Cars leaving Houghton terminus **FIVE MINUTES AFTER THE HOUR** up to 10:05 P. M. are scheduled to connect with Lake Linden at Lake Linden Junction. Cars leaving Houghton terminus 35 minutes after the hour are scheduled to connect at Albion Station with the Mohawk as per above hour week day schedule. Cars leaving Houghton terminus 5 minutes after the hour are scheduled to connect at Albion Station with Wolve Car, as per above hour week day schedule. Saturday Afternoons and Sundays all day either 20 or 40 minutes service will be run on the Mohawk Line traffic demands. **SUBJECT TO CHANGE WITHOUT NOTICE.**

GARDNER ROGERS, Manager, Houghton.

JOHN RALPH, JR., Supt. Hancock.

ROBERT ROBINSON, Chief of Trans. Calumet.

This is a timecard showing a detailed schedule for January 1, 1910. It would take about an hour and 15 minutes to travel between Houghton and Red Jacket. (Houghton County Historical Society.)

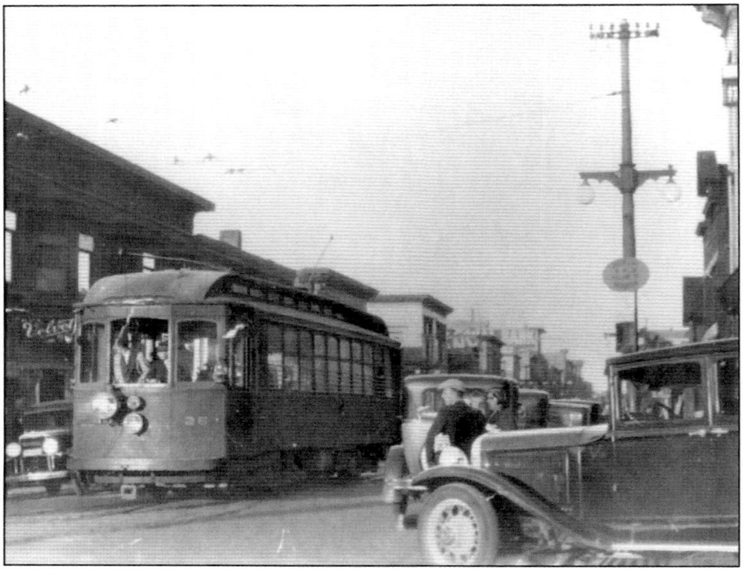

Streetcars would make frequent stops for passenger boarding and alighting in the urban areas and were typically manned by two-person crews comprising a motorman and a conductor. This photograph shows streetcar No. 26 operating on Shelden Street in downtown Houghton in the 1920s. (Houghton County Historical Society.)

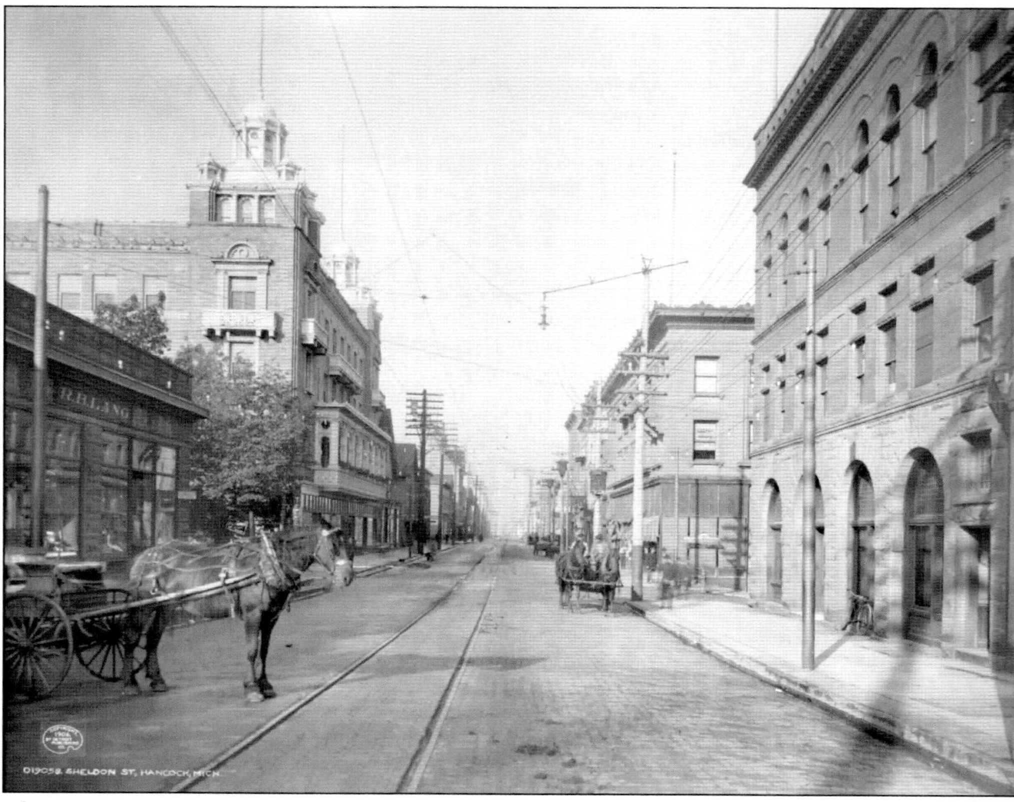

This is a 1906 view of Shelden Avenue in downtown Houghton looking west. Except for short sections of double track in Red Jacket, Laurium, and Hancock, and on the Portage Lake Bridge, the line was constructed as a single track. (Library of Congress.)

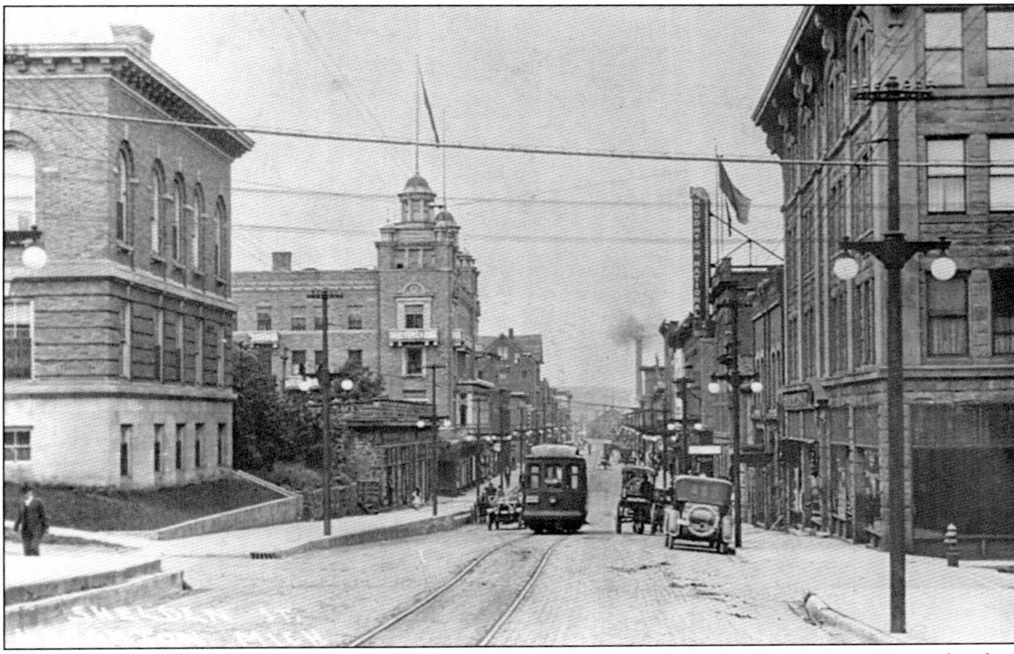

This is another view of Shelden Avenue in downtown Houghton looking west. Note the four means of transportation: streetcar, automobile, horse and buggy, and pedestrian. The building on the left is the Houghton Club, a private men's club constructed in 1906 where men could retreat for billiards, cards, and dining. (Houghton County Historical Society.)

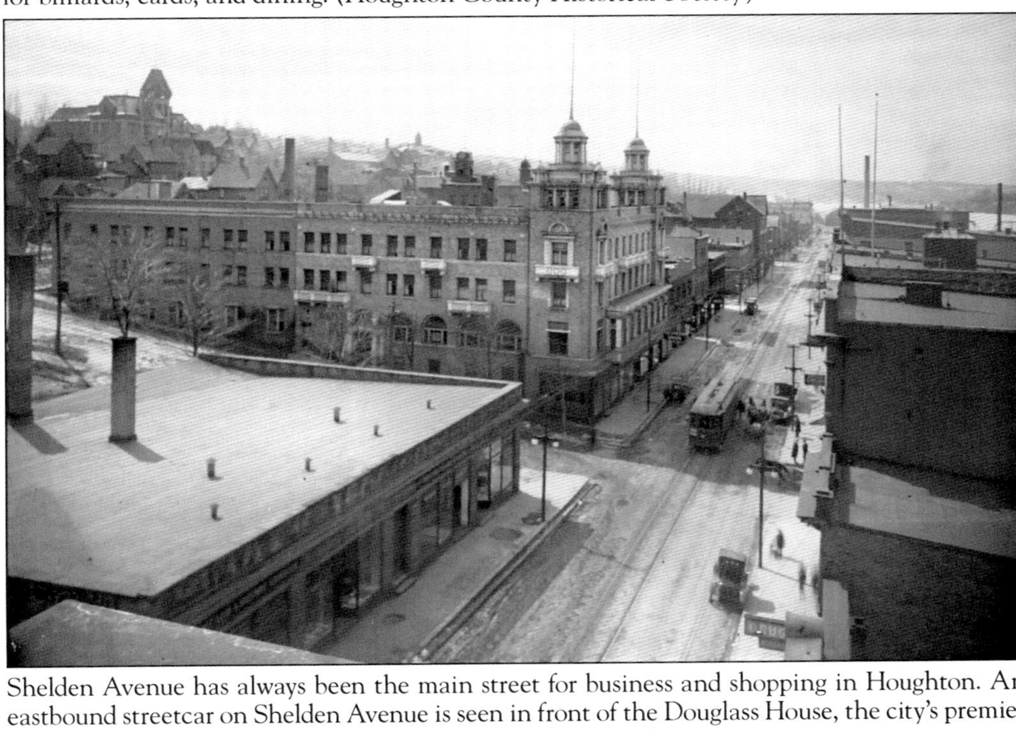

Shelden Avenue has always been the main street for business and shopping in Houghton. An eastbound streetcar on Shelden Avenue is seen in front of the Douglass House, the city's premier hotel for many years. (Houghton County Historical Society.)

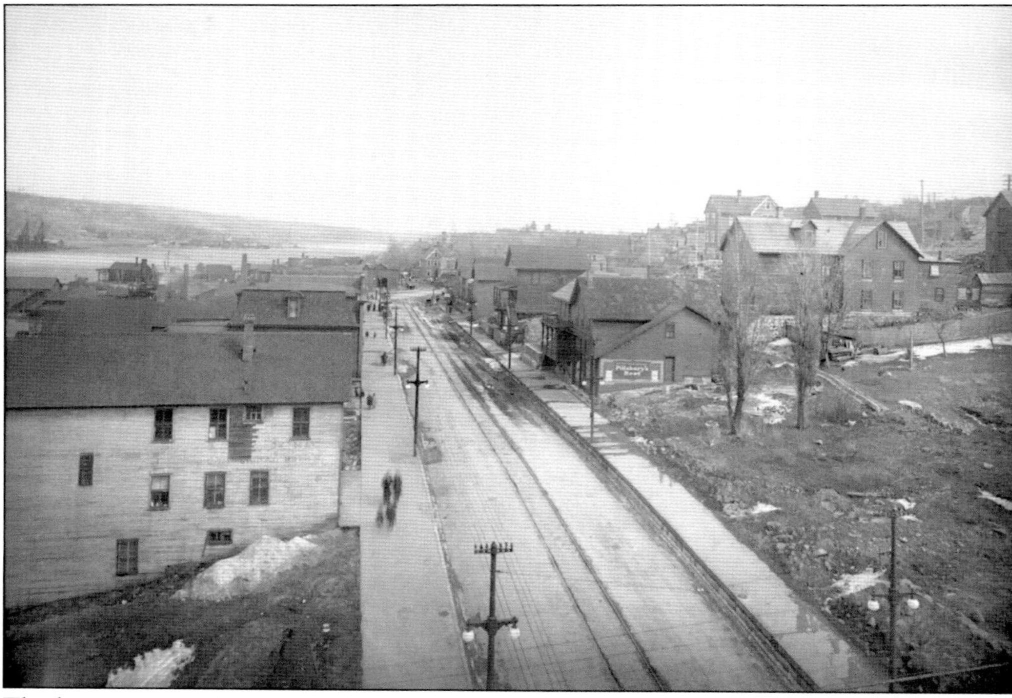

The line ran east of downtown Houghton to the Michigan College of Mines. It was extended from Franklin Square to Forest Hill Road in 1901. This is a view of Shelden Avenue looking east toward East Houghton. (Michigan Technological University Archives/Copper Country Historical Collection.)

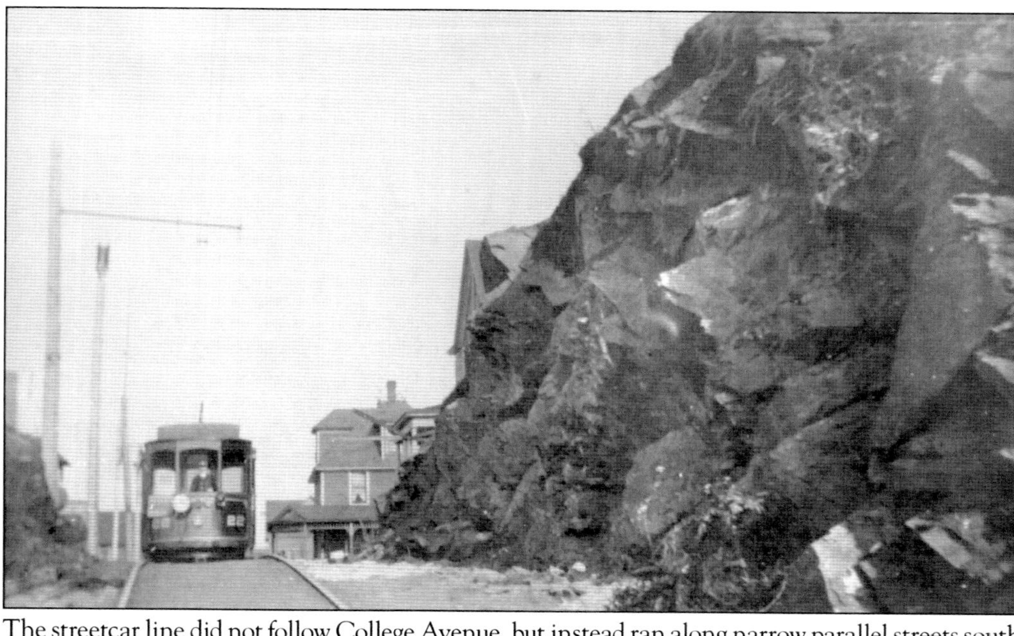

The streetcar line did not follow College Avenue, but instead ran along narrow parallel streets south of College Avenue. Here, streetcar No. 22 operates westbound on Ruby Street in East Houghton. (Michigan Technological University Archives/Copper Country Historical Collection.)

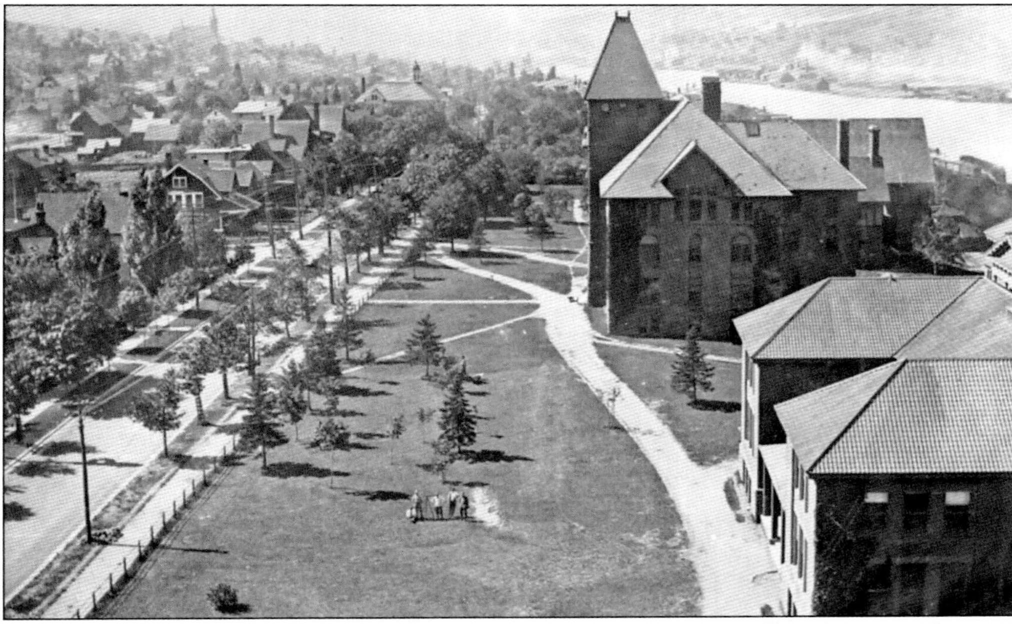

This is a view of the Michigan College of Mines campus looking west. College Avenue is the main street linking the campus to downtown Houghton. In the early years, all of the campus buildings were located north of College Avenue. Hubbell Hall (upper right) and the Shops Building are seen in this 1910s photograph. (Michigan Technological University Archives/Copper Country Historical Collection.)

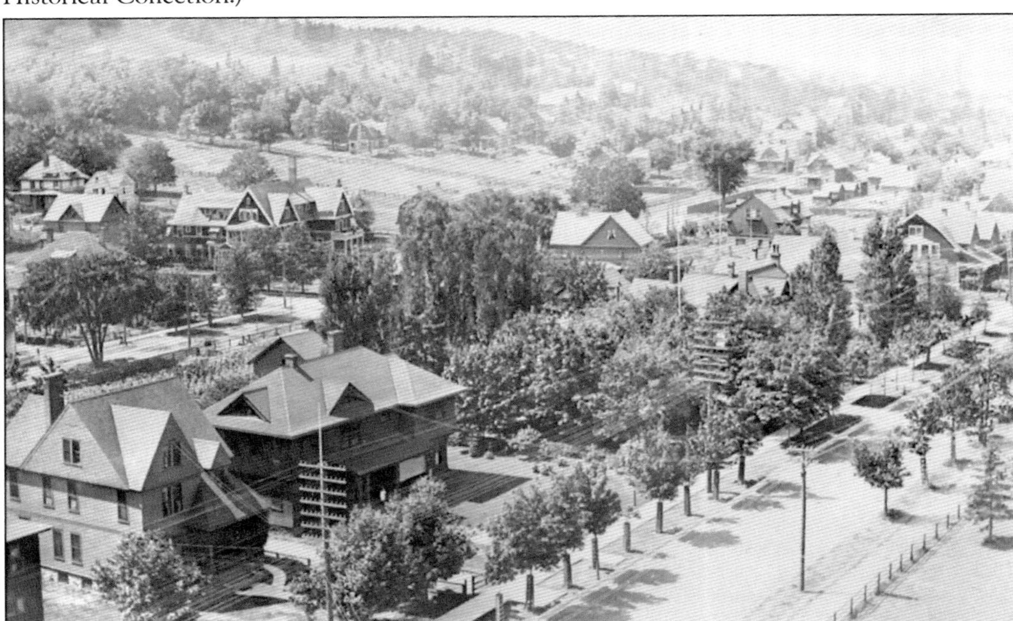

This is a view of homes on the south side of College Avenue near the MCM campus. Many of the homes on College Avenue were built for the wealthier residents of Houghton. As a result, the streetcar line was located one block south of College Avenue on Jasper and Houghton Avenues. (Michigan Technological University Archives/Copper Country Historical Collection.)

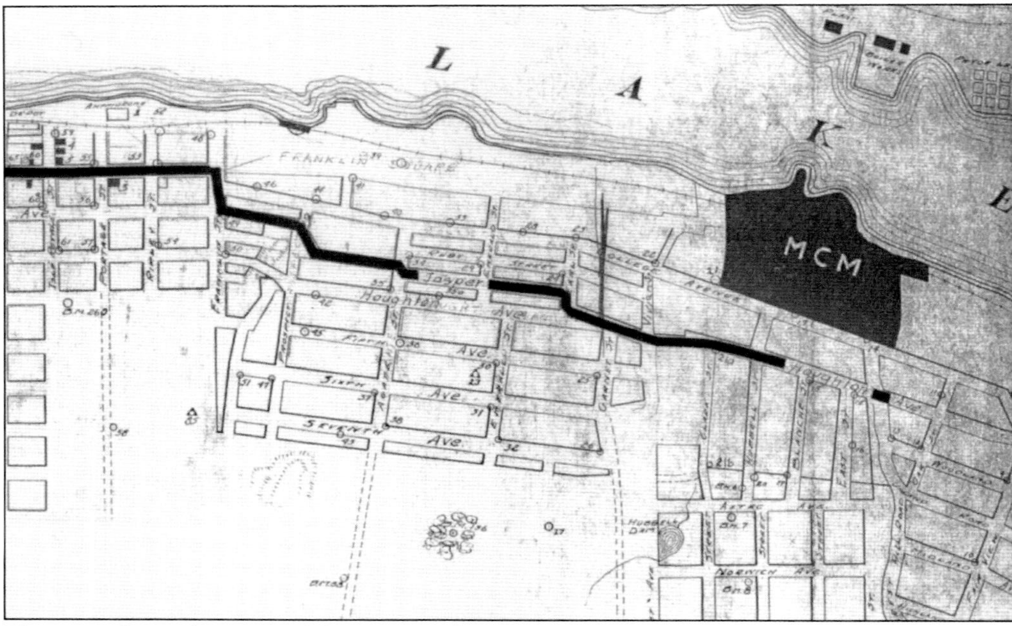

This map shows the route of the streetcar line through East Houghton. The end of the line was located south of the existing Michigan Tech library near MacInnes Drive. (Houghton County Historical Society.)

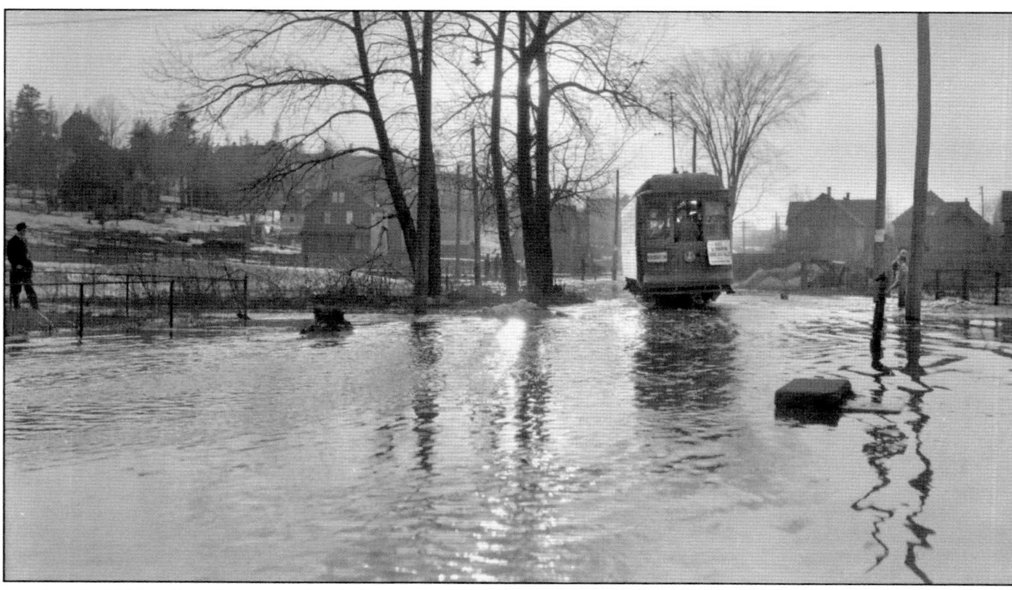

In April 1912, flooding resulted from the overflow of the old Hubbell Dam in East Houghton. Luckily, it was not severe enough to stop streetcar service in the area. (Michigan Technological University Archives/Copper Country Historical Collection.)

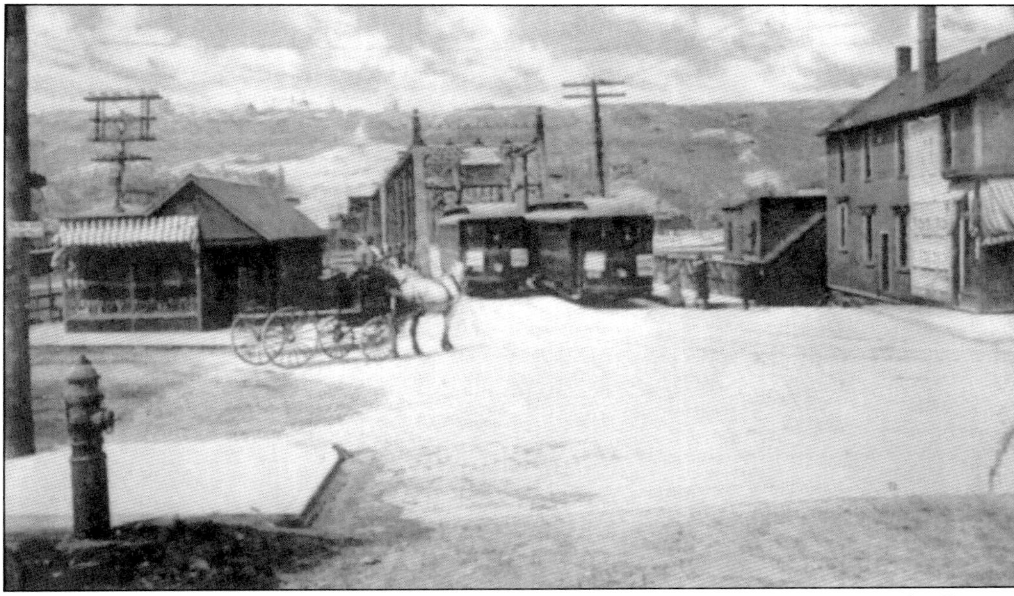

This postcard of Houghton, looking to the north, shows two streetcars passing on the Portage Lake Bridge. A problem with an initial streetcar order arose because a few of the cars were too wide to cross the bridge. As a solution, one set of tracks was moved to accommodate two-way operations. (Houghton County Historical Society.)

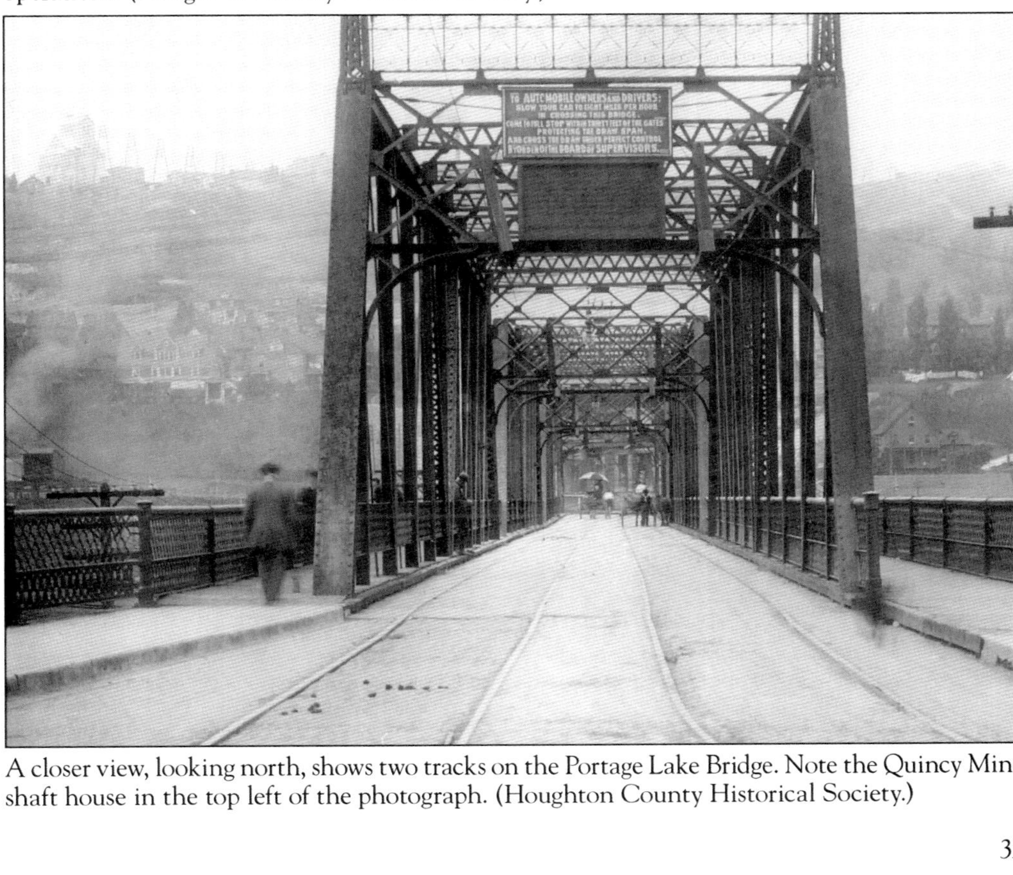

A closer view, looking north, shows two tracks on the Portage Lake Bridge. Note the Quincy Mine shaft house in the top left of the photograph. (Houghton County Historical Society.)

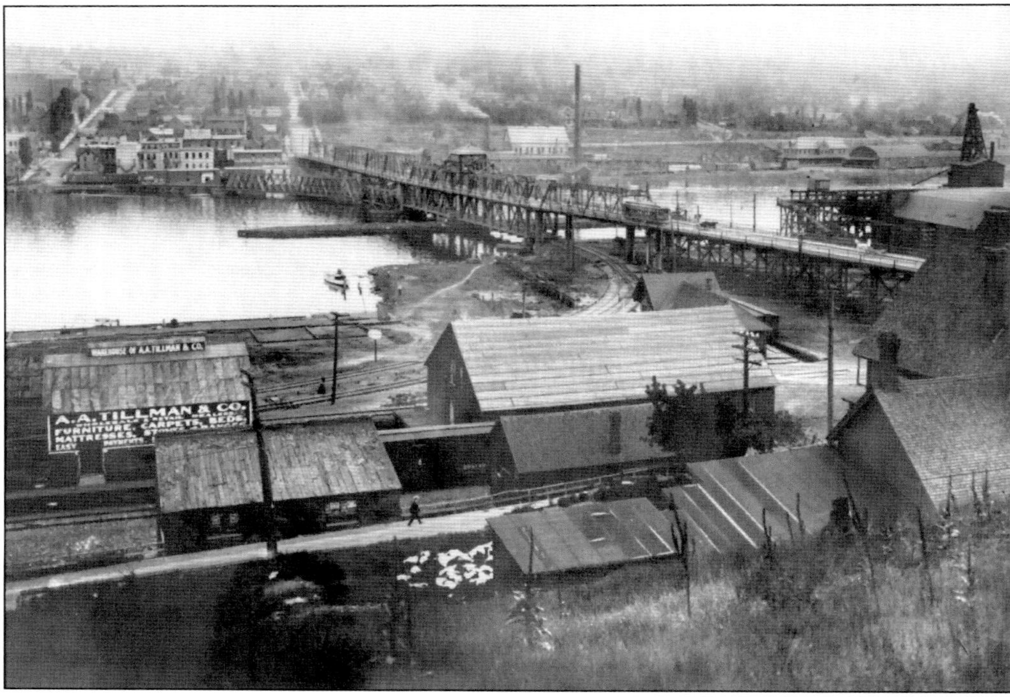

This is the Portage Lake Bridge as seen from Hancock looking south. The streetcars crossed on the top level of the bridge, and railroad traffic operated on the lower level. (Michigan Technological University Archives/Copper Country Historical Collection.)

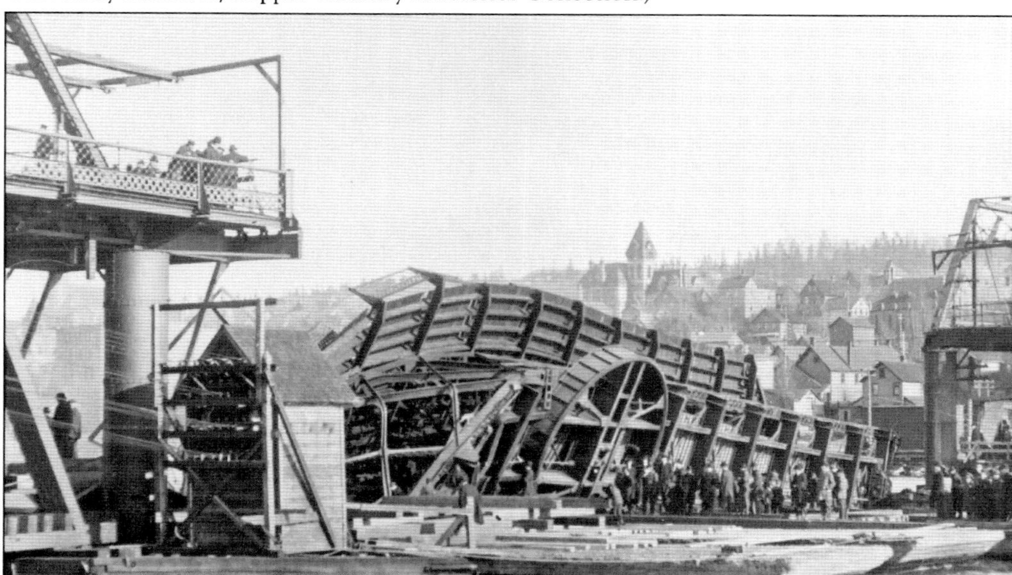

In April 1905, the middle section of the Portage Lake Bridge collapsed after being struck by the steamer *Northern Wave*. Luckily, a streetcar was trapped in Houghton when the bridge collapsed, so local service was able to continue. Ferries were used to carry passengers across the canal during the eight-month bridge reconstruction. (Michigan Technological University Archives/Copper Country Historical Collection.)

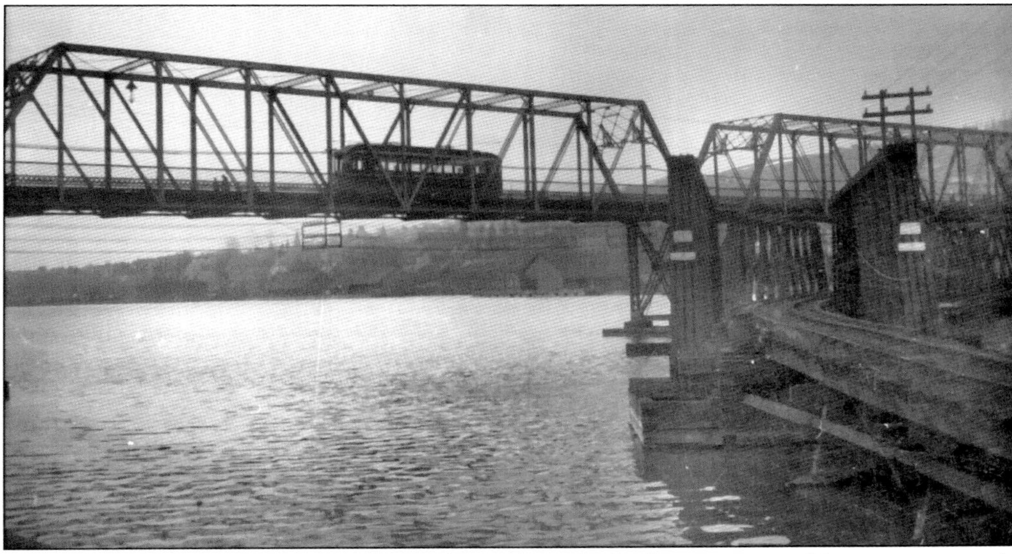

A streetcar crosses the Portage Lake Bridge. When the bridge was opened for passing vessels, streetcar service was disrupted, and long delays would occur. (Michigan Technological University Archives/Copper Country Historical Collection.)

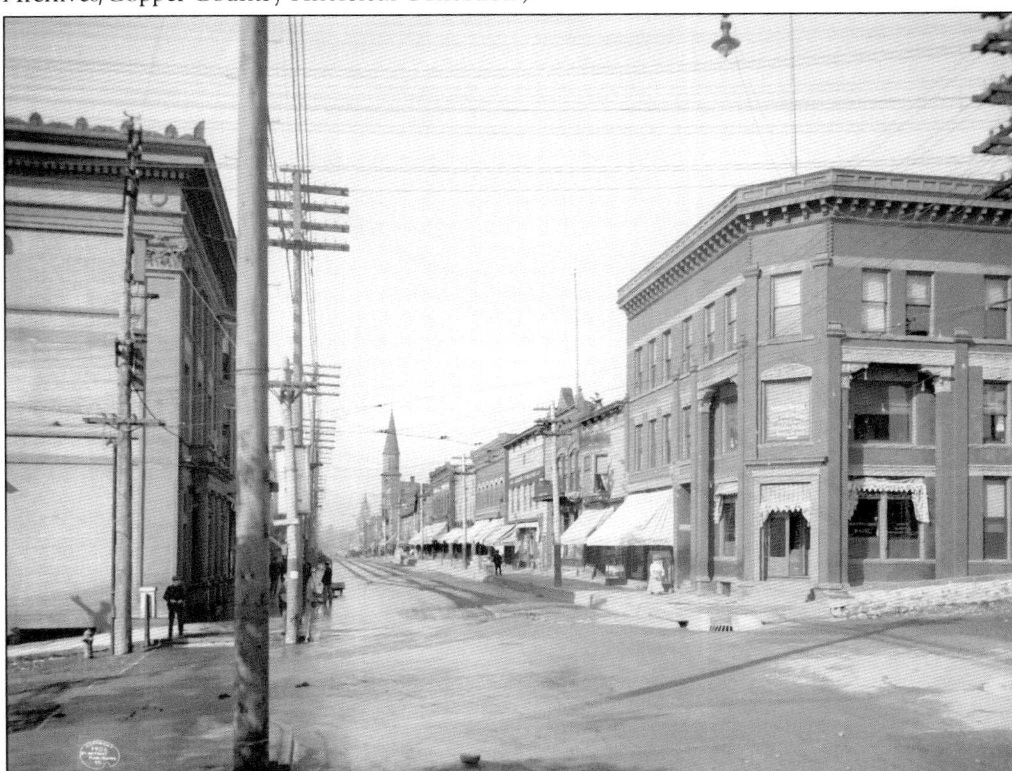

There were two tracks in downtown Hancock that allowed oncoming streetcars to pass. This is a view of Quincy Street looking west. In the foreground is the intersection of Quincy and Reservation Streets. (Library of Congress.)

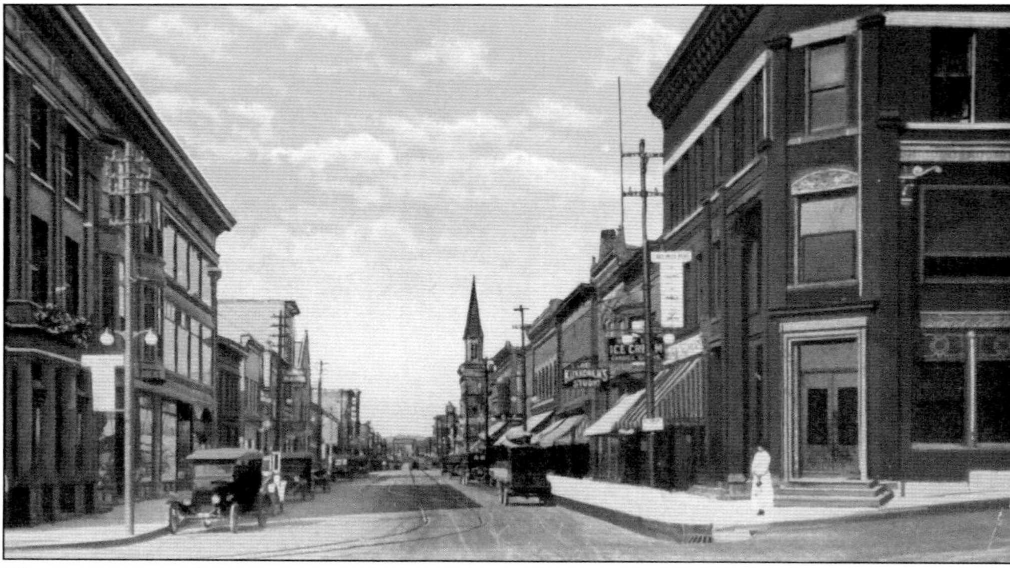

This is a postcard view of Quincy Street looking west. Note how the streetcar line has two tracks in downtown Hancock. (Michigan Technological University Archives/Copper Country Historical Collection.)

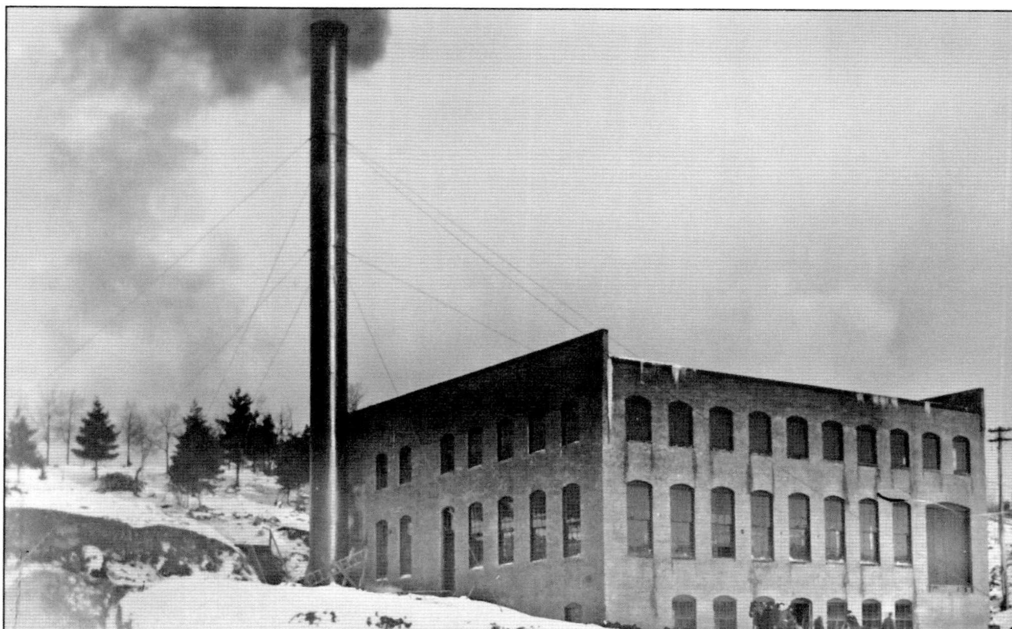

The main powerhouse for the Houghton County Traction Company, built in 1900, was located in Hancock on the Portage Lake waterfront. The Peninsula Electric Light & Power Company was the parent company, so electricity was also produced for local customers. In the building were boilers and generators to supply power to the rail network as well as the necessary switching equipment for power distribution. Coal for the plant's boilers was shipped and received at the company's dock on the waterway. (Michigan Technological University Archives/Copper Country Historical Collection.)

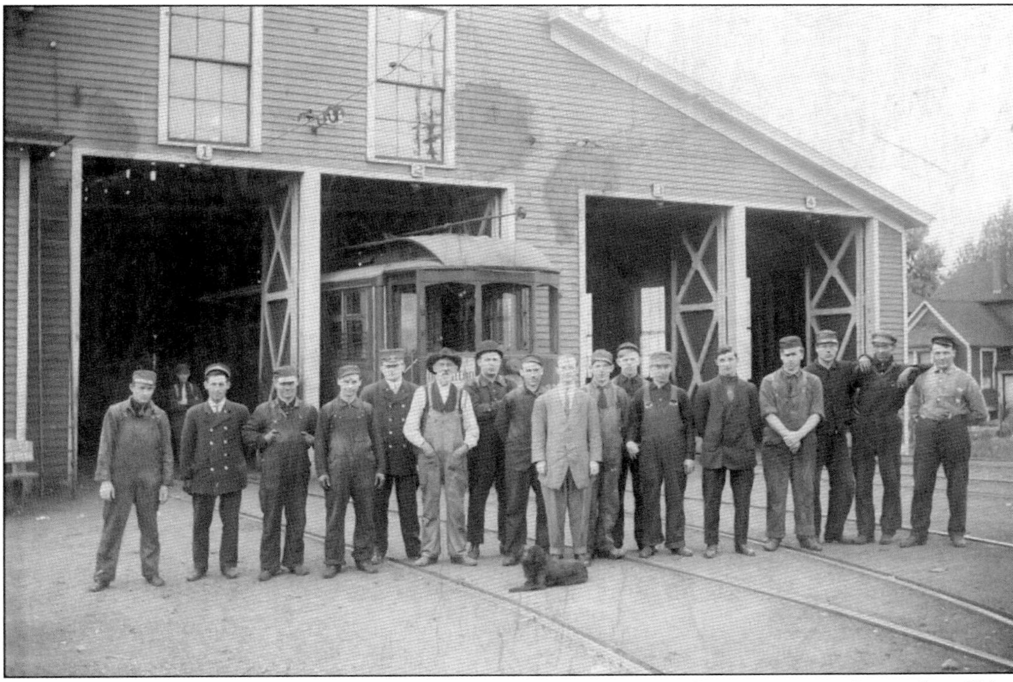

The main carbarn and offices for the Houghton County Traction Company were located on Ethel Street in West Hancock. Here, some of the employees stand in front of that carbarn. During the peak years of operations, there were over 100 company employees. The workforce grew to 140 during summer months for maintenance and construction projects. (Houghton County Historical Society.)

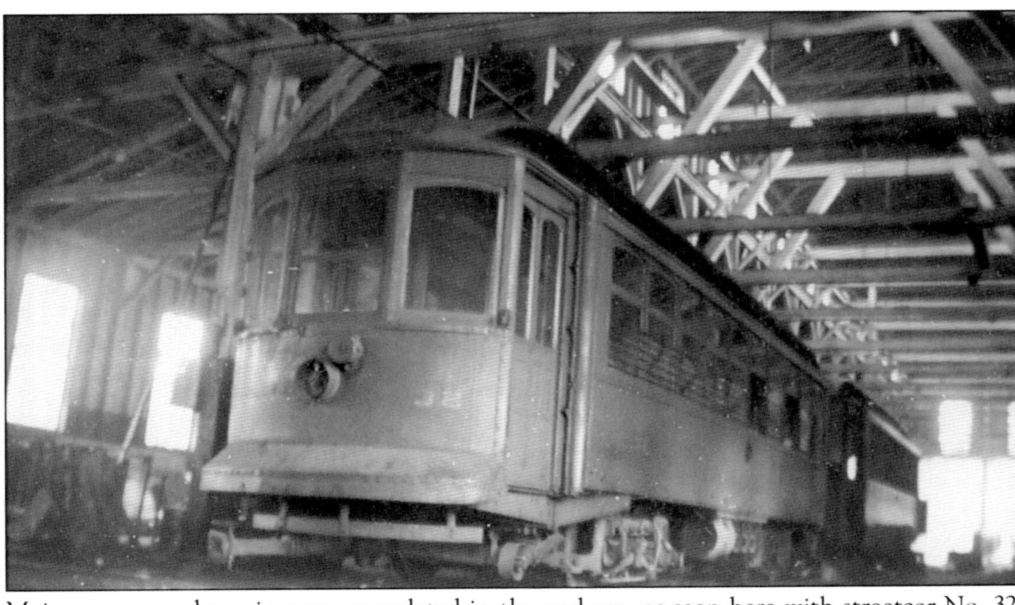

Maintenance and repairs were completed in the carbarn, as seen here with streetcar No. 32. Streetcars were also stored in the building or on the Ethel Street property when not in service. (Houghton County Historical Society.)

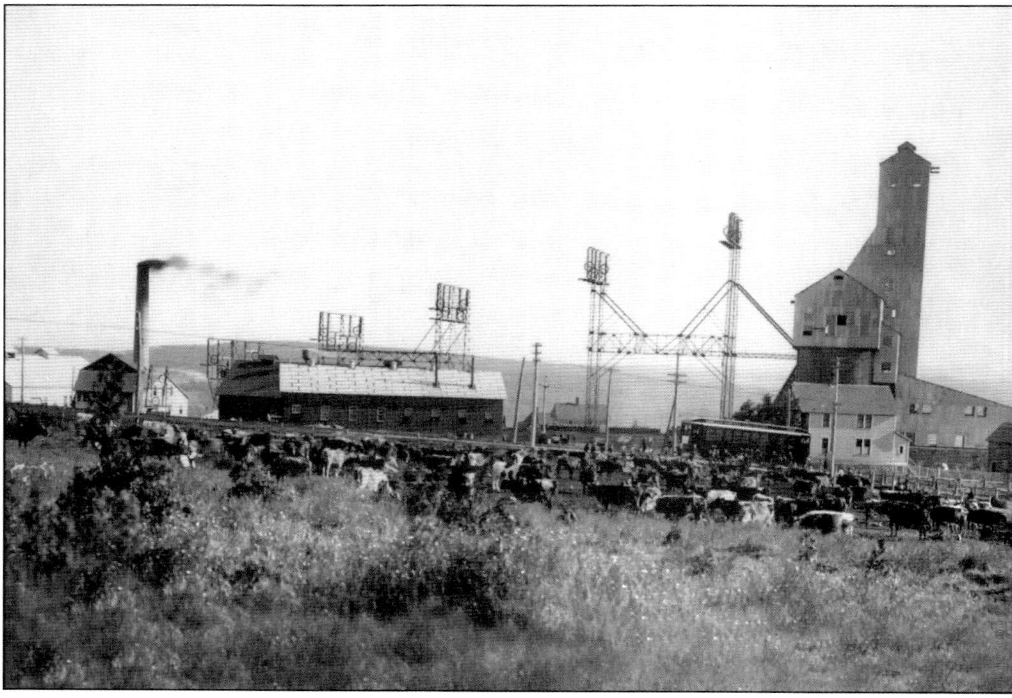

As the line headed north from Hancock, it followed Ingot Street to Frenchtown and the Quincy Hill area. This photograph shows a streetcar near the Hancock Mine No. 2 shaft at Ingot and Elevation Streets halfway up Quincy Hill. This section of the line was probably the greatest challenge for operations, as there was a steep 7.5-percent grade. For the downbound direction, the line was extended past the carbarn on Ingot Street to provide a runaway safety track. (Michigan Technological University Archives/Copper Country Historical Collection.)

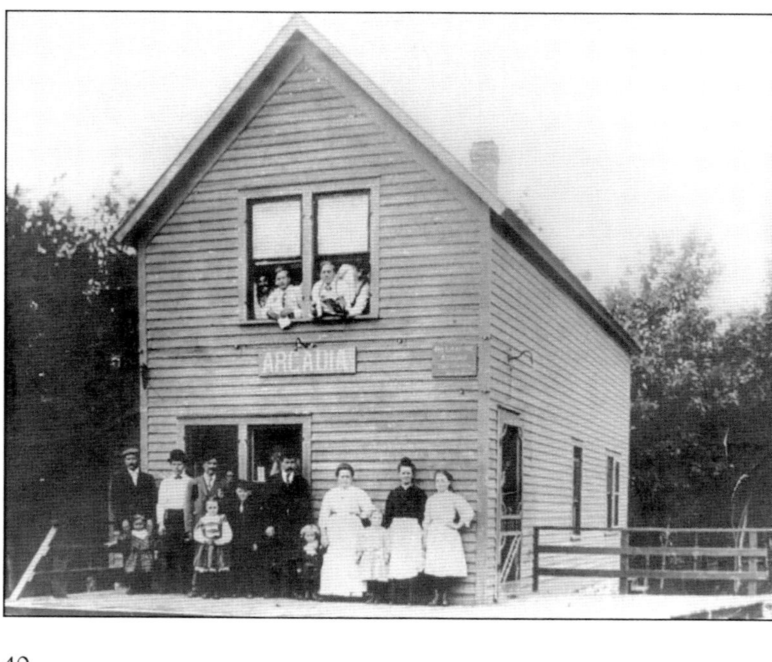

Established stations were located every one to two miles in the countryside for passengers to board and alight streetcars. The Arcadia station is shown here, but it was replaced by the Mesnard station in 1910. The Mesnard station can still be seen today as one travels northbound on US 41. It was relocated but it is on the left side of the highway, north of the Quincy mine shaft house. (Houghton County Historical Society.)

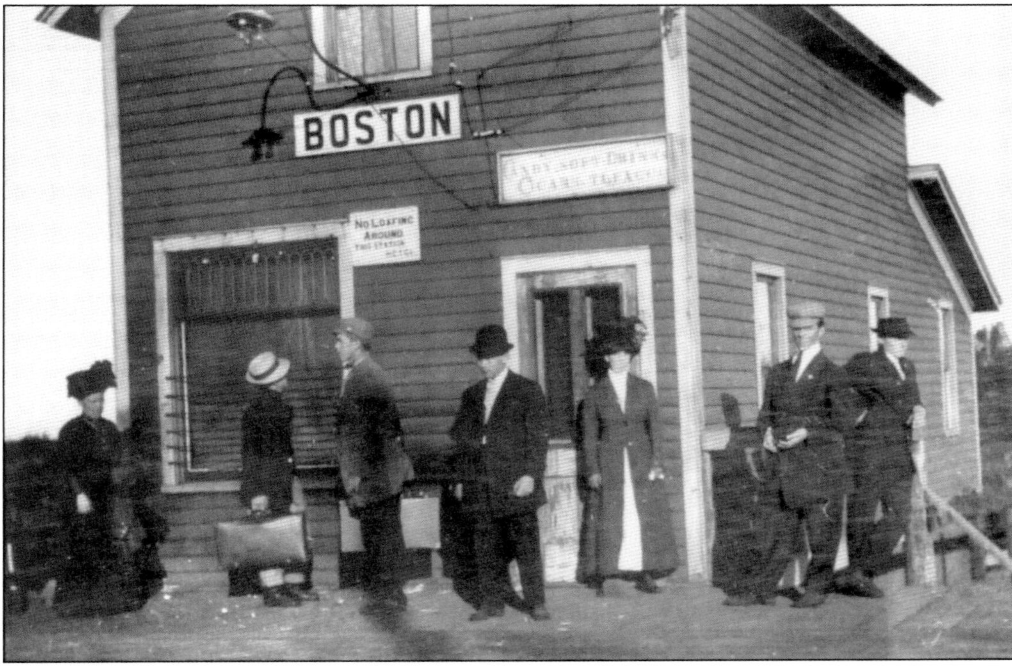

Another established station was in Boston. In 1909, the Boston Post Office was renamed Demmon due to confusion with mail destined for Boston, Massachusetts. The name of the town, however, remained Boston. (Houghton County Historical Society.)

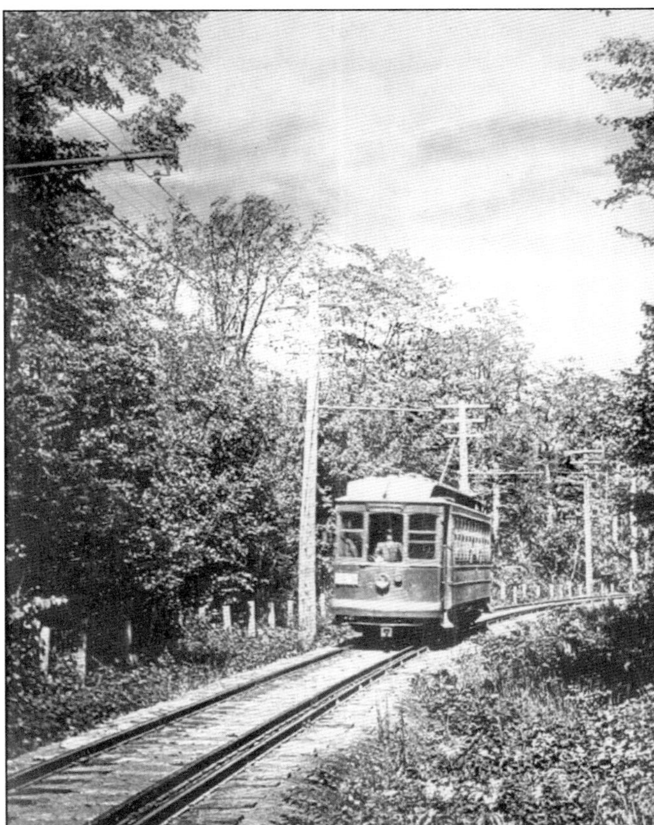

Streetcar No. 40 is seen operating through a heavily forested area north of Boston. Streetcars running between towns were often called interurbans. (Houghton County Historical Society.)

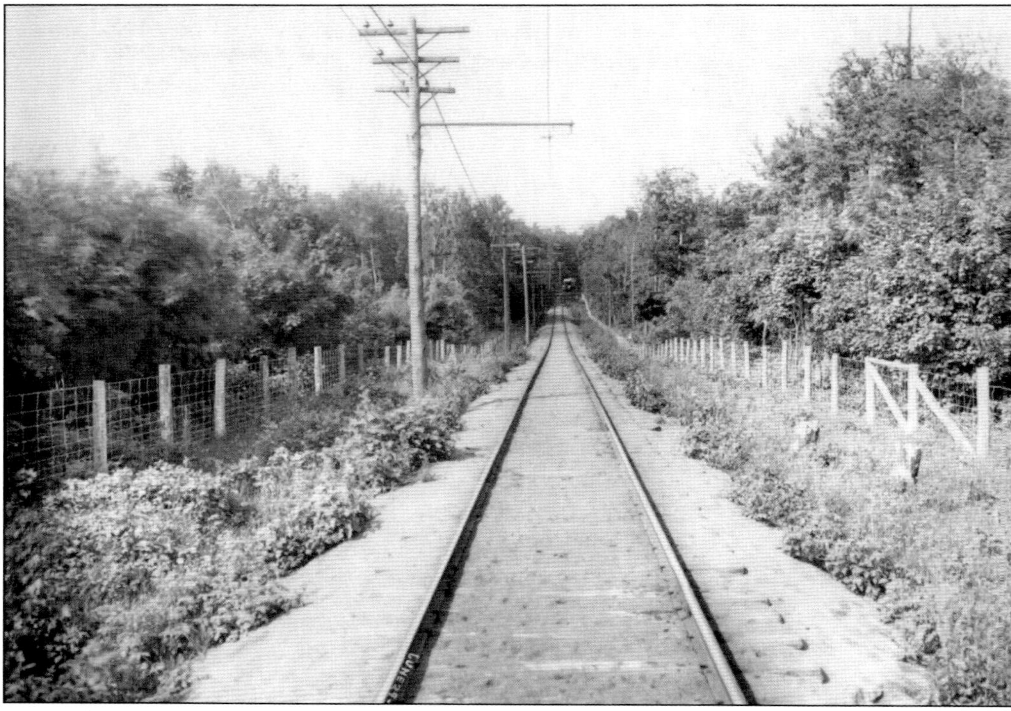

A standard railroad gauge (four feet, eight and a half inches) was used for track, and waste stamp sand from mining operations was used for ballast. In this 1911 photograph of the tracks between Hancock and Calumet, a streetcar is visible in the distance. Due to heavy winter snowfall, the designers avoided cut sections in the rural areas, or they elevated the track bed above the surrounding countryside to minimize snow drifting. Snow fences were also placed along the line for the winter months. (Michigan Technological University Archives/Copper Country Historical Collection.)

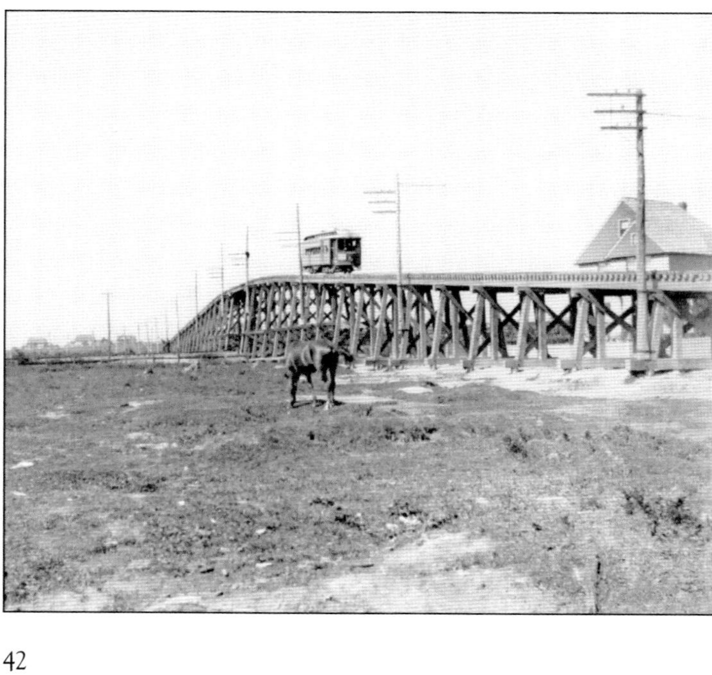

Trestles, like the one seen here, allowed streetcar lines to cross over railroads. Regulations of the Michigan Railroad Commission did not permit at-grade crossings of interurban cars and steam railroads. As a result, all crossings on the line were done with overpasses or wooden trestles. There were eight trestles between Hancock and Mohawk. (Michigan Technological University Archives/ Copper Country Historical Collection.)

This map shows the lines in the Calumet area. Transfers were made at the Albion station or in Laurium. There were basically five routes: Houghton to Red Jacket, Red Jacket to Laurium via the Albion station, Laurium to Lake Linden and Hubbell, Albion to Mohawk, and Albion to Wolverine. (Houghton County Historical Society.)

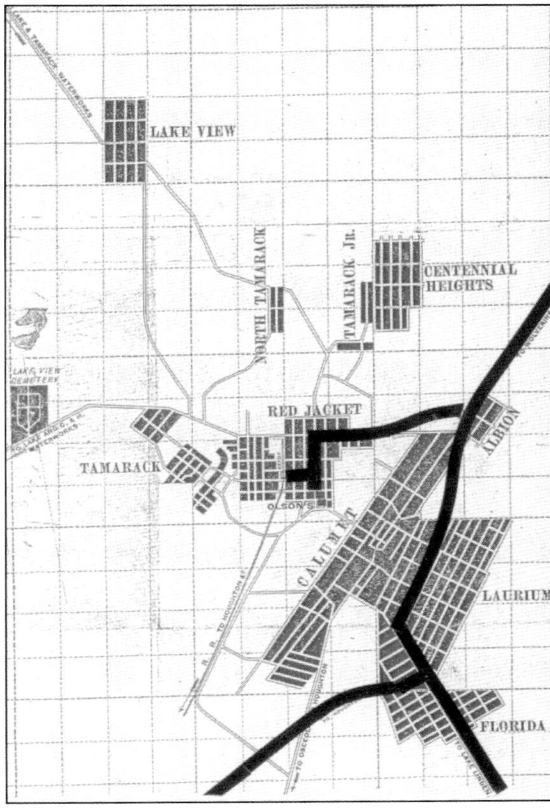

A second carbarn and a substation were located on the south side of Laurium. The carbarn was used for the storage of cars on the north end of the line, while all maintenance and repairs were done at the main carbarn in West Hancock. (Houghton County Historical Society.)

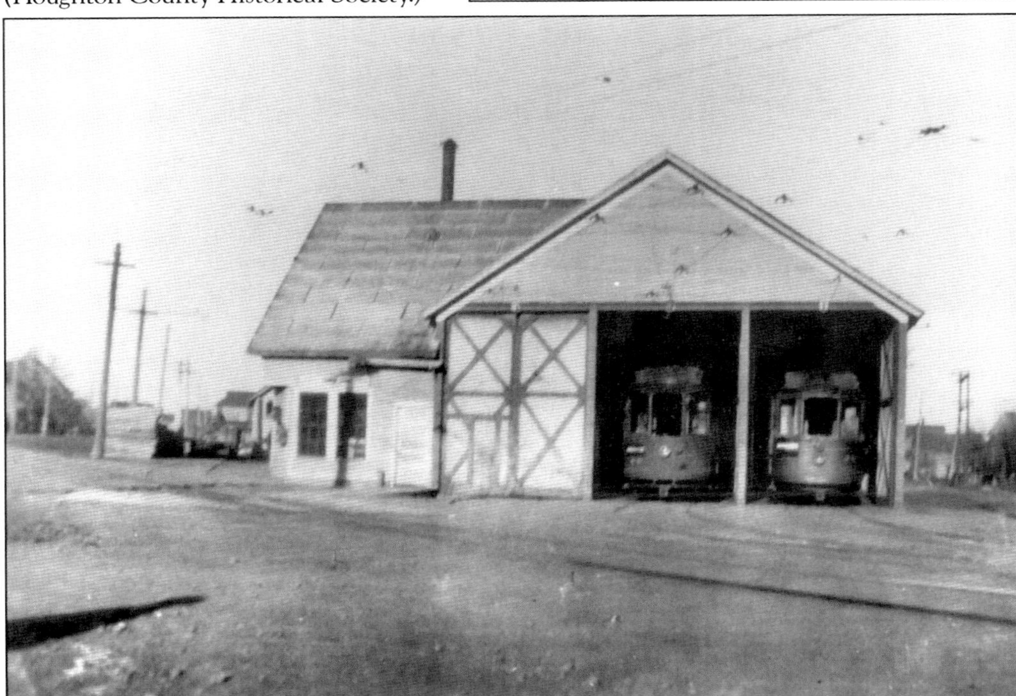

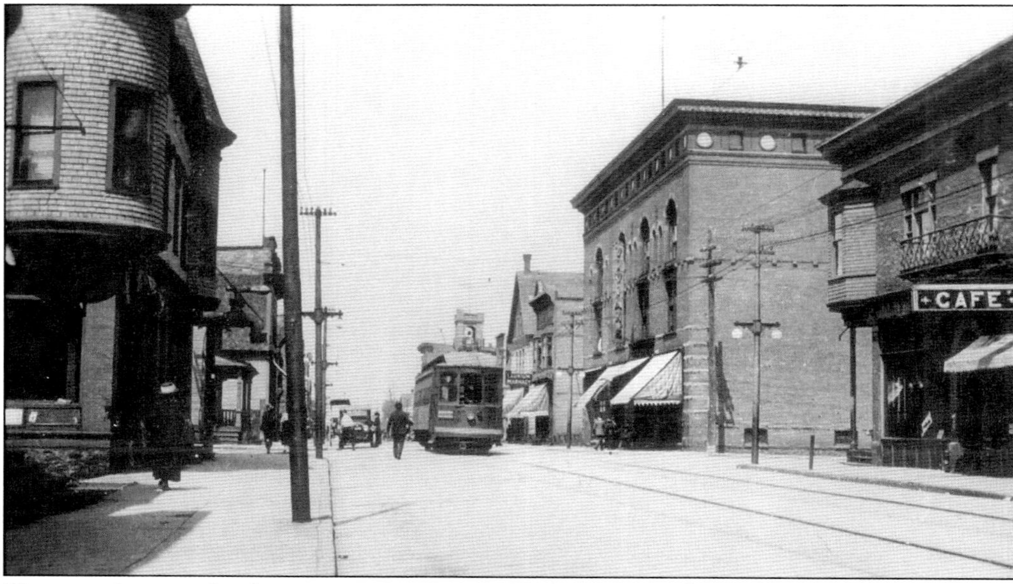

This is a photograph of a streetcar running on Hecla Street in downtown Laurium. (Houghton County Historical Society.)

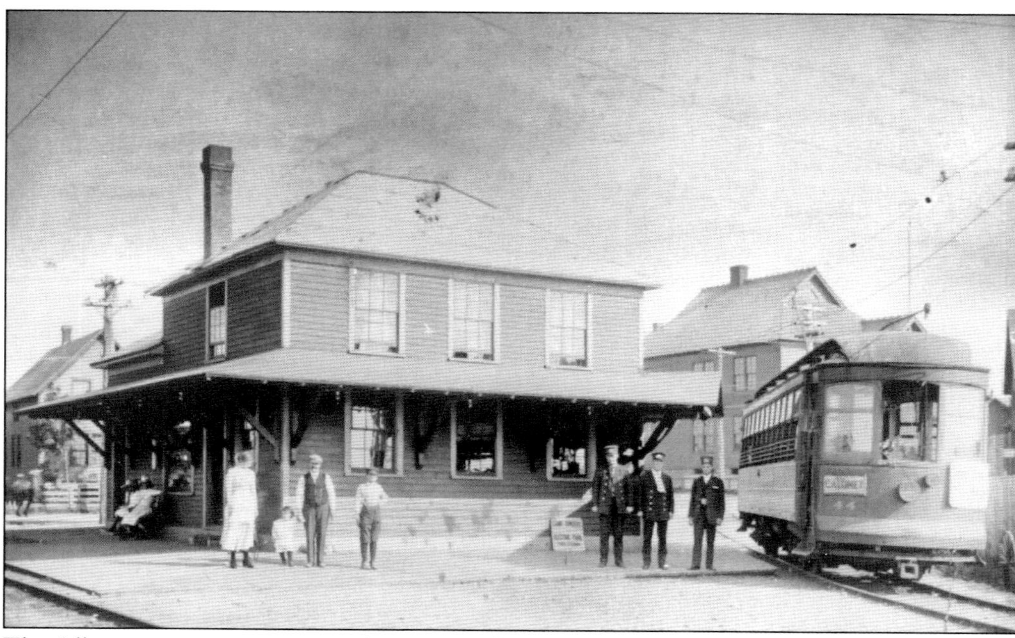

The Albion station, a major transfer junction for passengers, was operated by August Buralli. He had a confectionery store and made and sold ice cream (Peninsula brand). Today, the site is a bottle museum and glass-blowing shop. (Houghton County Historical Society.)

Another section with a steep grade (five percent) was the Lake Linden hill between Laurium and Lake Linden. Two locations on this section crossed railroad lines, but instead of trestles, underpasses were used. (Houghton County Historical Society.)

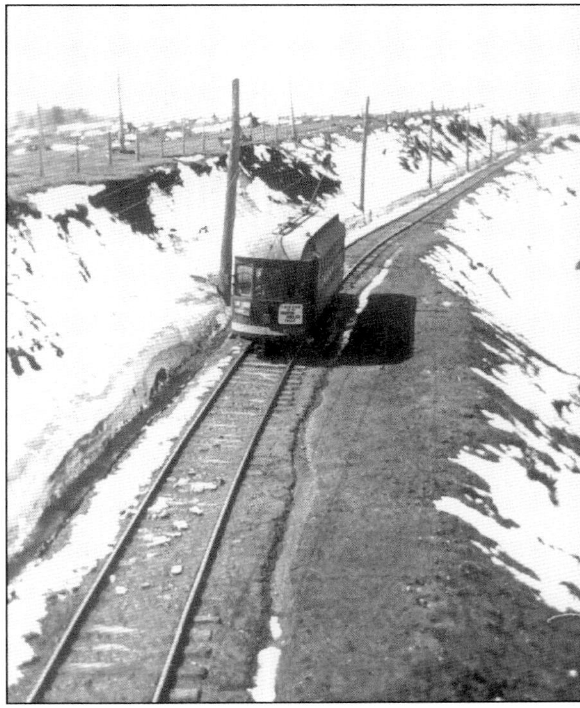

These two streetcars appear to have collided, as streetcar No. 10 jumped the track at a switch point north of Calumet. The event attracted several spectators and a photographer. (Michigan Technological University Archives/Copper Country Historical Collection.)

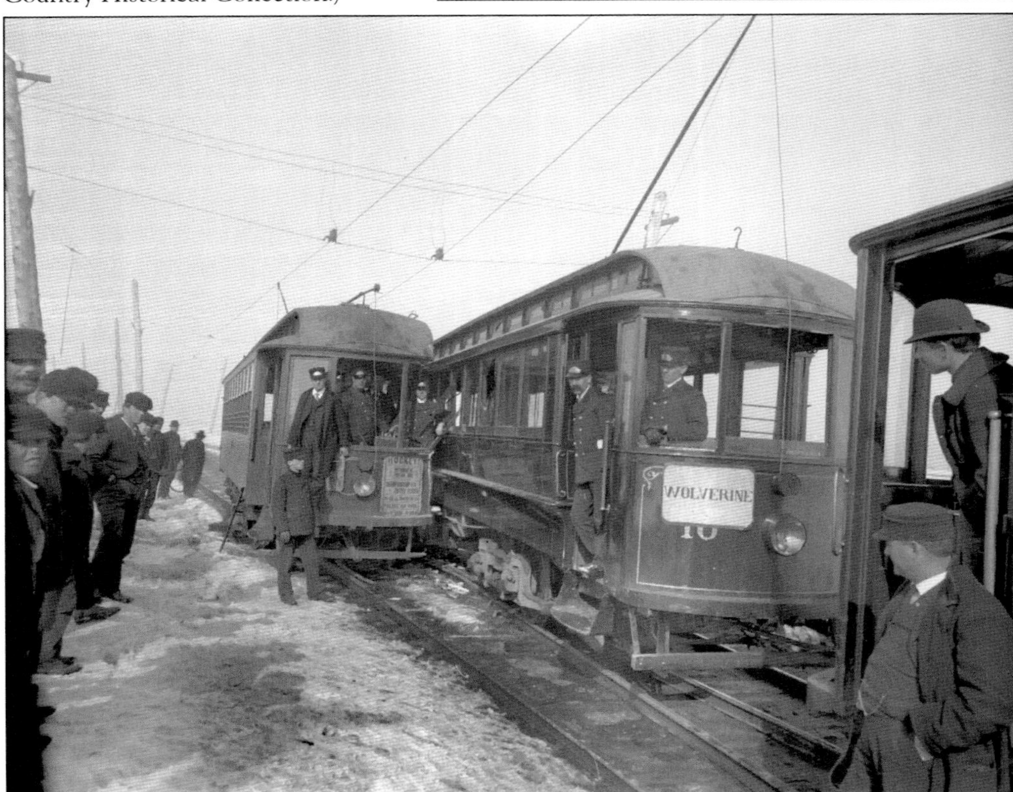

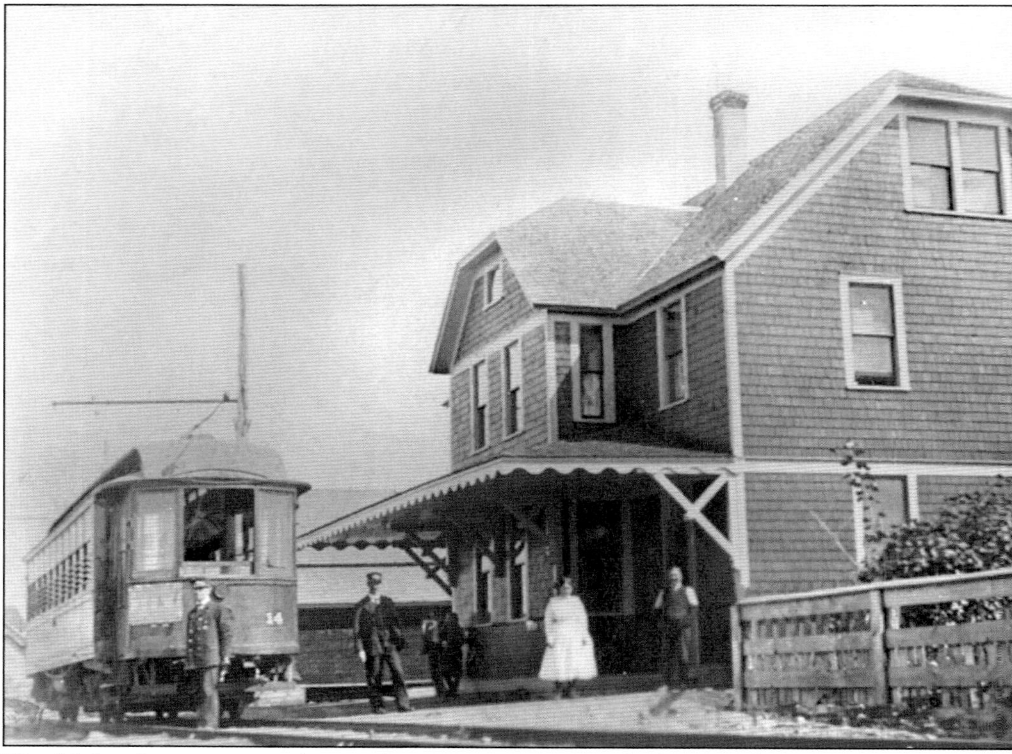

The Mohawk station was the northernmost station on the line. Mohawk was the site of the Mohawk Mining Company operations. (Houghton County Historical Society.)

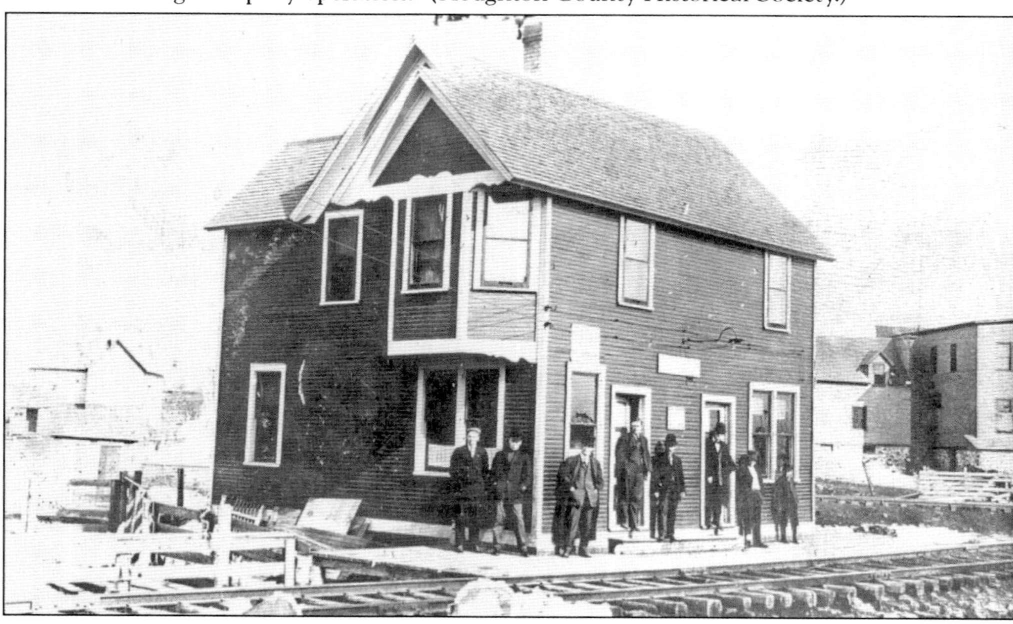

The Wolverine station was another stop on the north end of the line. Wolverine was the home for operations of the Wolverine Mining Company, one of the major copper producers in the region. (Houghton County Historical Society.)

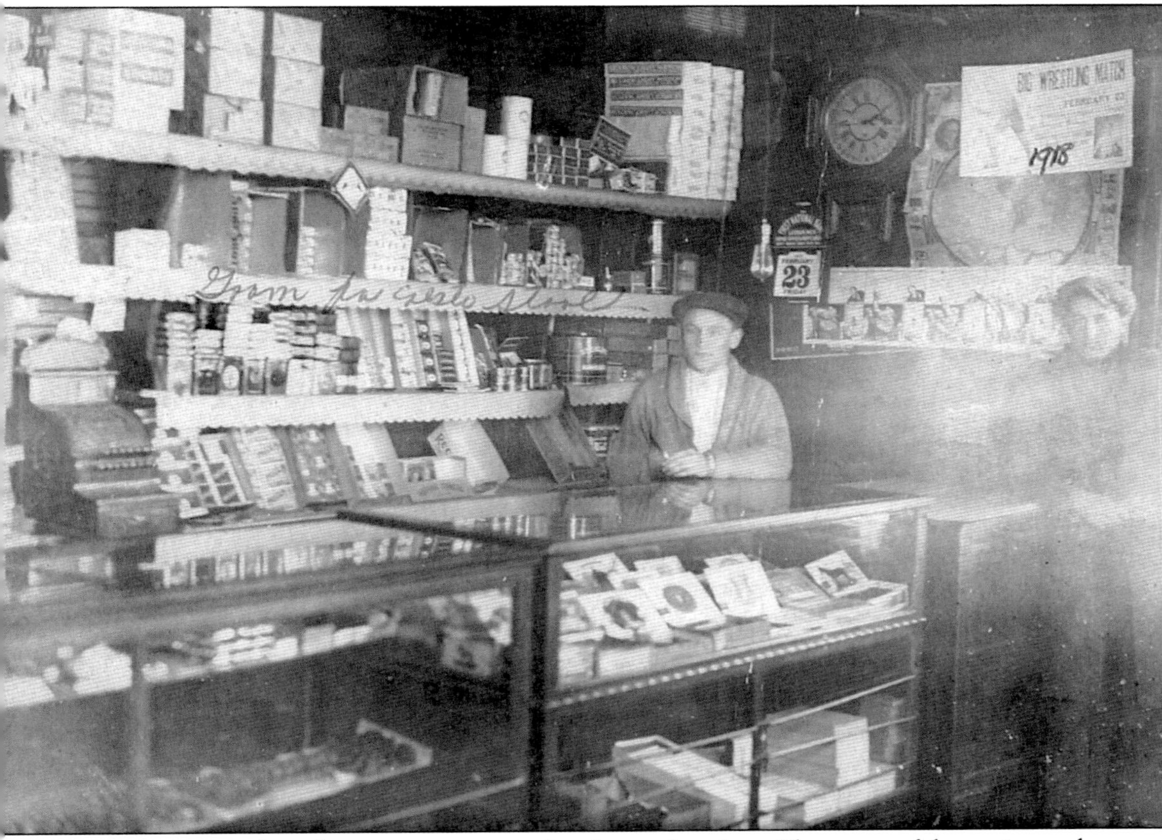

A waiting area and confectionery were typical at the rural stations. The owner of the station and his family would usually live on the second floor of the building. In the store at the Wolverine station in 1918, Albert Bullock (left) and John Marchetti pose for a photographer. (Houghton County Historical Society.)

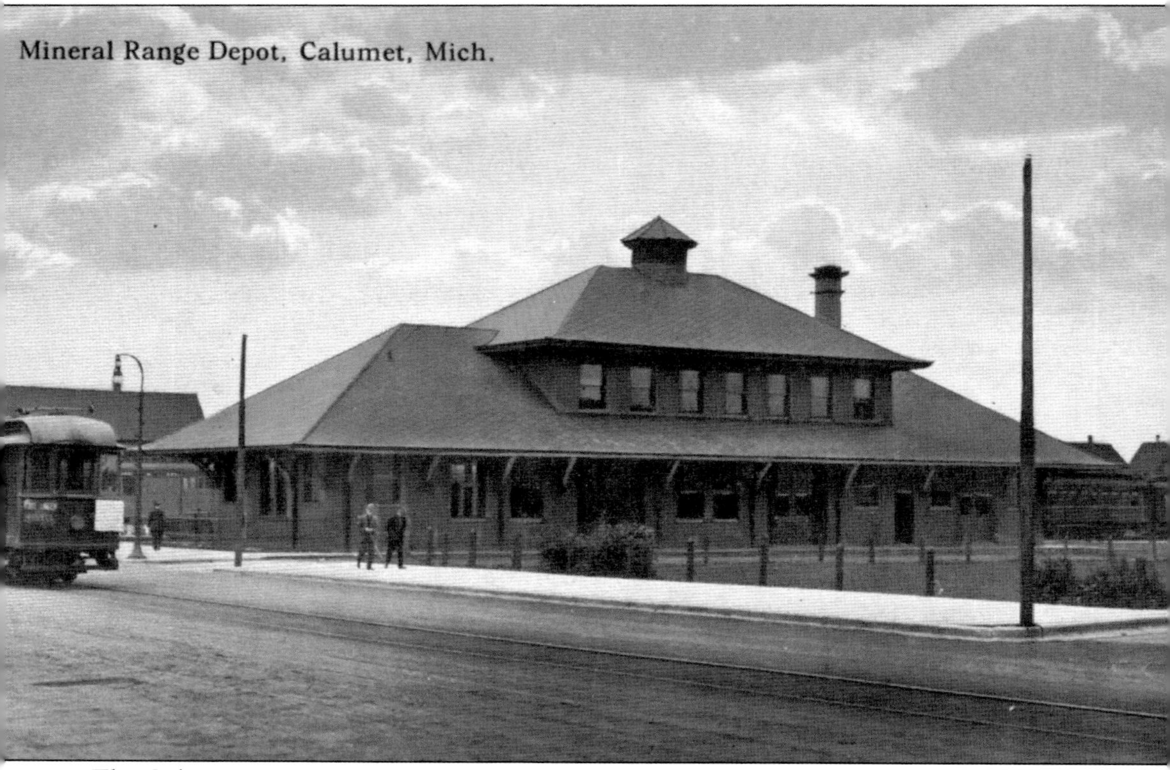

The Calumet Union station was originally built by the Mineral Range Railroad (a subsidiary of the Duluth, South, and Atlantic Railroad) and was located on Oak Street in Red Jacket. Streetcars operating on Oak Street provided service to the downtown area. A second Calumet railroad station, built by the Copper Range Railroad, was located on Pine Street. (Keweenaw National Historical Park.)

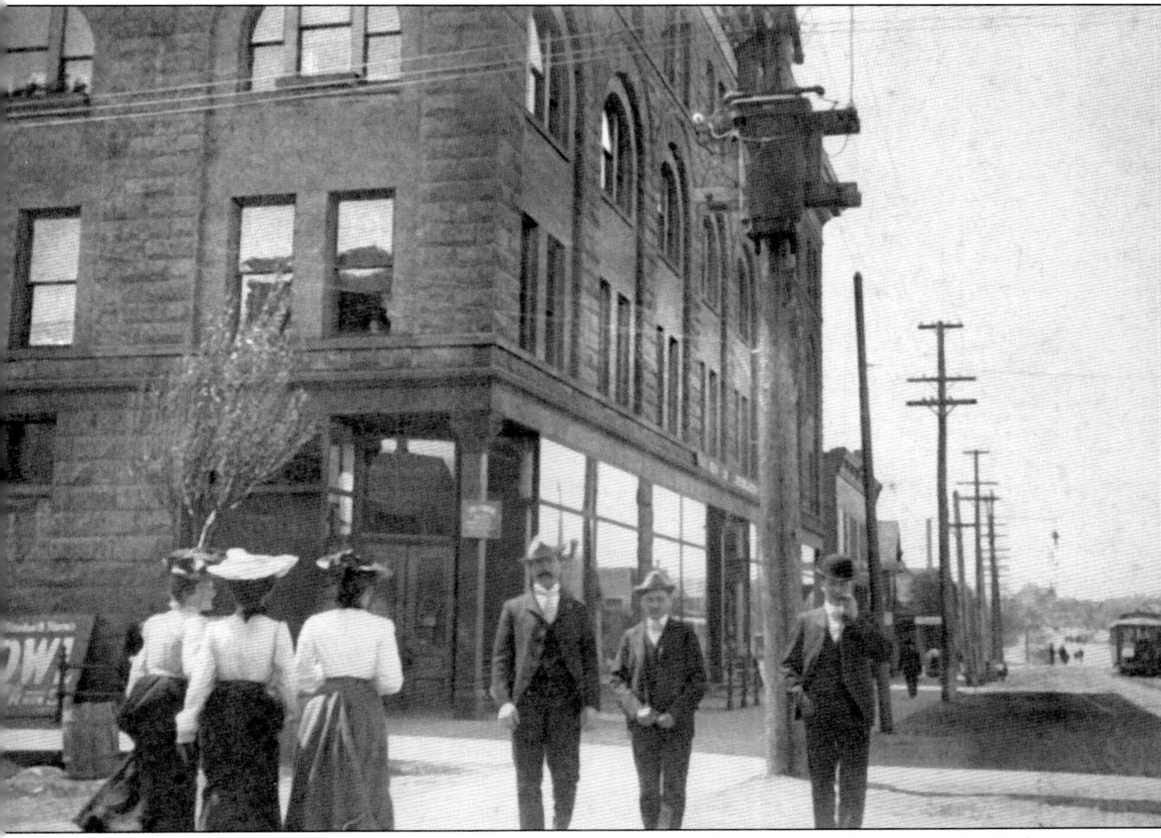

On the far right in this photograph, a streetcar operates on Oak Avenue between the Calumet Mineral Range Station and Sixth Street in Red Jacket. It ran through Red Jacket. (Michigan Technological University Archives/Copper Country Historical Collection.)

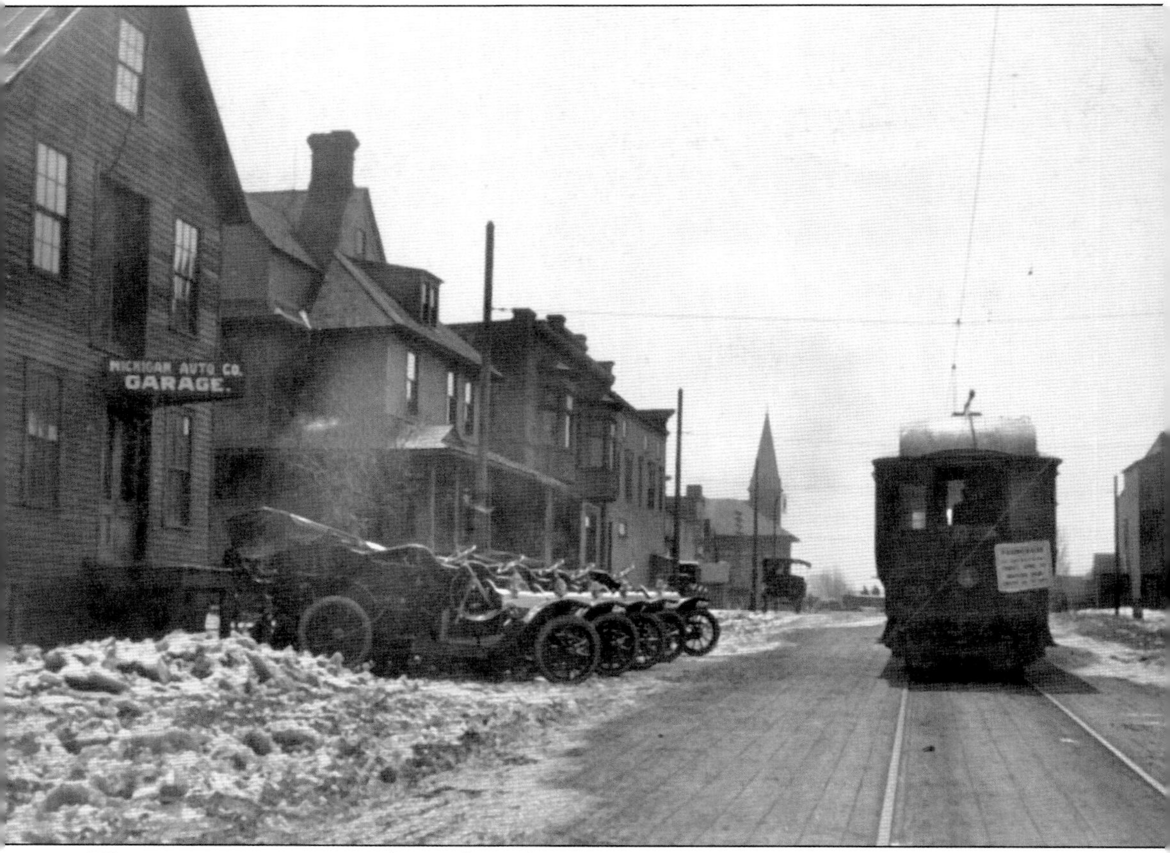

The streetcar was very popular in the Calumet area. Here, a streetcar passes the Michigan Auto Company garage in Red Jacket. (Michigan Technological University Archives/Copper Country Historical Collection.)

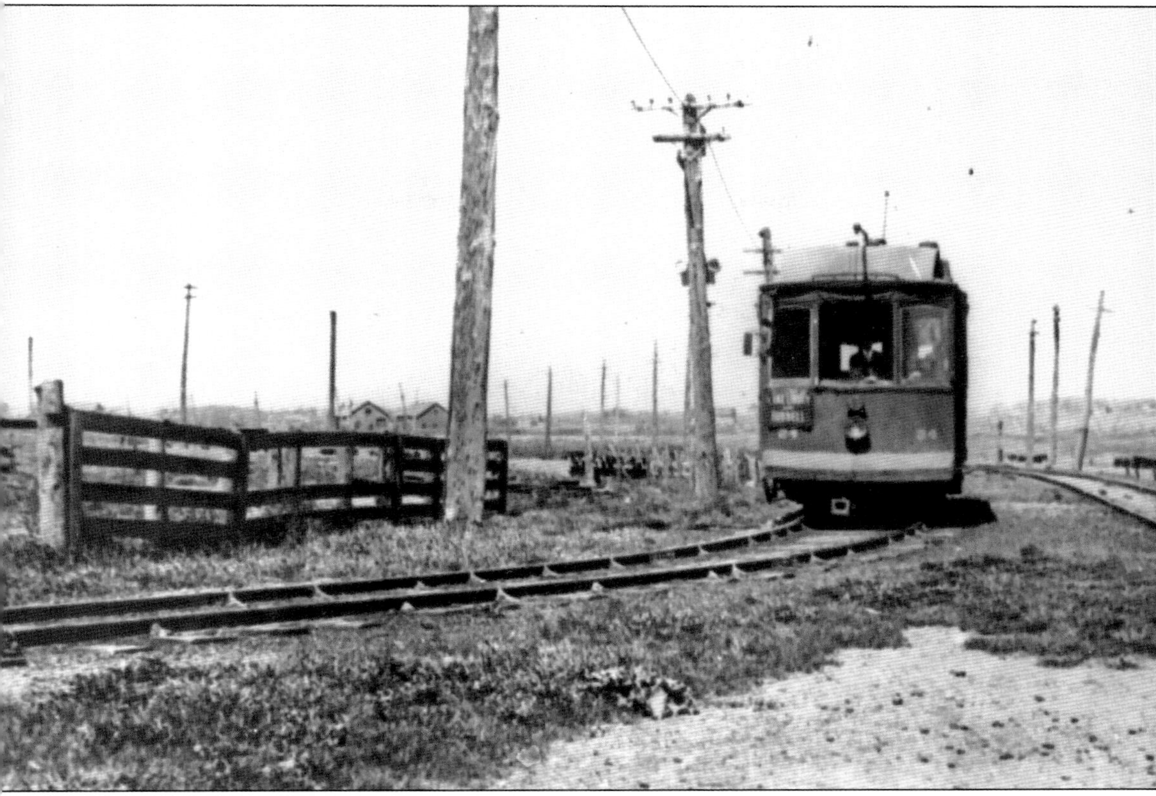

A dispute over responsibility for snow removal and fees in Lake Linden and Hubbell slowed the development of the extension of the line. It was eventually built, and service began between Calumet and Lake Linden and Hubbell in 1903. In this 1920 photograph, a streetcar on the line heads to Lake Linden and Hubbell. (Houghton County Historical Society.)

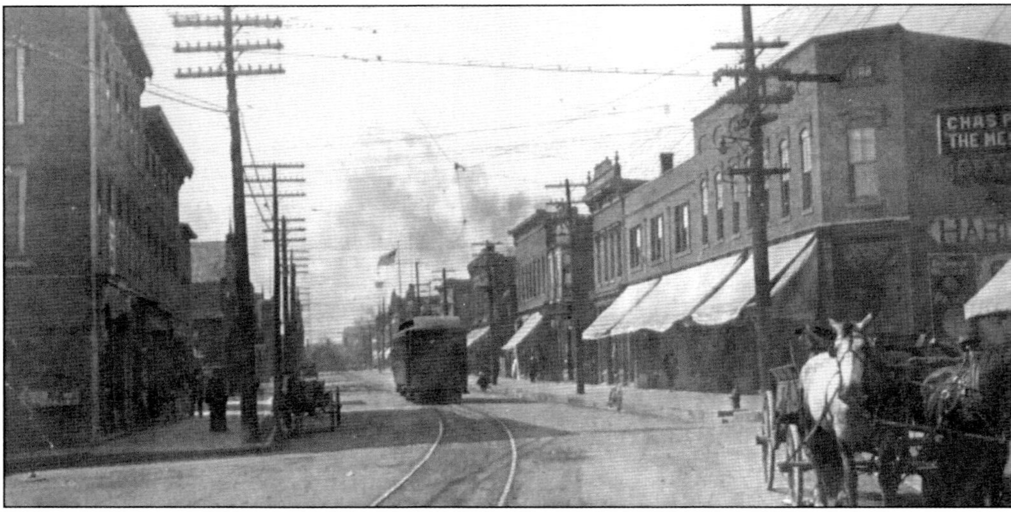

Here, a streetcar operates on Main Street in downtown Lake Linden. (Michigan Technological University Archives/Copper Country Historical Collection.)

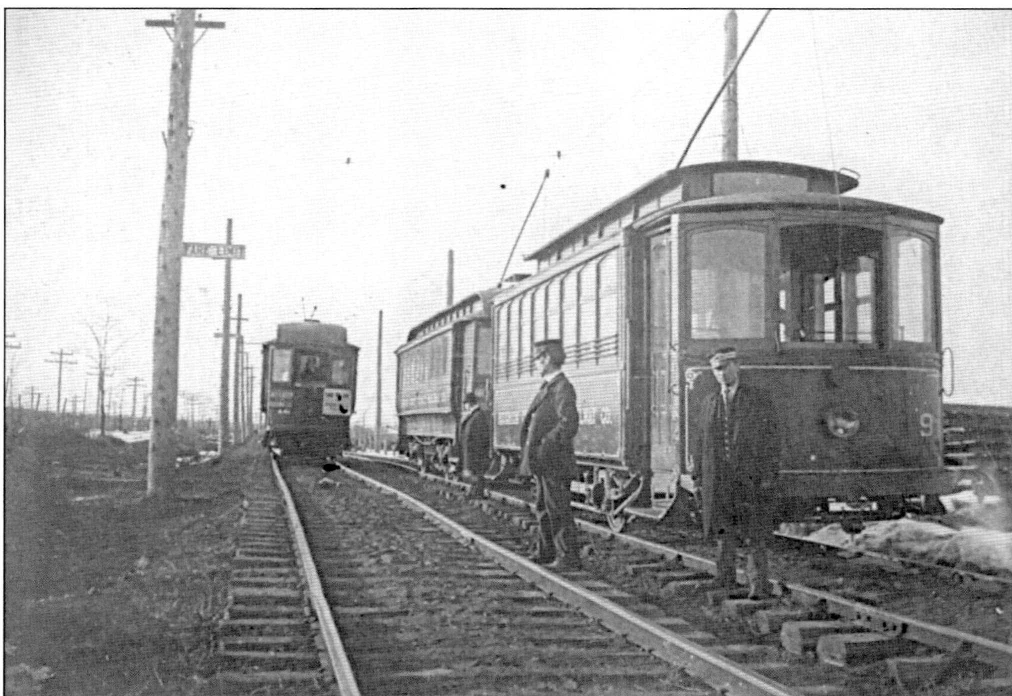

The system had a fare structure based on zones. This photograph shows streetcars at the fare limit area. Beyond this, passengers would cross into a new zone, and an additional fare would be required. Initially, adult fares were 5¢ per zone. Passengers could ride between Houghton and Hancock or between Laurium and Red Jacket for 5¢. A ride from Houghton to Red Jacket would pass through several zones, and the fare was 30¢. By the time service was abandoned in 1932, the fare had crept up to 8¢ per zone. Children could ride free on the system. (Houghton County Historical Society.)

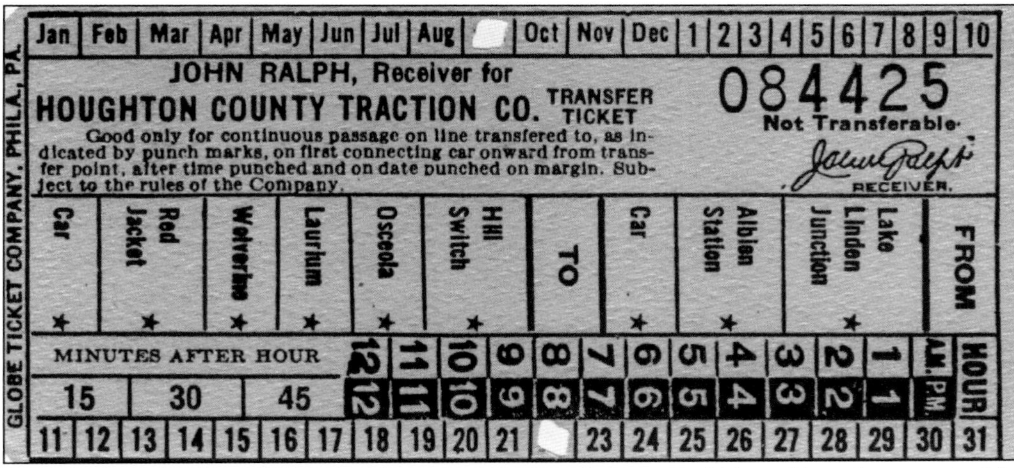

Passengers could use cash, paper tickets, or tokens, and these would be collected or punched by the conductor. Paper transfers were also available to passengers to transfer between routes for some destinations. The system also carried mail, small packages, and newspapers. (Keweenaw National Historical Park.)

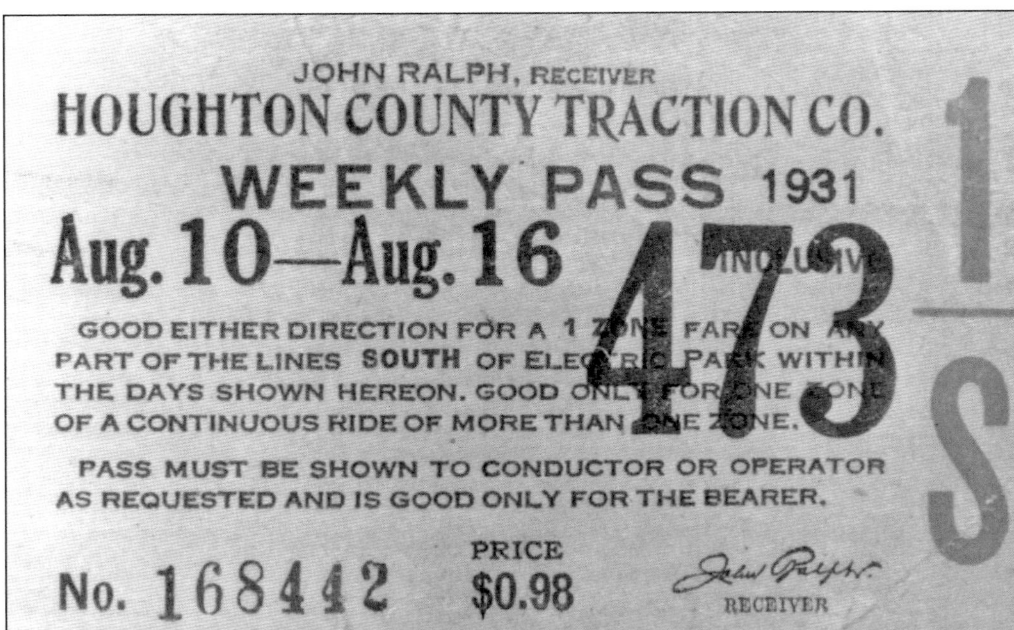

In later years, weekly passes were introduced to encourage ridership. Although they were a good idea, there was no means of verification, and riders could easily share a pass with friends or use it more than once on the same trip by passing it through the window to another rider waiting to board the car. (Houghton County Historical Society.)

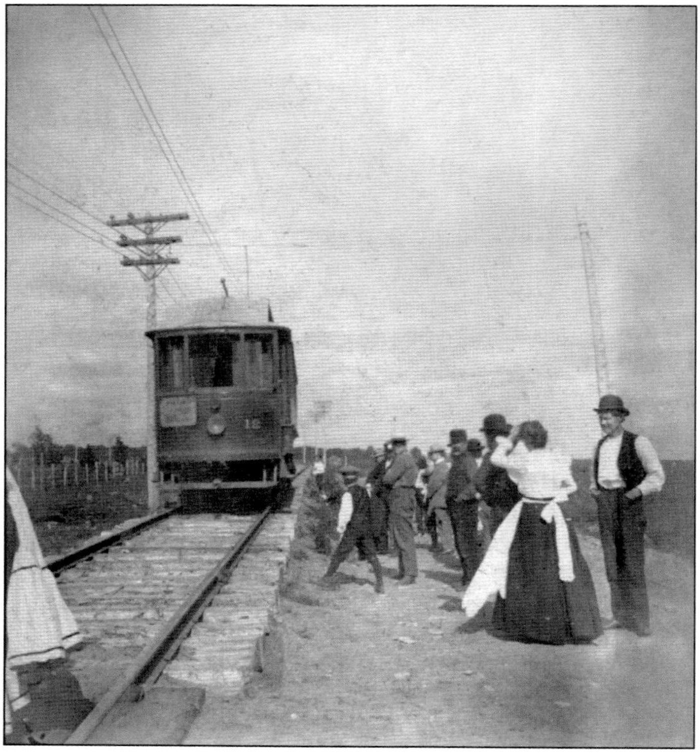

A group could rent a streetcar for $15 to $30, depending on the trip. This photograph shows a group getting ready to board streetcar No. 12. (Keweenaw National Historical Park.)

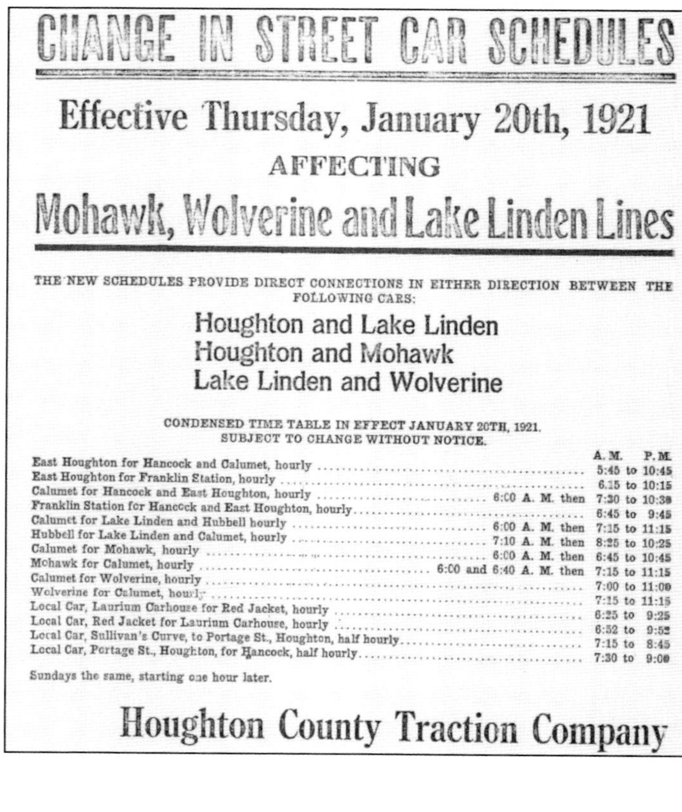

CHANGE IN STREET CAR SCHEDULES

Effective Thursday, January 20th, 1921

AFFECTING

Mohawk, Wolverine and Lake Linden Lines

THE NEW SCHEDULES PROVIDE DIRECT CONNECTIONS IN EITHER DIRECTION BETWEEN THE FOLLOWING CARS:

Houghton and Lake Linden
Houghton and Mohawk
Lake Linden and Wolverine

CONDENSED TIME TABLE IN EFFECT JANUARY 20TH, 1921.
SUBJECT TO CHANGE WITHOUT NOTICE.

		A. M.	P. M.
East Houghton for Hancock and Calumet, hourly		5:45 to	10:45
East Houghton for Franklin Station, hourly		6.15 to	10:15
Calumet for Hancock and East Houghton, hourly	6:00 A. M. then	7:30 to	10:30
Franklin Station for Hancock and East Houghton, hourly		6:45 to	9:45
Calumet for Lake Linden and Hubbell hourly	6:00 A. M. then	7:15 to	11:15
Hubbell for Lake Linden and Calumet, hourly	7:10 A. M. then	8:25 to	10:25
Calumet for Mohawk, hourly	6:00 A. M. then	6:45 to	10:45
Mohawk for Calumet, hourly	6:00 and 6:40 A. M. then	7:15 to	11:15
Calumet for Wolverine, hourly		7:00 to	11:00
Wolverine for Calumet, hourly		7:15 to	11:15
Local Car, Laurium Carhouse for Red Jacket, hourly		6:25 to	9:25
Local Car, Red Jacket for Laurium Carhouse, hourly		6:52 to	9:52
Local Car, Sullivan's Curve, to Portage St., Houghton, half hourly		7:15 to	8:45
Local Car, Portage St., Houghton, for Hancock, half hourly		7:30 to	9:00

Sundays the same, starting one hour later.

Houghton County Traction Company

This is a 1921 newspaper advertisement announcing a change in schedules; three lines were affected. (Houghton County Historical Society.)

Three

Equipment

The Houghton County Traction Company owned 25 pieces of passenger rolling stock. There were two types of cars: two-axle (single truck) small cars, called "dinkies," which were used on local or shuttle service between Houghton and Hancock and between Laurium and Red Jacket; and larger, four-axle (double truck) cars used for longer interurban distances or for operations between towns. There were four dinkies and 21 larger cars, and each was identified by a number. The cars were ordered from prominent car builders of the era: the J.G. Brill Company, the Laconia Car Company, and the G.C. Kulman Company. The original car No. 22 was damaged in a fire, so the shop combined the shorter car nos. 3 and 5 to produce the largest car in the fleet and renumbered it 22. Despite the difference in builders and length, all cars were built to the same mechanical and structural specifications. All cars were double-ended with control stands at either end of the car, allowing the car operator, when the end of the line was reached, to simply walk to the other end of the car and begin operations in the opposite direction. This feature eliminated the need for loops or turntables. All cars were powered from an overhead electric wire, and the motors were General Electric models 67 or 80 that produced top speeds of 30 to 40 miles per hour. The seating in a car was arranged either longitudinal, along the sides of the car, or coach seating, in which passengers were seated in the direction of travel. Larger cars were designed to seat about 50 passengers, but during special events 60 to 100 riders were common in a car. The longitudinal seating was popular for local operations. The initial cars were heated by coal stoves, while later orders had electric heaters. Most of the cars had wooden bodies, and all cars were painted olive green with white lettering. In addition to passenger cars, there were six pieces of equipment for handling snow and keeping lines open during the winter months.

Passenger Car Equipment Roster								
No.	Builder	Trucks	Motors	Controls	Length	Speed	Purchase Date	Price
3	Brill	Brill 21E	2 GE67	K-10	30' 0"	25	08/01/01	$3,505.50
5	Brill	Brill 21E	2 GE67	K-10	30' 0"	25	08/01/01	$3,505.50
6	Laconia	Peck 14B3	4 GE67	C-6	39' 0"	32	10/01/00	$7,085.00
7	Brill	Brill 21E	2 GE67	K-10	30' 0"	25	08/01/01	$3,505.50
8	Laconia	Peck 14B3	4 GE67	C-6	39' 0"	32	10/01/00	$7,085.00
9	Brill	Brill 21E	2 GE67	K-10	30' 0"	25	08/01/01	$3,505.50
10	Laconia	Peck 14B3	4 GE67	C-6	39' 0"	32	10/01/00	$6,235.00
12	Laconia	Peck 14B3	4 GE67	C-6	39' 0"	32	10/01/00	$6,235.00
14	Laconia	Peck 14B3	4 GE67	K-6	39' 0"	32	01/01/01	$6,235.00
16	Laconia	Peck 14B3	4 GE67	K-6	39' 0"	32	01/01/01	$7,085.00
18	Laconia	Peck 14B3	4 GE67	K-6	39' 0"	32	01/01/01	$7,085.00
20	Laconia	Peck 14B3	4 GE67	K-6	39' 0"	32	01/01/01	$6,235.00
22	Brill	Brill 27G	4 GE67	C-6	40' 6"	32	08/01/01	$7,185.00
24	Brill	Brill 27G	4 GE67	C-6	40' 6"	32	08/01/01	$7,185.00
26	Brill	Brill 27G	4 GE67	C-6	40' 6"	32	08/01/01	$7,185.00
28	Brill	Brill 27G	4 GE67	C-6	40' 6"	32	08/01/01	$7,185.00
30	Brill	Brill 27G	4 GE67	C-6	40' 6"	32	08/01/03	$7,185.00
32	Brill	Brill 27G	4 GE67	C-6	40' 6"	32	08/01/03	$7,185.00
34	Brill	Brill 27G	4 GE67	C-6	40' 6"	32	08/01/03	$7,185.00
36	Brill	Brill 27G	4 GE80	K-28J	42' 9"	32	NA	NA
38	Brill	Brill 27G	4 GE80	K-28J	42' 9"	32	NA	NA
40	Brill	Brill 27G	4 GE80	K-28J	42' 9"	32	NA	NA
42	Brill	Brill 27G	4 GE80	K-28J	42' 9"	32	NA	NA
44	Kuhlman	Brill 27G	4 GE80	K-28J	42' 9"	32	NA	NA
48	Kuhlman	Brill 27G	4 GE80	K-28J	42' 9"	32	NA	NA
22 (2nd)	CO. Shops	Brill 27G	4 GE67	NA	44' 6"	32	NA	NA

Snow Fighting Equipment Roster							
No.	Builder	Trucks	Motors	Controls	Speed	Purchase Date	Price
1	Taunton	Taunton	2 GE67	K-10	15	NA	$2,995.80
2	Taunton	Taunton	2 GE67	K-10	15	NA	$2,995.80
3	Taunton	Taunton	2 GE67	K-10	15	NA	$2,995.80
4	Taunton	Taunton	4 GE57	2 K-14	20	01/01/01	$2,995.80
5	Ruggles	Peck 14B6	4 GE57	2 K-14	20	08/01/03	$6,325.52
6	Ruggles	Peck S.T.	2 GE57	2 K-11	20	10/01/00	$3,844.00

This list identifies the equipment used by the company. Specifications for each piece of equipment included purchase date, price, and builder. (Chad Hewitt.)

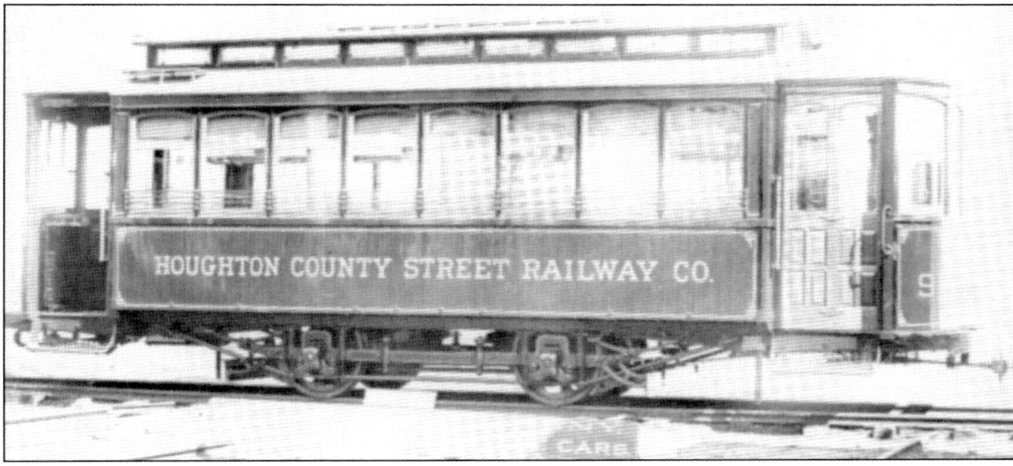

Smaller cars, called "dinkies," were used for local or shuttle operations. They had two axles and could be handled by one man. There were four dinkies, Nos. 3, 5, 7, and 9, all manufactured by the Brill Company. This photograph shows dinky streetcar No. 9. (Houghton County Historical Society.)

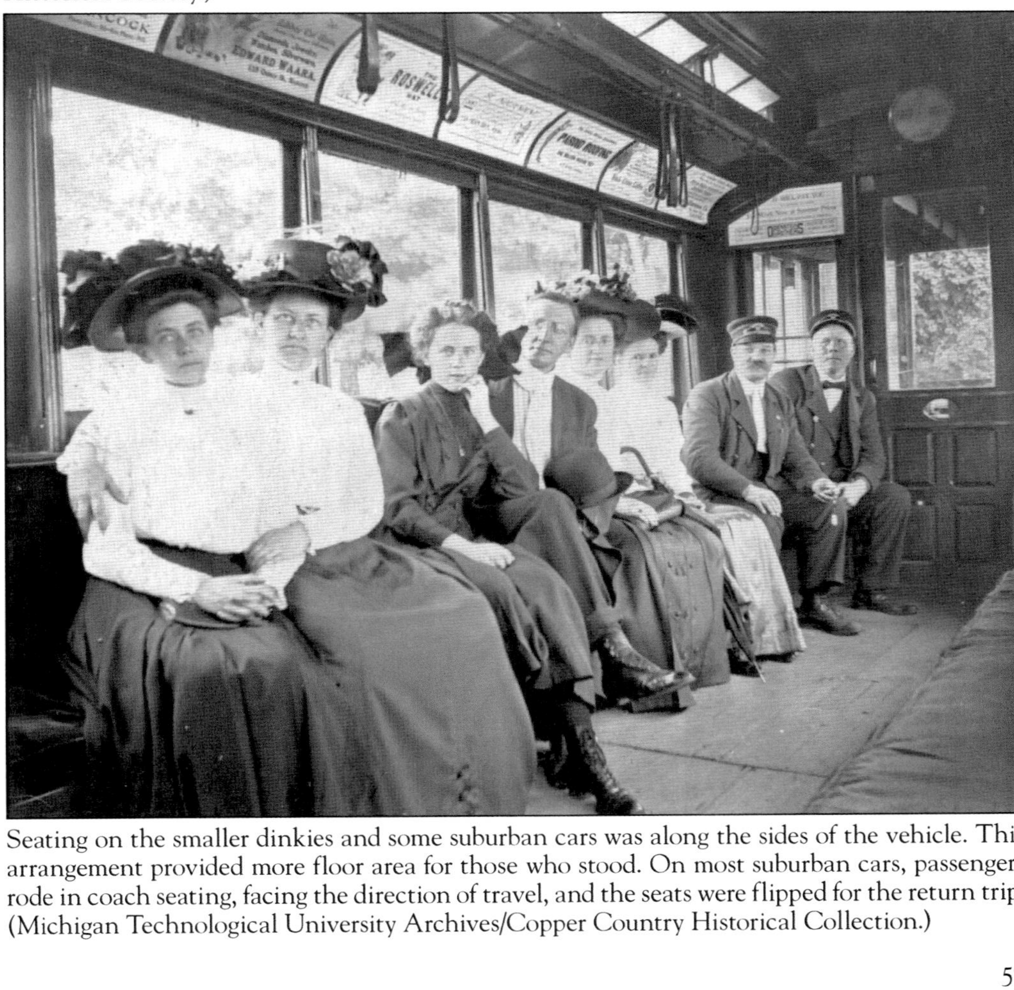

Seating on the smaller dinkies and some suburban cars was along the sides of the vehicle. This arrangement provided more floor area for those who stood. On most suburban cars, passengers rode in coach seating, facing the direction of travel, and the seats were flipped for the return trip. (Michigan Technological University Archives/Copper Country Historical Collection.)

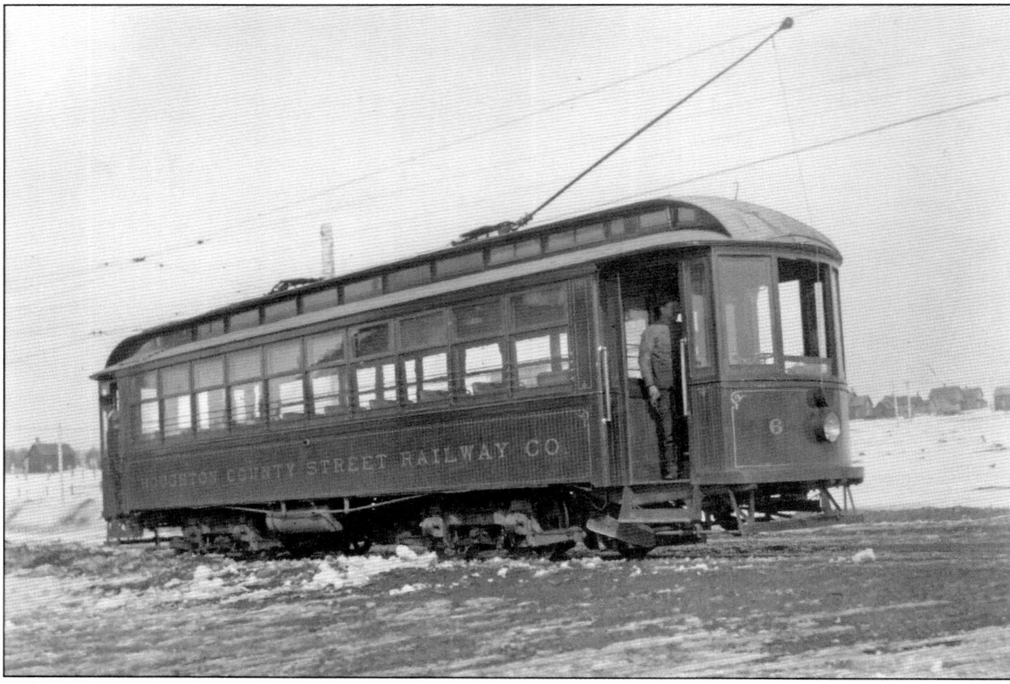

All cars were powered from an overhead electric source suspended from adjacent poles and could be operated in both directions. No. 6 is an example of an interurban car that was used for trips between towns. A person could board this car in Houghton and travel to the Calumet area. (Michigan Technological University Archives/Copper Country Historical Collection.)

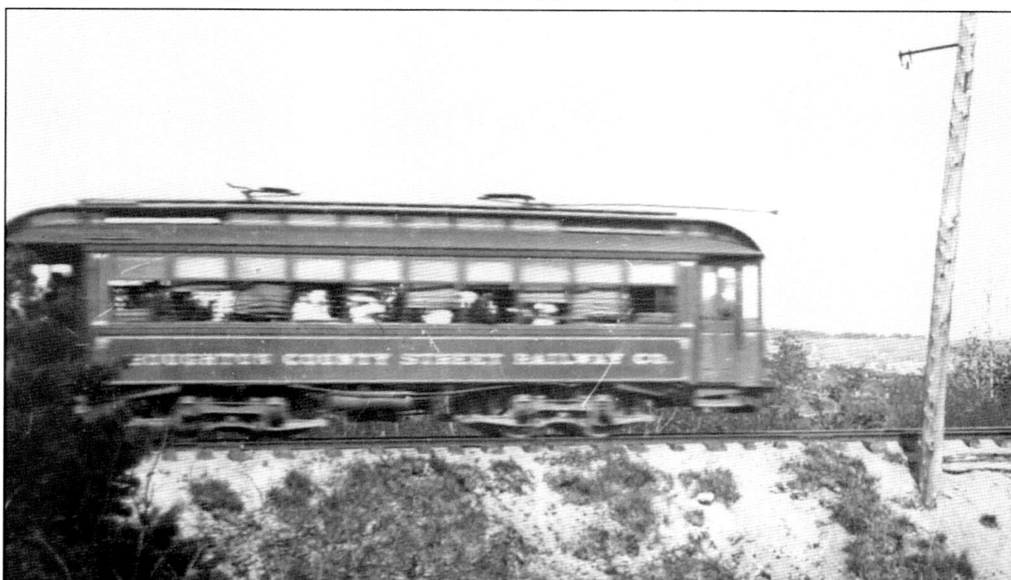

In the early years, the system was known as the Houghton County Street Railway Company. Streetcar No. 6, seen here speeding between Hancock and Calumet, was manufactured by Laconia. Interurbans were about 40 feet long and could operate at top speeds approaching 40 miles per hour. (Houghton County Historical Society.)

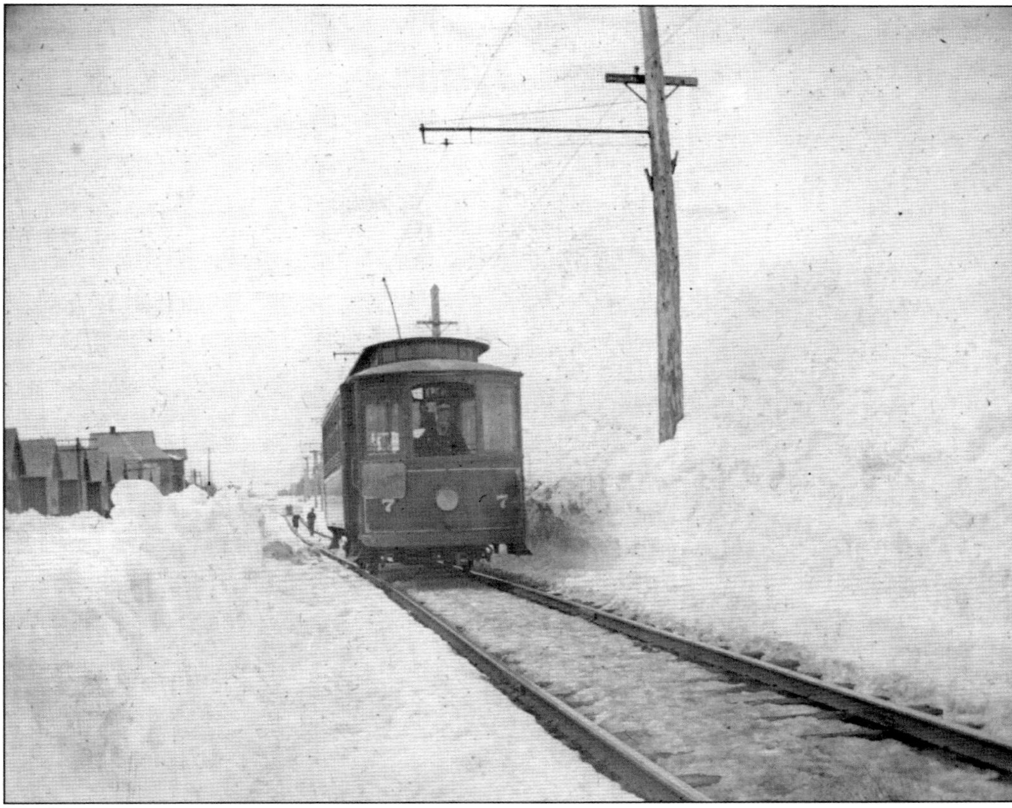

Streetcar No. 7 was a dinky manufactured by Brill. Dinkies were about 30 feet long and could operate at a top speed of 25 to 30 miles per hour. (Keweenaw National Historical Park.)

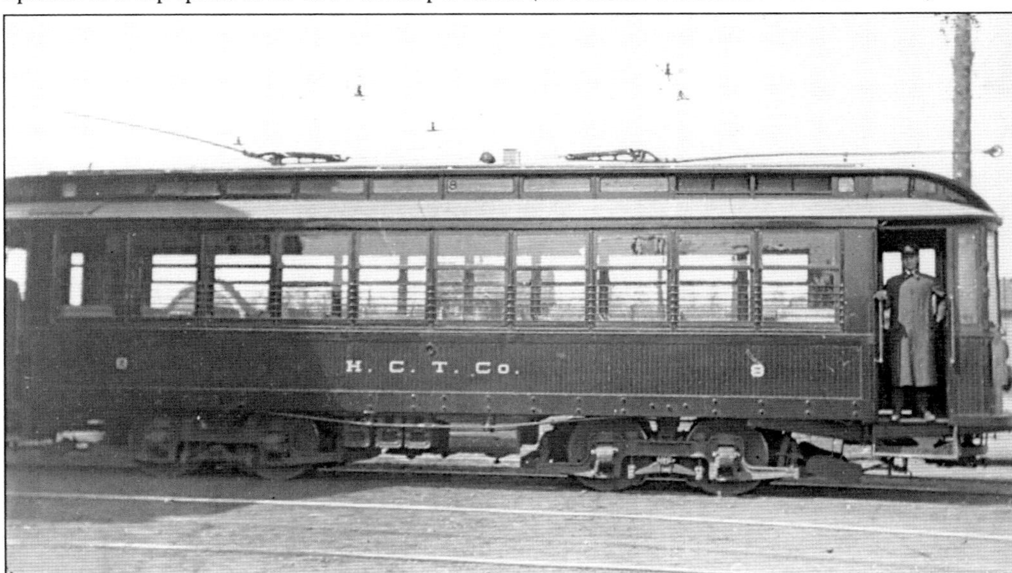

No. 8 was an interurban car manufactured by Laconia. Interurban cars had four axles and were be manned by two-person crews. (Houghton County Historical Society.)

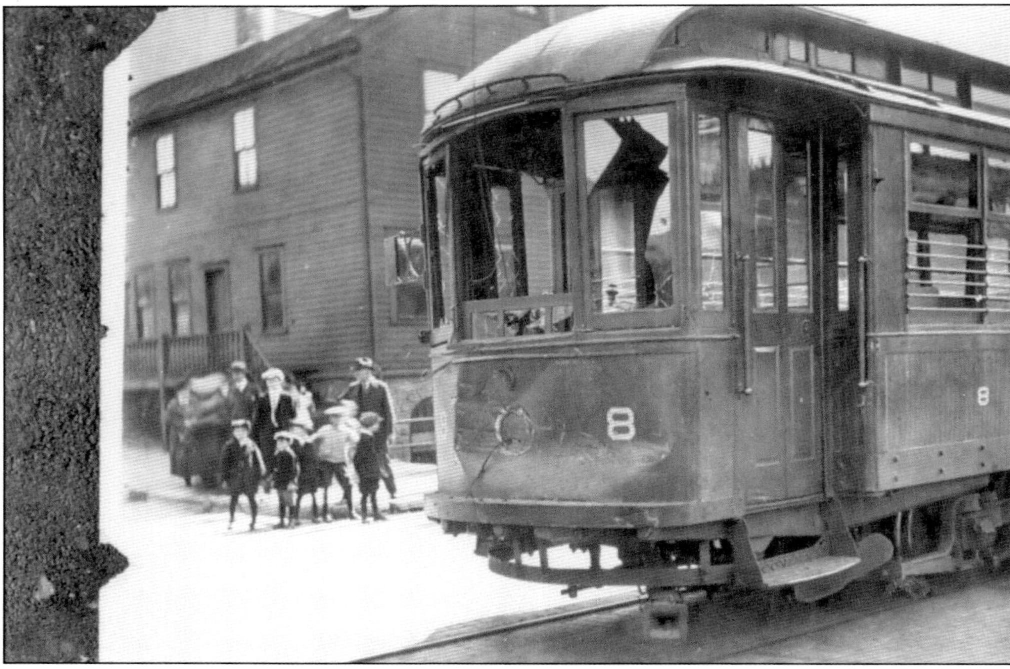

Streetcar No. 8 was damaged during a strike by employees in 1908. The strike lasted a few days before the dispute was resolved. (Houghton County Historical Society.)

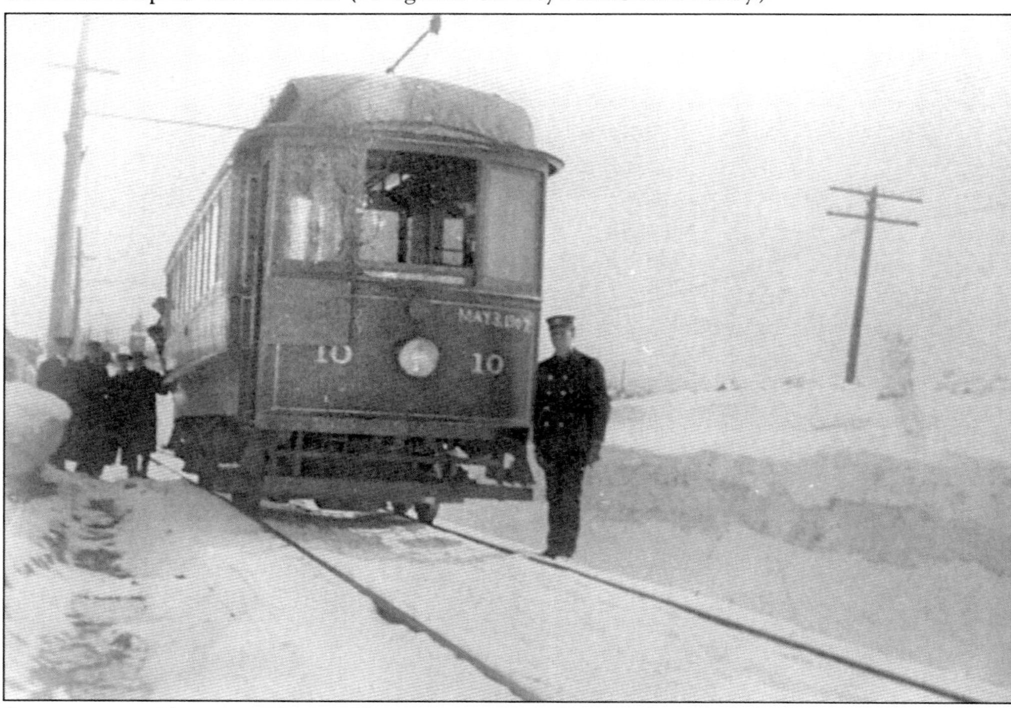

Streetcars could stop on demand between stations for boarding and alighting of passengers. A system of bells and whistles was used to notify passengers of stops. This photograph shows streetcar No. 10 stopped on a winter day to pick up passengers. (Houghton County Historical Society.)

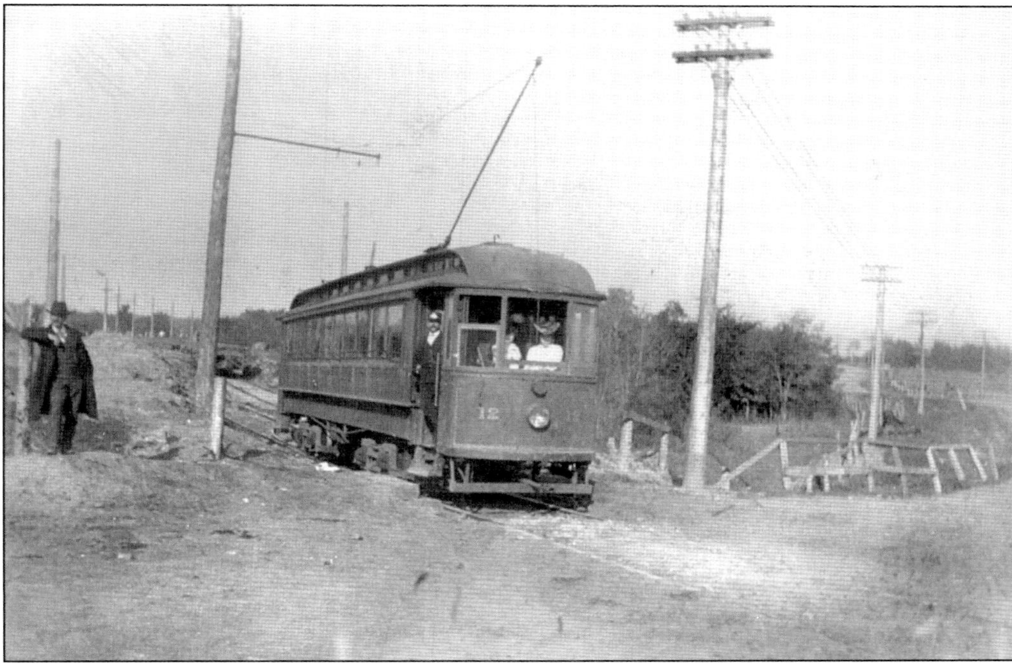

No. 12, an interurban car manufactured by Laconia, was one of the original vehicles purchased in 1900. In rural areas outside of towns, vehicles operated on tracks with *T*-section rails laid on native cedar ties similar to a typical railroad. (Houghton County Historical Society.)

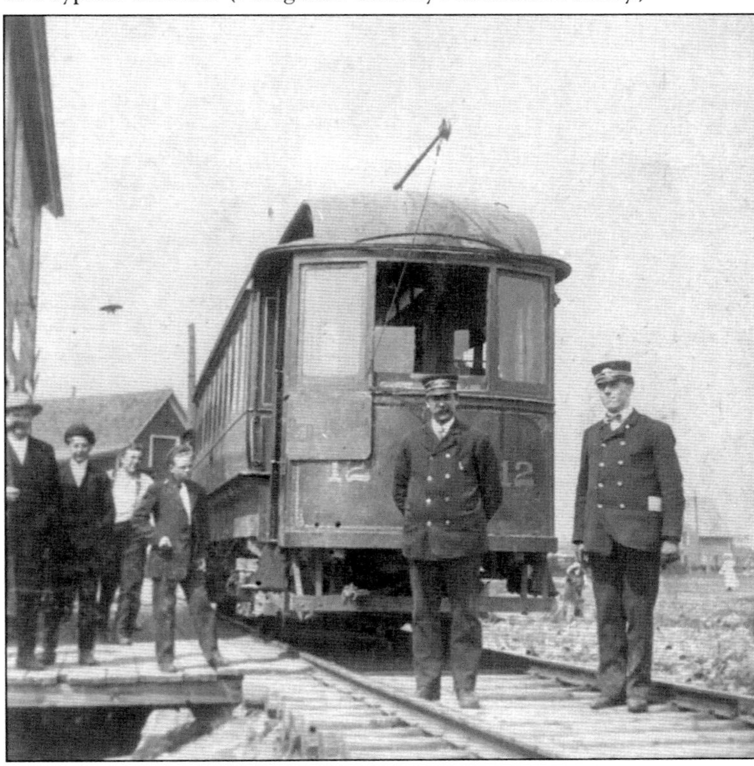

Streetcar No. 12 is seen here with its motorman and conductor. The motorman drove the car, and the conductor punched tickets, handled fares, and assisted passengers as needed. A typical daily shift was 10 hours. A second conductor was often added during special-event service. (Houghton County Historical Society.)

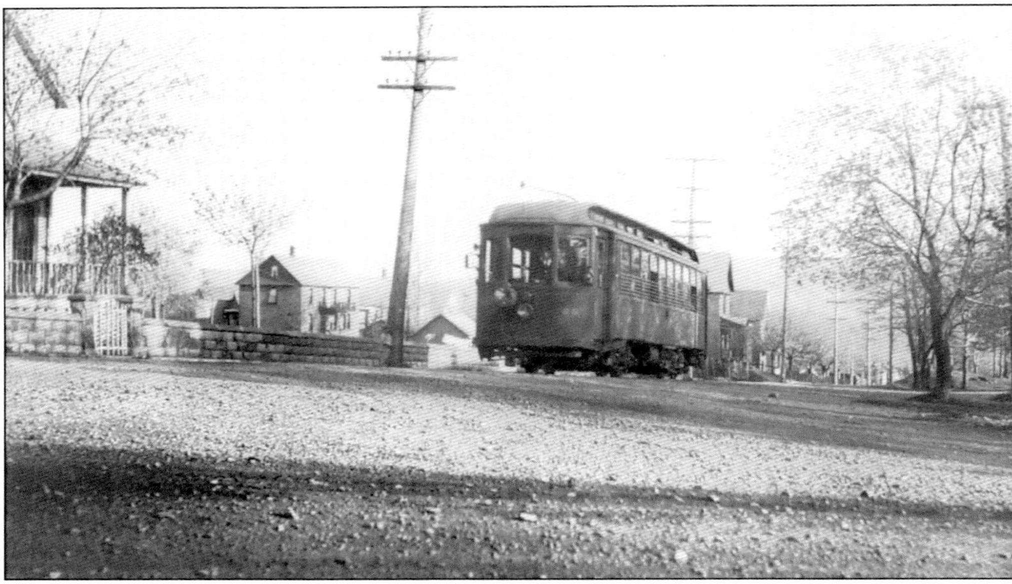

No. 26, an interurban car manufactured by Brill, is shown running on city streets. Initially, T-section rails were used, since most streets were not paved. Within a few years, however, girder section rail was used, and streets were paved with bricks. (Houghton County Historical Society.)

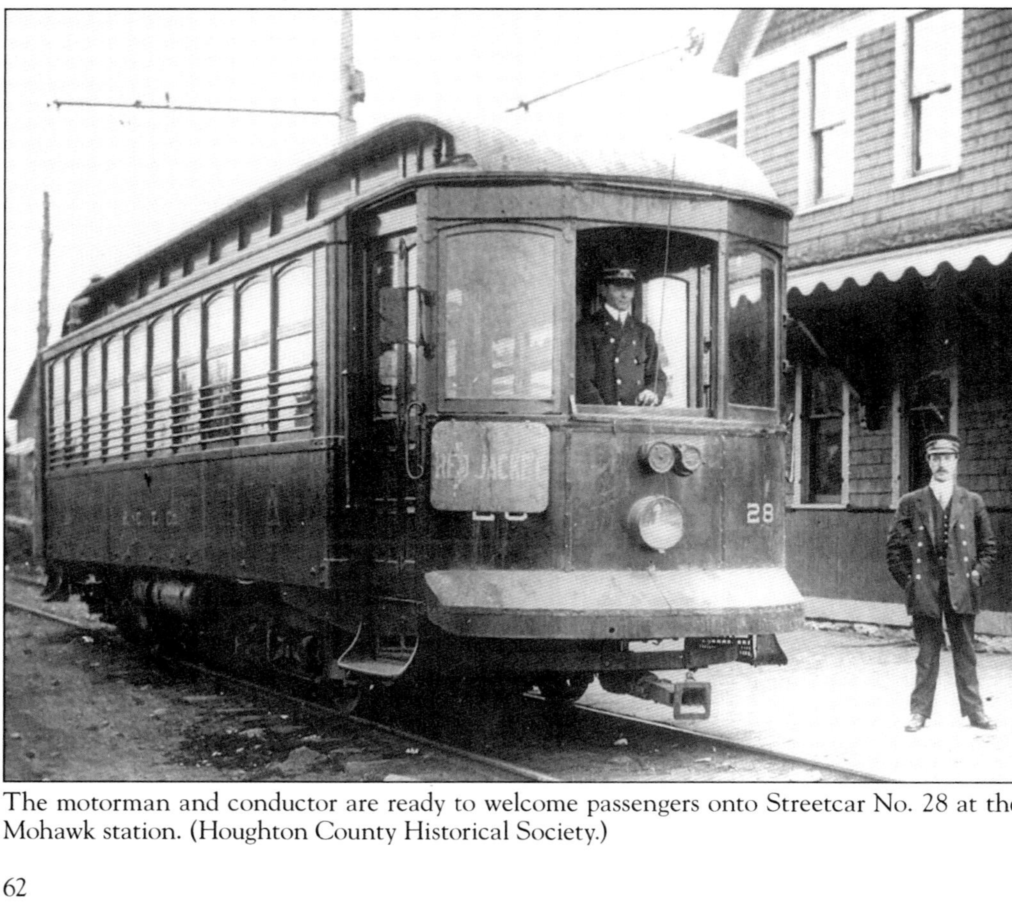

The motorman and conductor are ready to welcome passengers onto Streetcar No. 28 at the Mohawk station. (Houghton County Historical Society.)

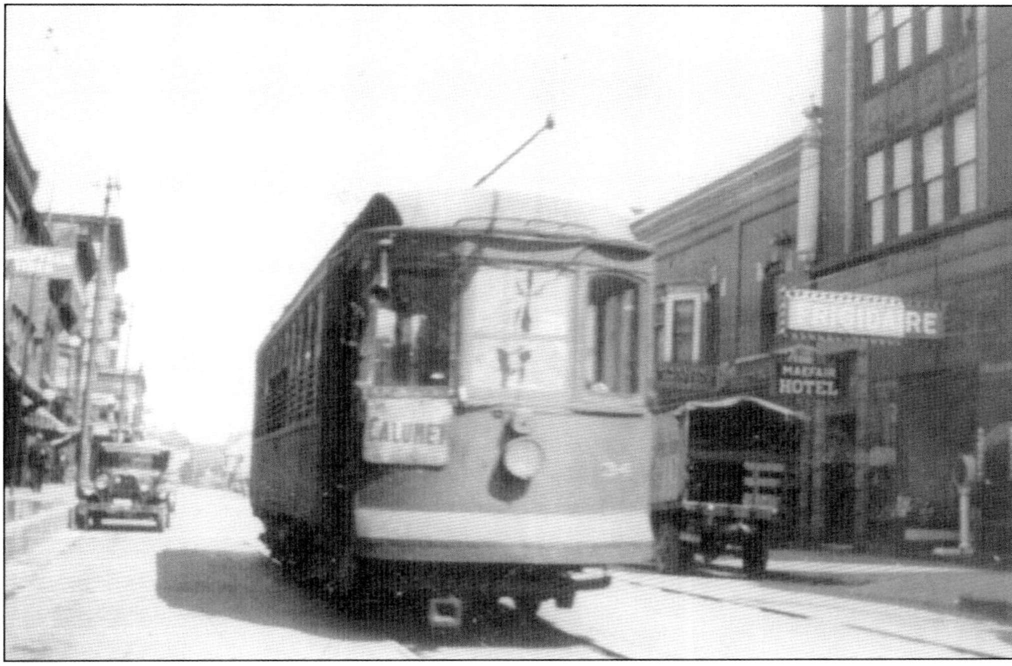

Interurban streetcar No. 34 was manufactured by Brill. It is seen here in street operations. (Houghton County Historical Society.)

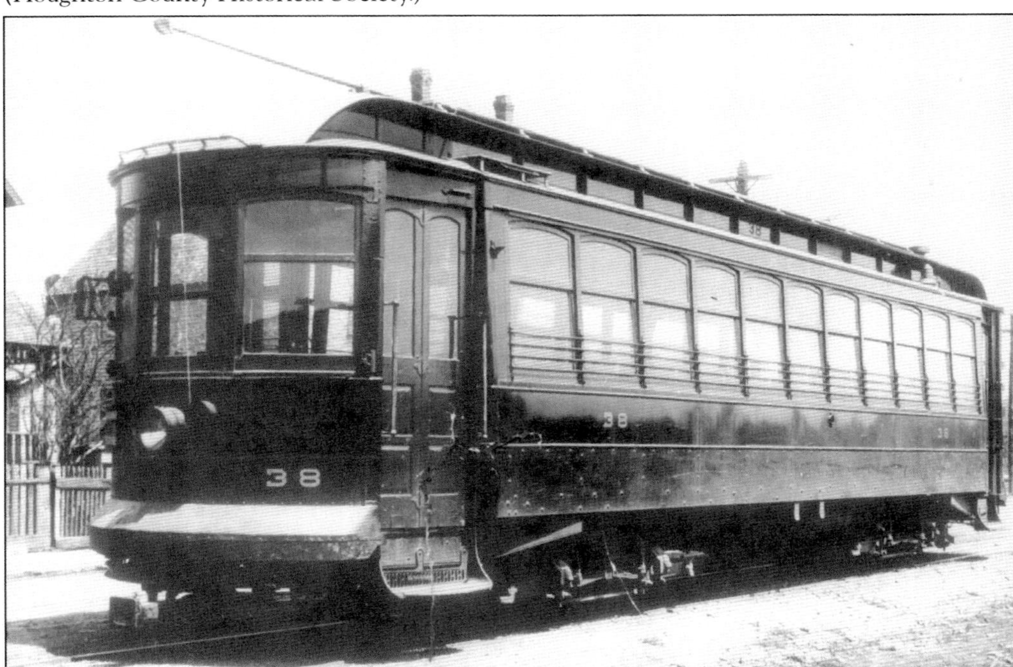

Also manufactured by Brill, No. 38 was one of the longest interurban cars at almost 43 feet. The dual trolley poles and controls on both ends, typical of interurbans, facilitated running in either direction. (Houghton County Historical Society.)

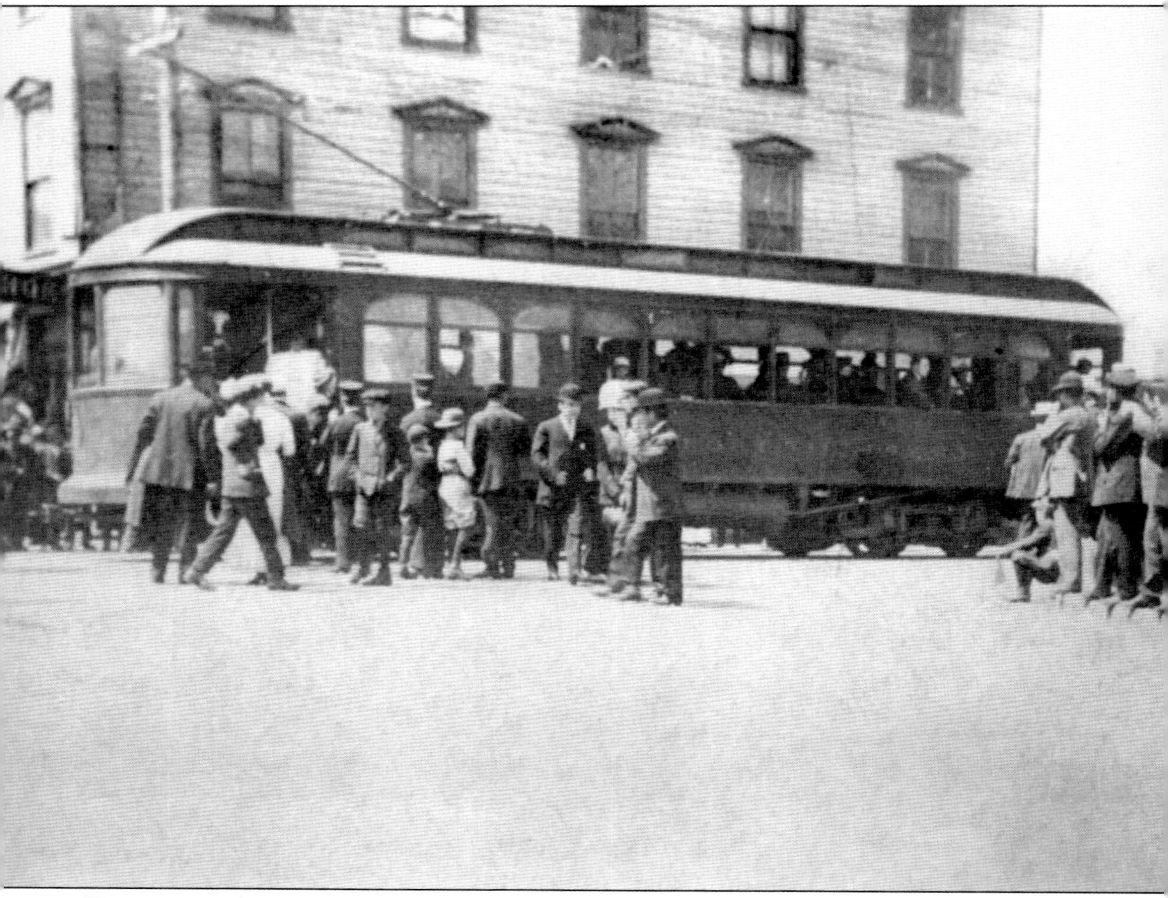

During special-event service, two conductors were necessary to permit loading from two doors. (Houghton County Historical Society.)

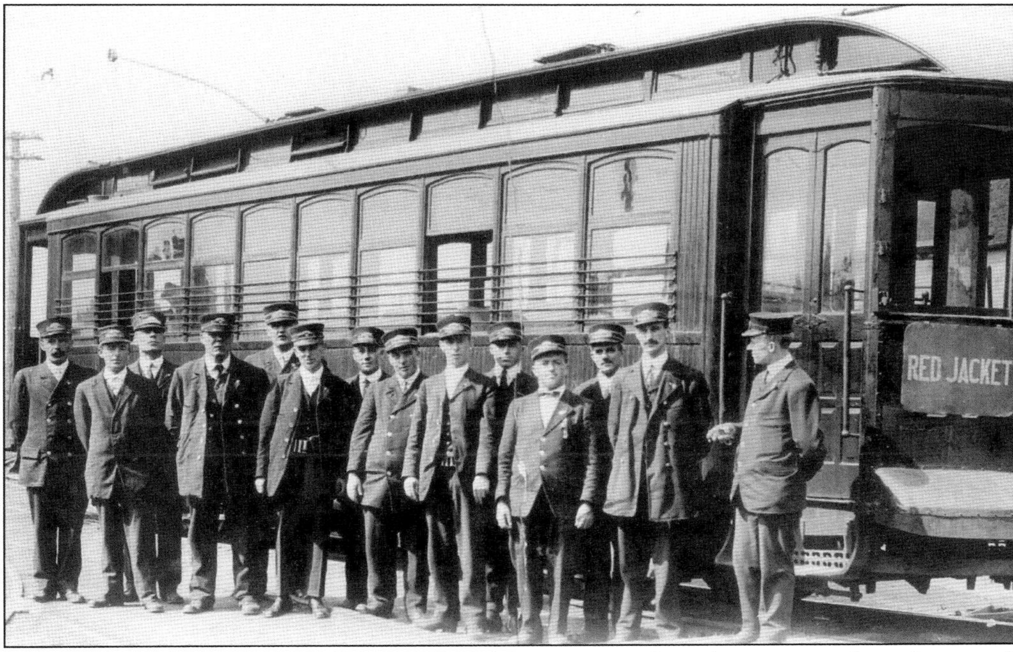

Houghton County Traction Company (HCTC) motormen and conductors pause for a photograph at the Laurium carbarn. Everyone likes to have their picture taken. (Houghton County Historical Society.)

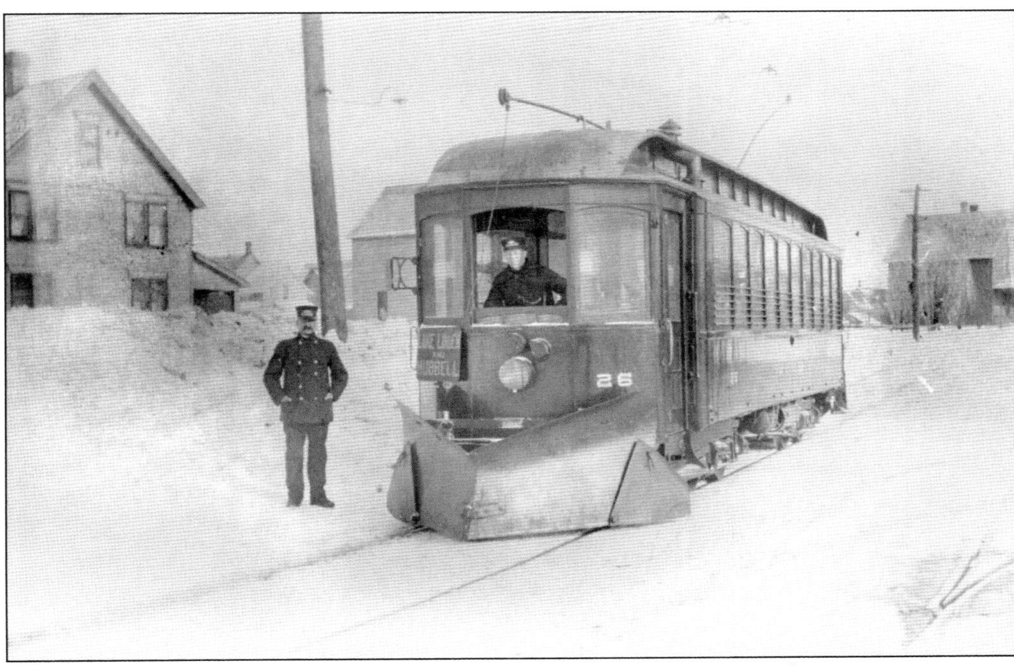

In the winter, small plows or scrapers were installed on a few of the Brill cars. Here, streetcar No. 26 is equipped with a small plow to keep the tracks clear of snow. (Houghton County Historical Society.)

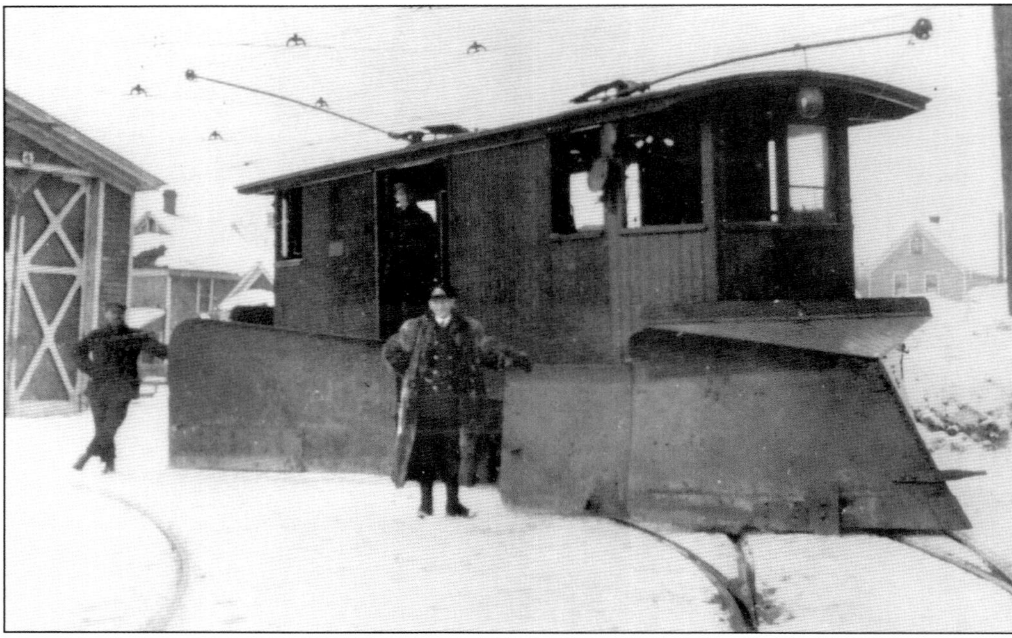

The company used four heavy snowplow vehicles manufactured by Taunton. The plows were used to push snow off of the tracks following heavier snowfalls. (Houghton County Historical Society.)

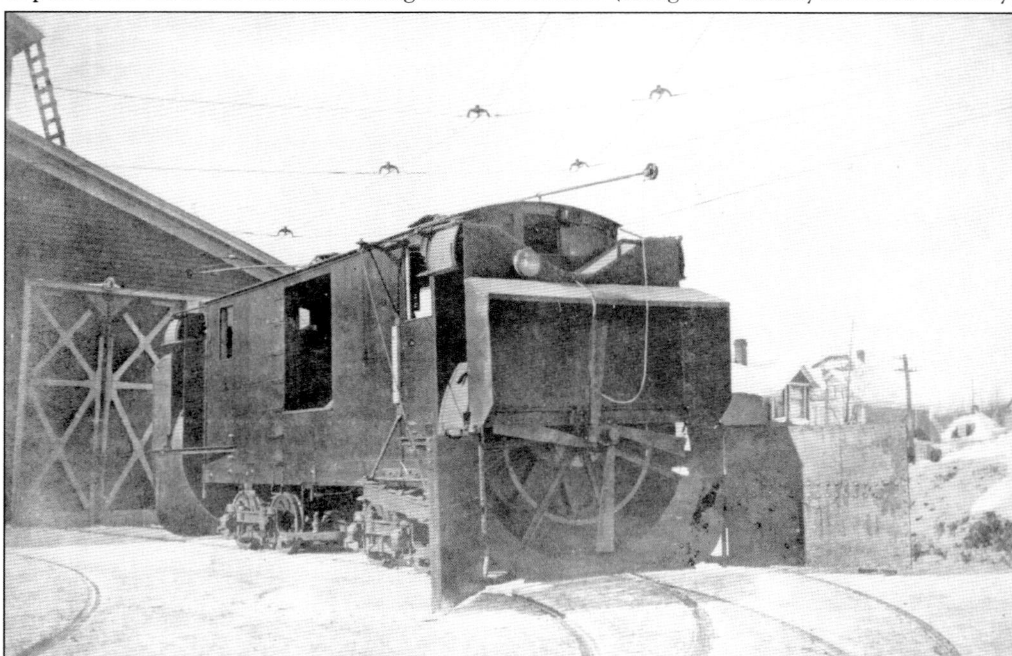

There were also two rotary plow units. These unique vehicles, manufactured by Ruggles, were essentially snowblowers. They were equipped with side wings to funnel the snow into the rotary blower. This photograph shows No. 5, a two-directional car with rotary plows on both ends, allowing it to be operated in either direction. No. 6 was a one-directional unit. (Michigan Technological University Archives/Copper Country Historical Collection.)

Four

Winter Operations

The Copper Country averages more snowfall than any part of the United States east of the Mississippi River and more snowfall than any non-mountainous region of the continental United States. Over 200 inches of snow blanket the area in an average winter, and during some winters the snowfall has exceeded 300 inches. The Houghton County Traction Company was prepared to battle the snow with proven and effective equipment. The heavy accumulation of snow, and at times blizzard conditions, certainly caused a standstill in other parts of the state. Reliable snow scrapers were used on some of the Brill interurban cars during the winter months, and four heavy snowplows and two giant rotary plows were used to tackle the heaviest snowfalls and drifting. The heavy snowplows pushed snow off of the tracks, while the rotary plows were essentially large snowblowers that would throw the snow from the track.

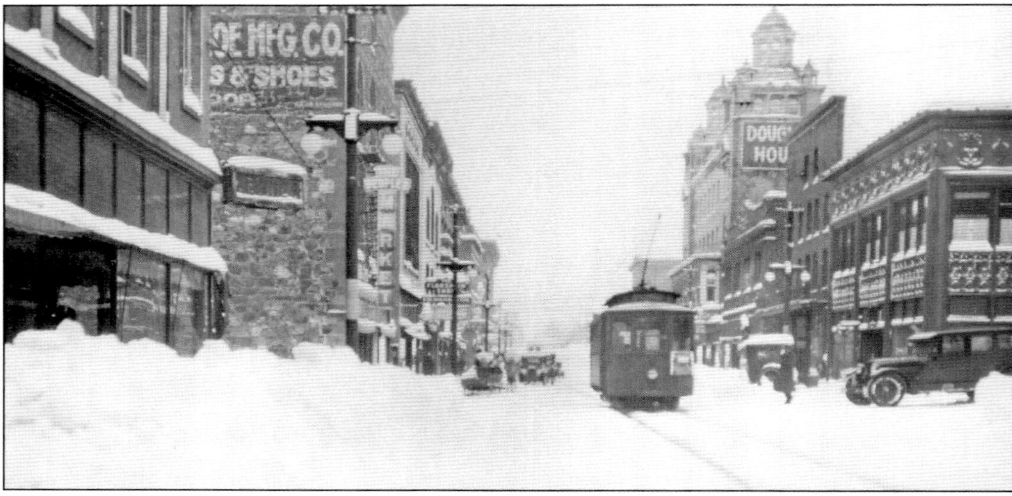

Here, a westbound streetcar operates on Shelden Avenue in downtown Houghton at Huron Street. Note the Douglass House on the right. (Michigan Technological University Archives/Copper Country Historical Collection.)

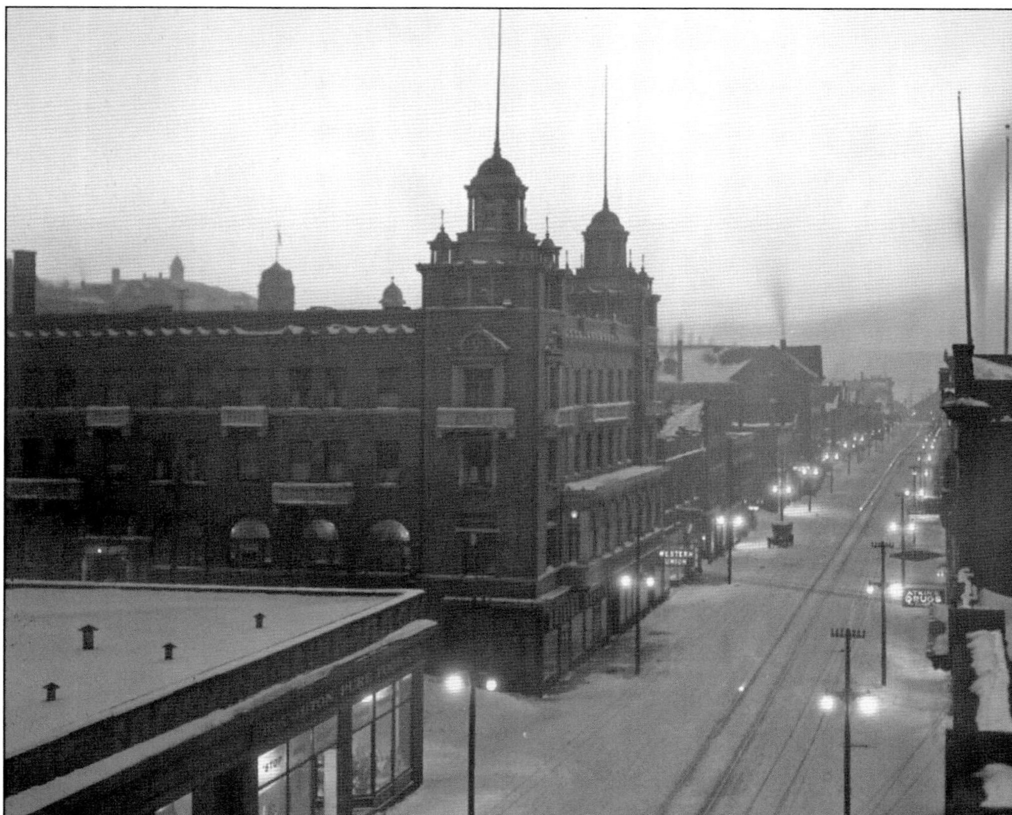

Looking west on Shelden Avenue, downtown Houghton is seen here on a winter night. The Douglass House is visible in the center. (Michigan Technological University Archives/Copper Country Historical Collection.)

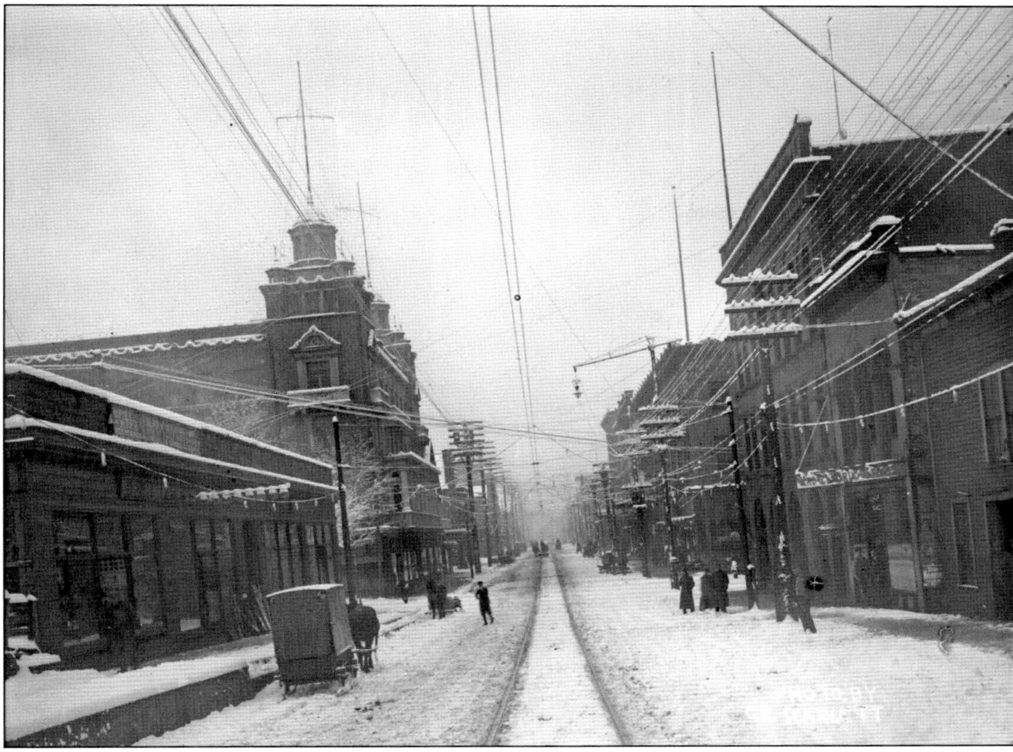

This is another view of downtown Houghton on a winter day looking west. Swift hardware store and the Douglass House are on the left. The streetcar track is visible in the snow, but there is not much activity. (Michigan Technological University Archives/Copper Country Historical Collection.)

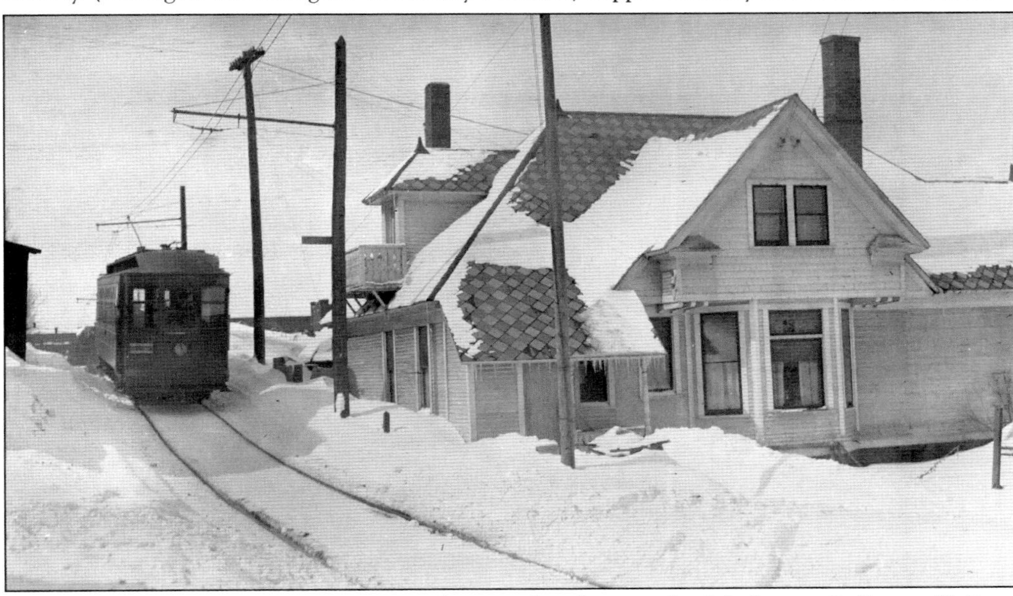

This streetcar, operating in East Houghton, is heading to the Michigan College of Mines. The streetcar was a dependable method for winter travel in the Copper Country. (Michigan Technological University Archives/Copper Country Historical Collection.)

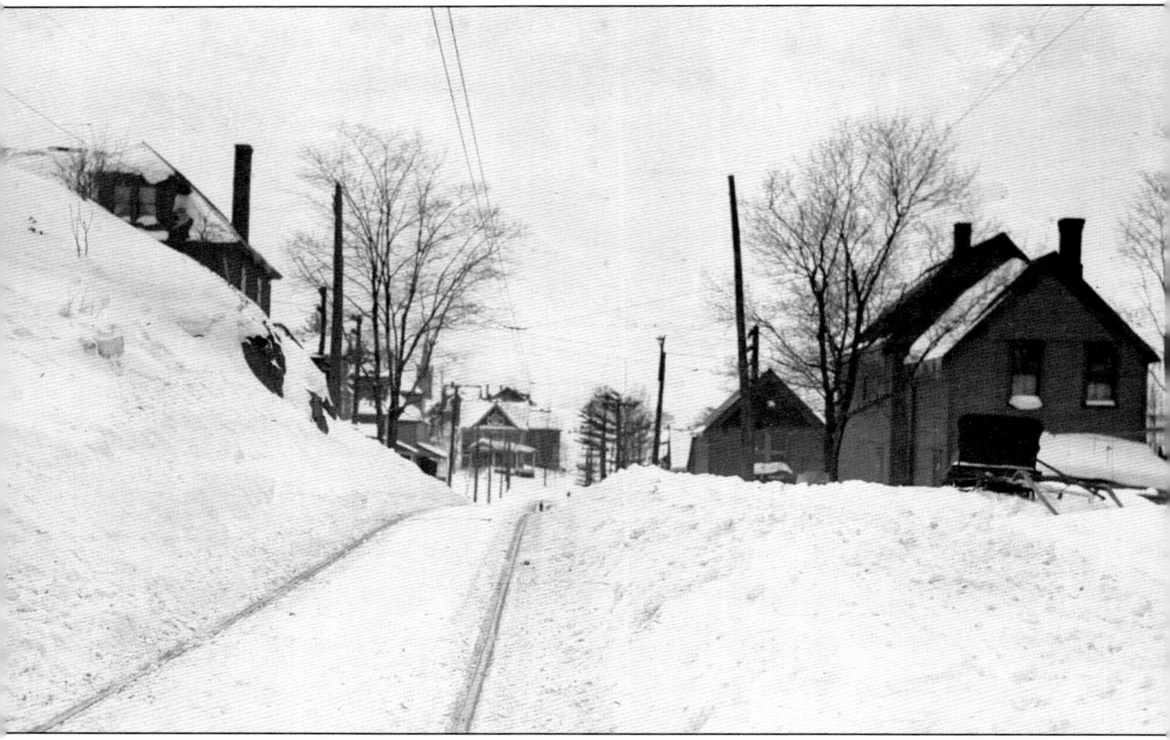

This is a view of the streetcar line on Jasper Avenue. The photographer is standing in East Houghton looking west. (Michigan Technological University Archives/Copper Country Historical Collection.)

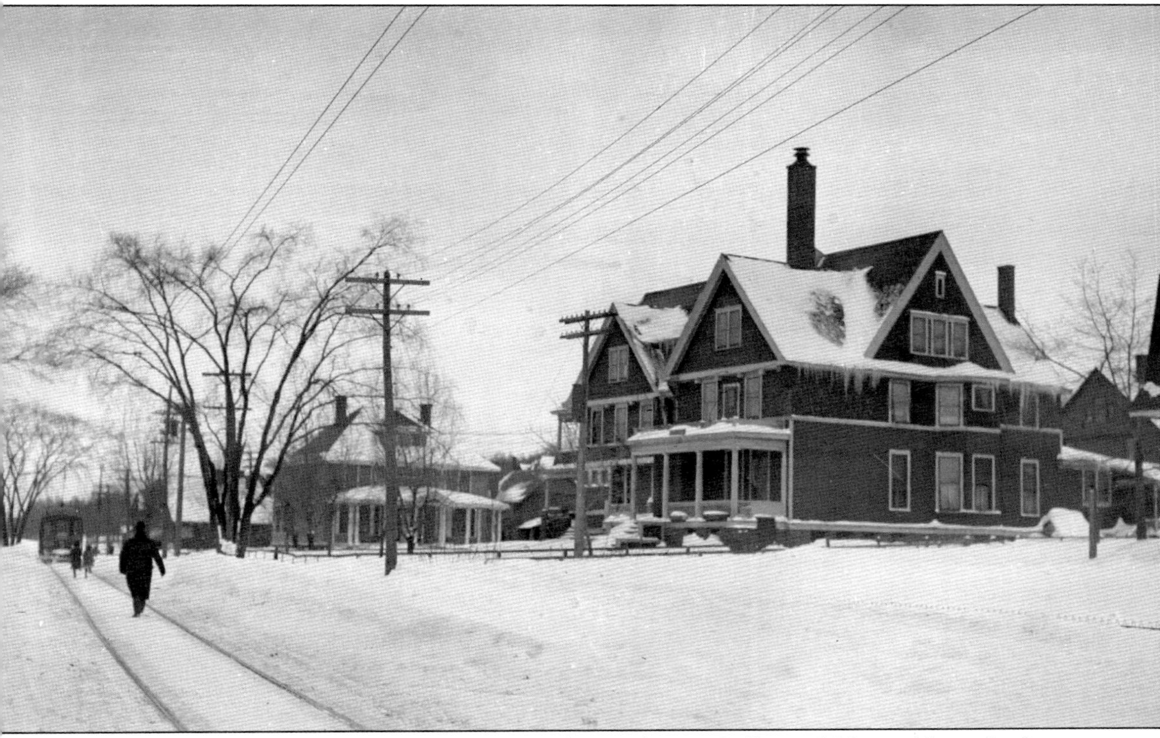

A streetcar runs on Houghton Avenue near the Michigan College of Mines. Note the larger homes of East Houghton near the college. (Michigan Technological University Archives/Copper Country Historical Collection.)

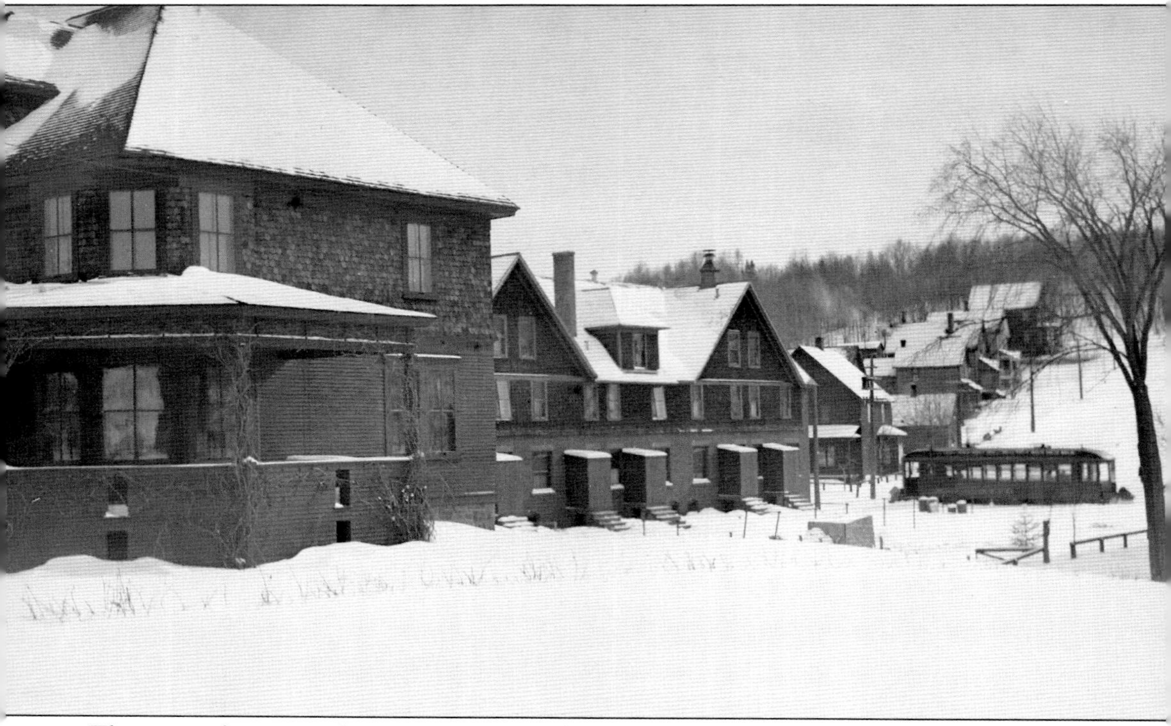

This is another view of a streetcar on Houghton Avenue. The photograph was taken near the Michigan College of Mines looking south from College Avenue. (Michigan Technological University Archives/Copper Country Historical Collection.)

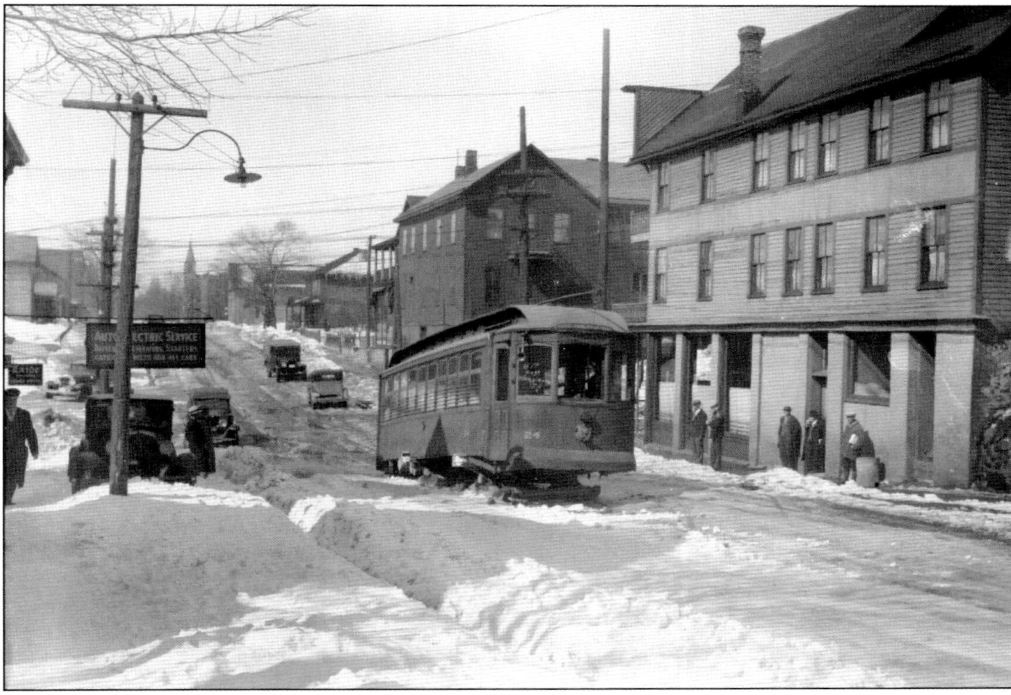

This photograph shows streetcar No. 24 in downtown Hancock. Onlookers view its passage from the sidewalk. (Michigan Technological University Archives/Copper Country Historical Collection.)

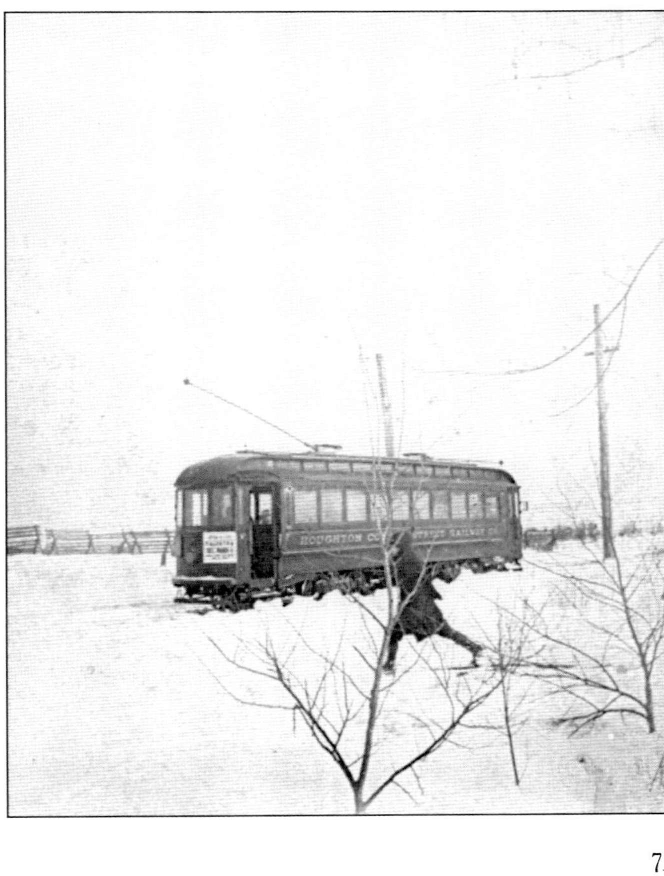

Passengers could board streetcars between stations. Here, a passenger runs to catch a winter streetcar. Note the sign on the front of the car advertising hockey at the Palestra. (Houghton County Historical Society.)

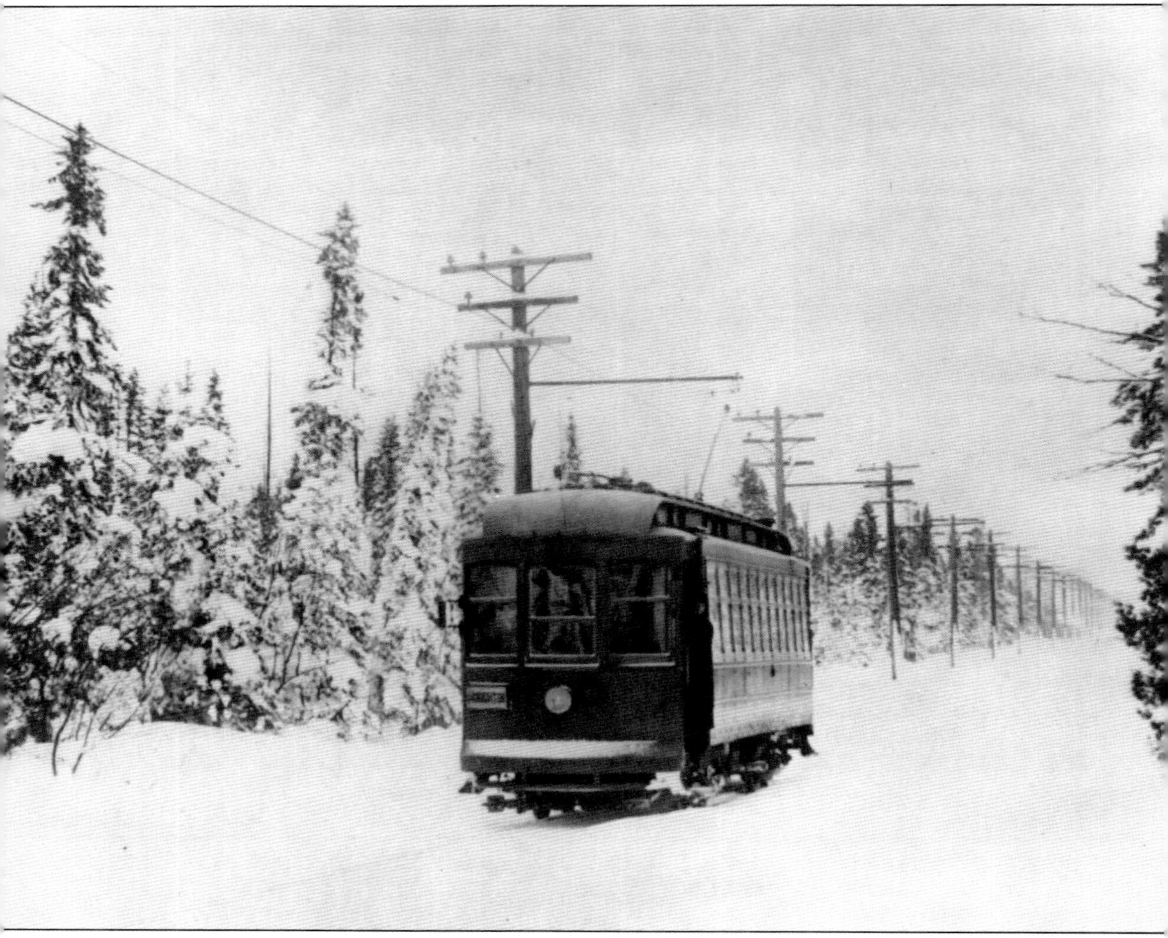

Streetcar No. 40 is seen here heading south on a winter day. It is pictured traveling between Hancock and Calumet near the Rhode Island station. (Keweenaw National Historical Park.)

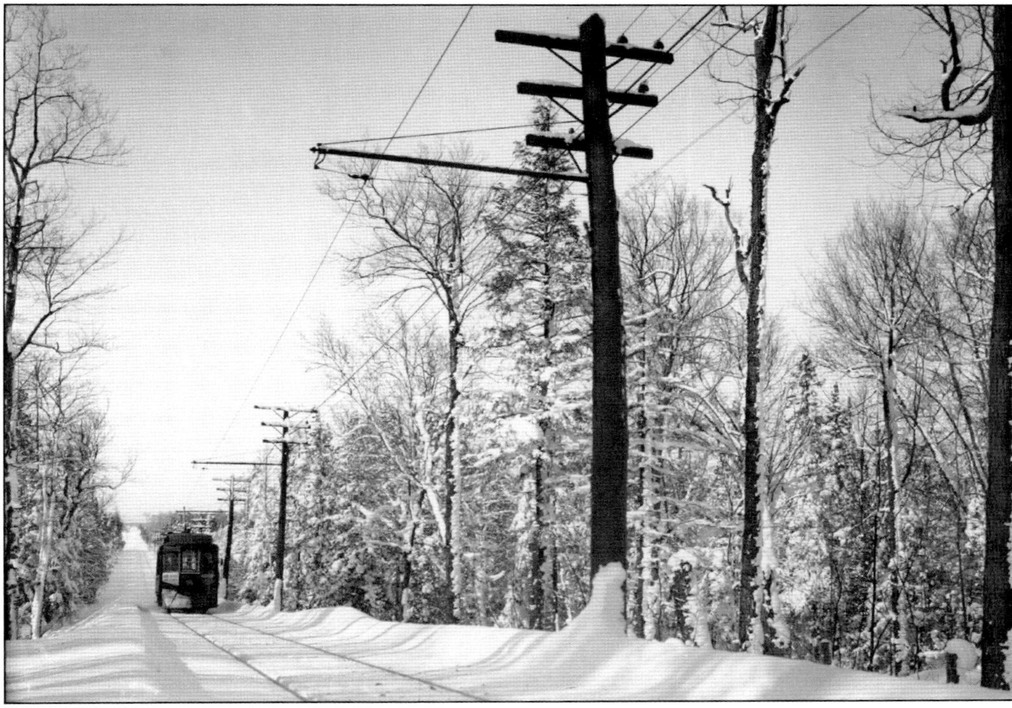

An interurban car operates between the Rhode Island station and Electric Park on a sunny winter day. Poles along the line were made from native cedar and stood about 35 feet tall, and each one carried three cross arms. The trolley wire was No. 00 and was made of local copper. (Michigan Technological University Archives/Copper Country Historical Collection.)

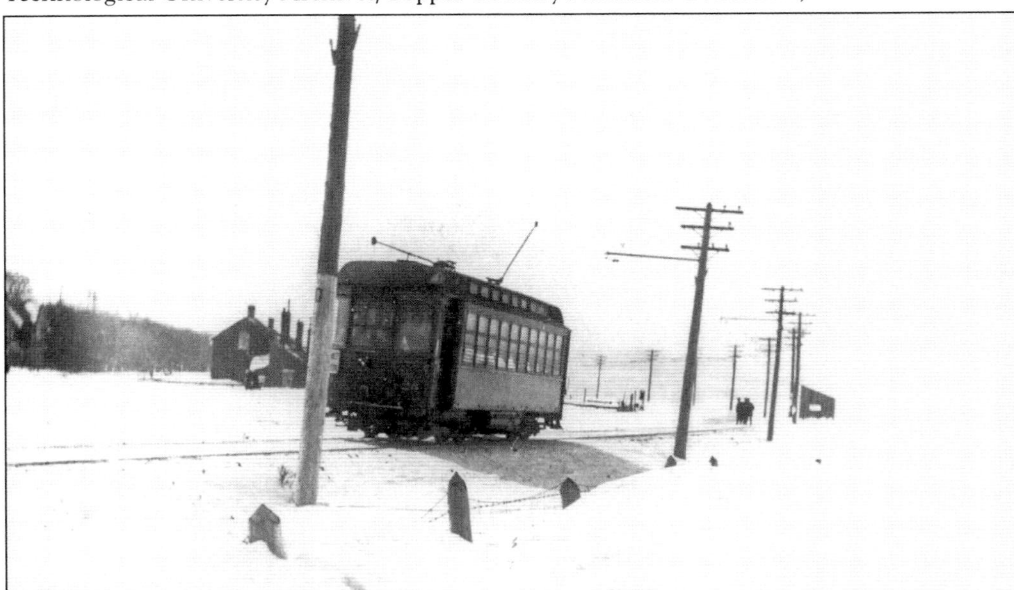

This is a 1915 photograph of a streetcar near the Frenchtown station on Quincy Hill. One can see the trolley pole on the car that draws power from the overhead electric wire. (Houghton County Historical Society.)

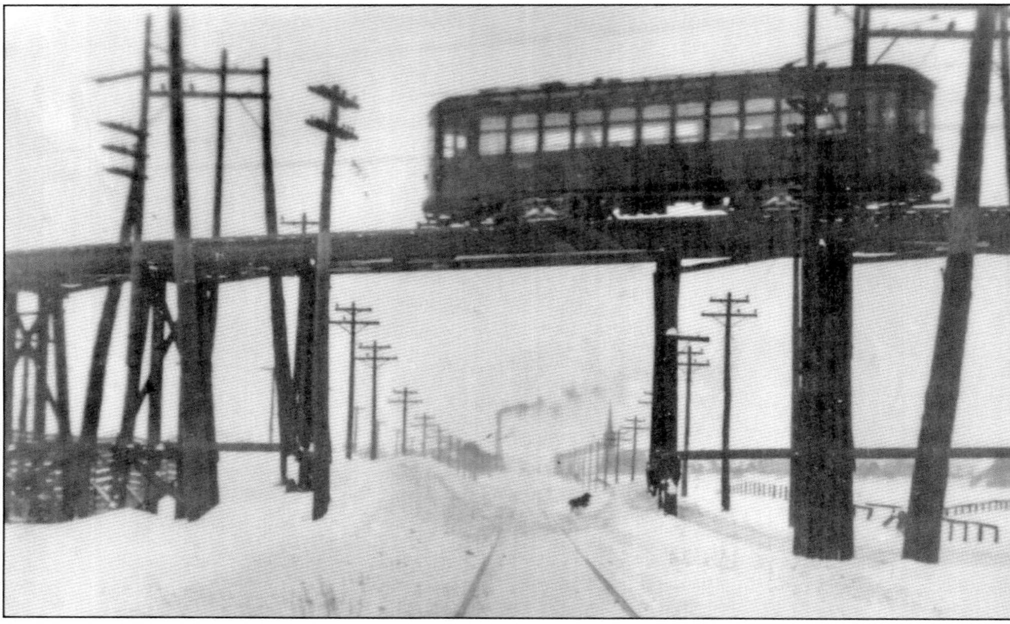

This view shows a streetcar heading southbound on a trestle near St. Mary's crossing a Mineral Range Railroad line. The wooden trestles were designed to clear a railroad line by 23 feet. (Houghton County Historical Society.)

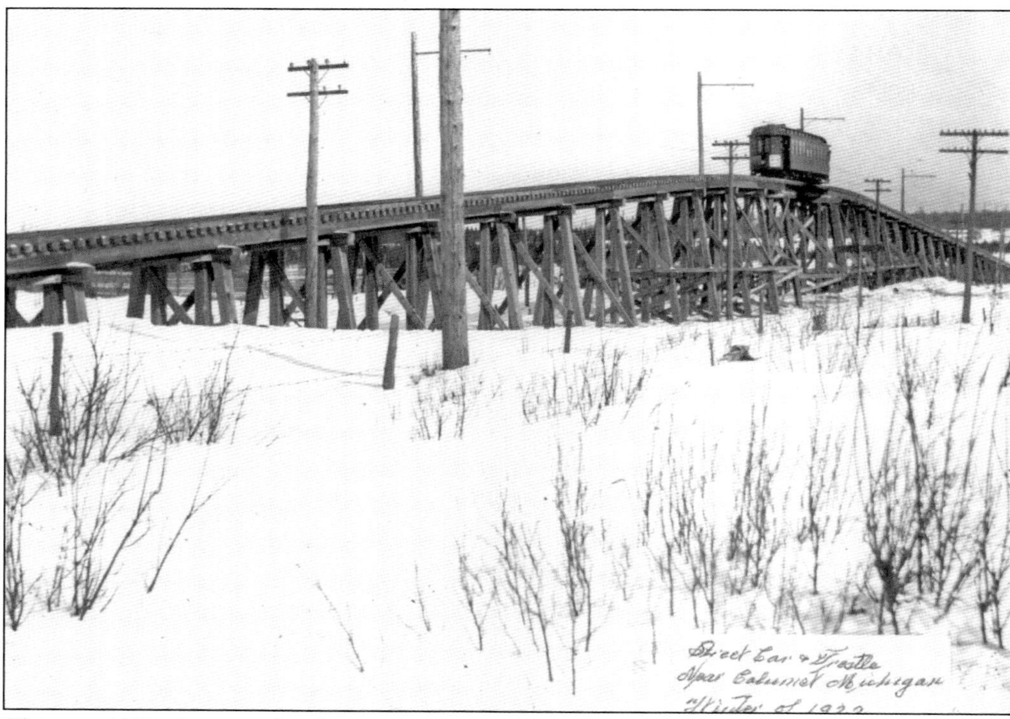

This is a 1922 photograph of a trestle near Calumet crossing a Mineral Range Railroad line. Each trestle was between 600 and 700 feet in length, with an eight-percent grade on each side. (Houghton County Historical Society.)

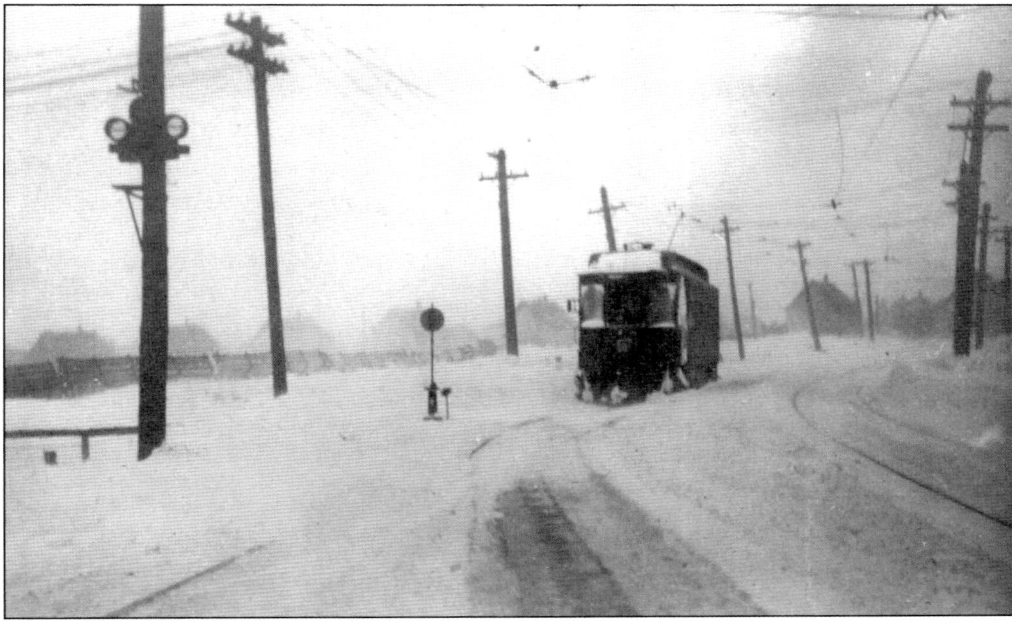

A snowy day in the Copper Country created many challenges for streetcar operations. In addition to the snow, sleet build-up on the overhead wires created problems on some winter days. (Houghton County Historical Society.)

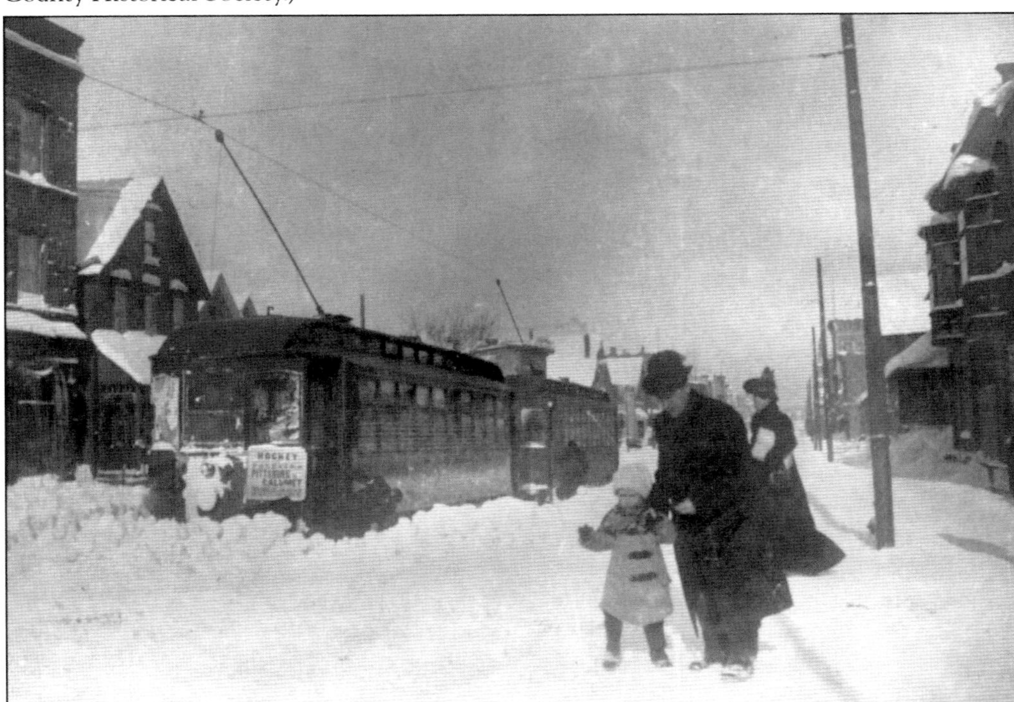

This photograph of a winter day was taken at the intersection of Sixth and Scott Streets in Red Jacket. Note the poster on the front of the first car for a hockey game between Pittsburgh and Calumet at the Palestra (in Laurium). (Keweenaw National Historical Park.)

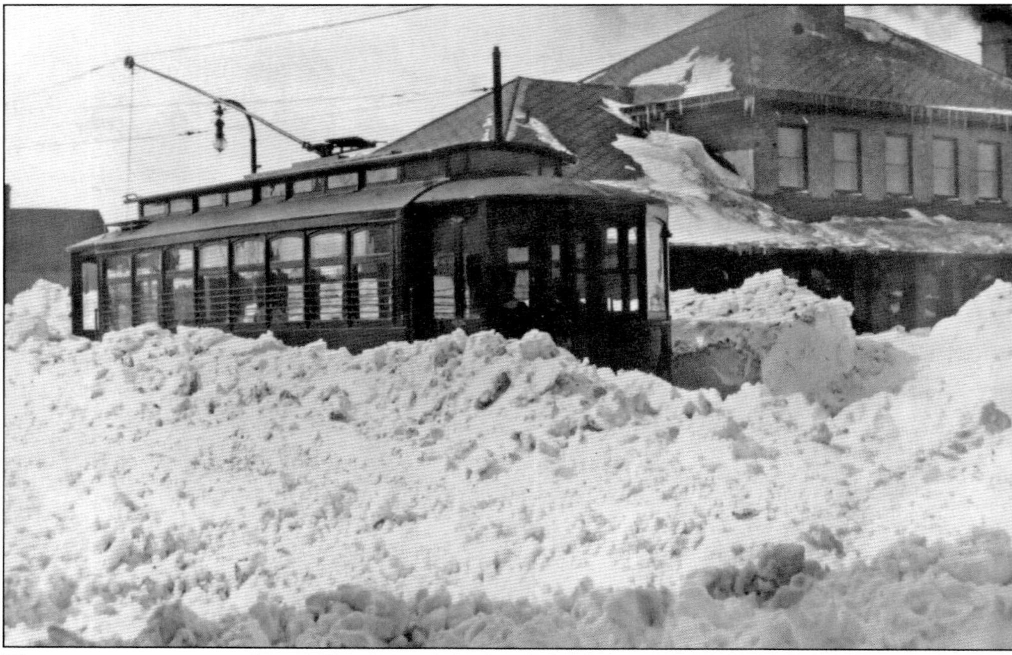

This streetcar was caught in the snow near the Calumet train station. The inclement weather brought it to a stop on Oak Street in Red Jacket. (Michigan Technological University Archives/ Copper Country Historical Collection.)

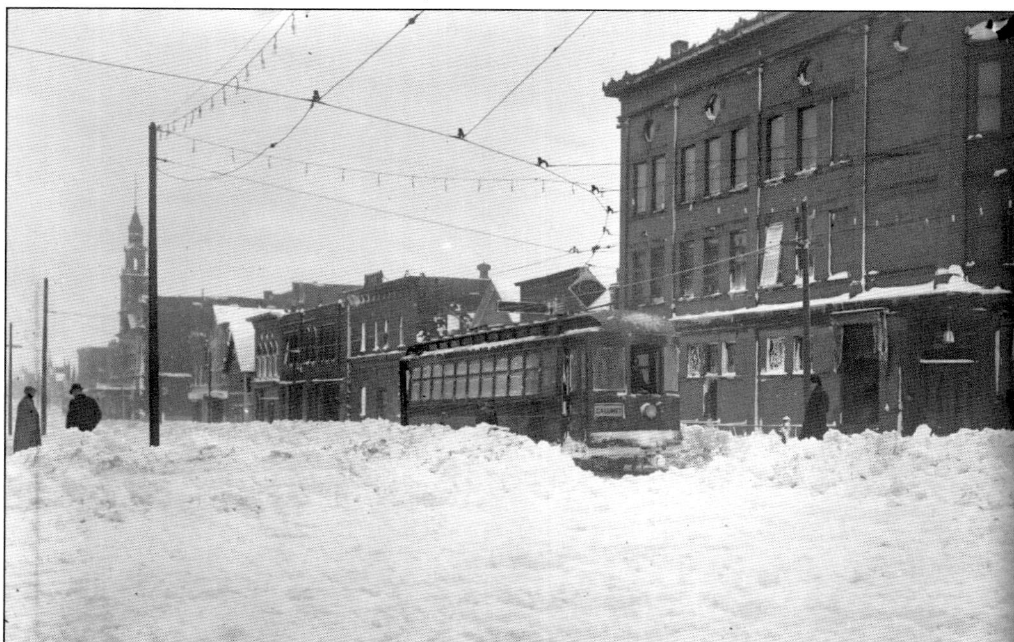

Southbound streetcar No. 38 is seen running on Sixth Street in Red Jacket near the Michigan House at Oak Street. George Gipp, the famous Notre Dame football star, worked at the Michigan House and was a frequent rider of the streetcar. (Michigan Technological University Archives/ Copper Country Historical Collection.)

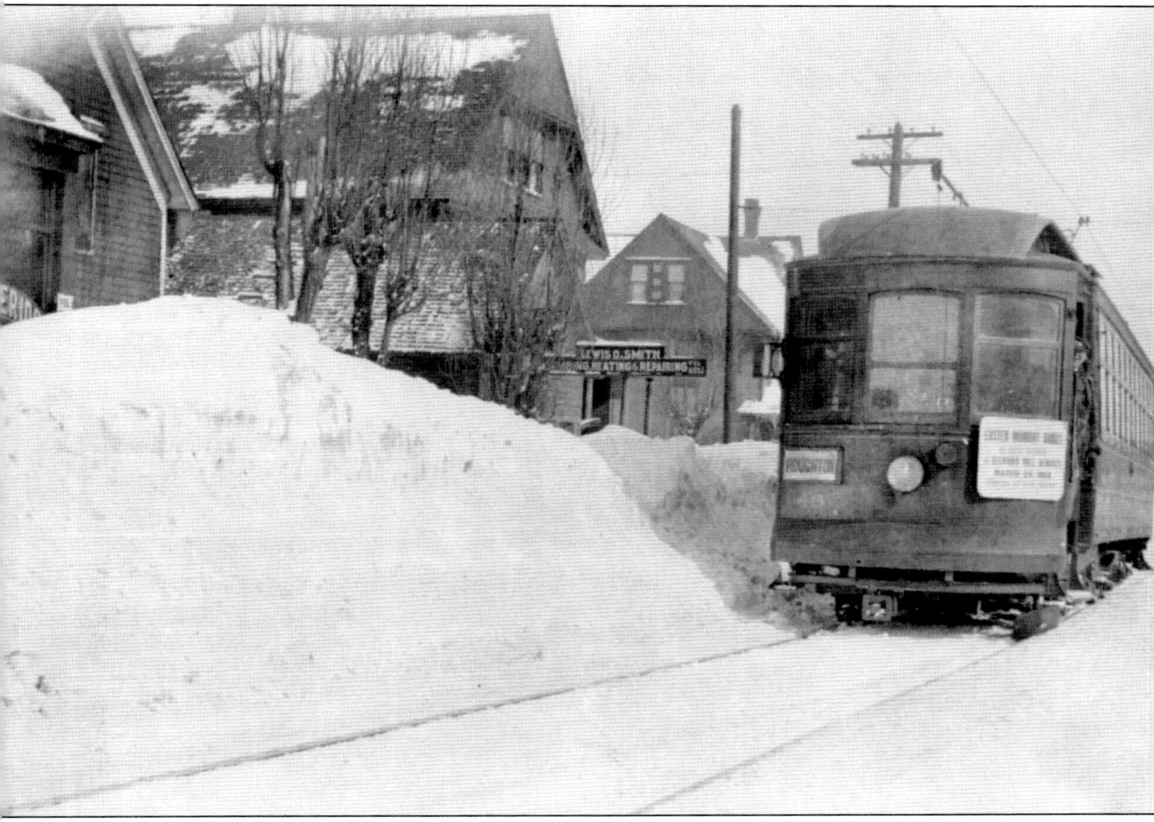

Streetcar No. 48 is heading to Houghton. The poster on the front of the car advertises a March Easter dance. (Michigan Technological University Archives/Copper Country Historical Collection.)

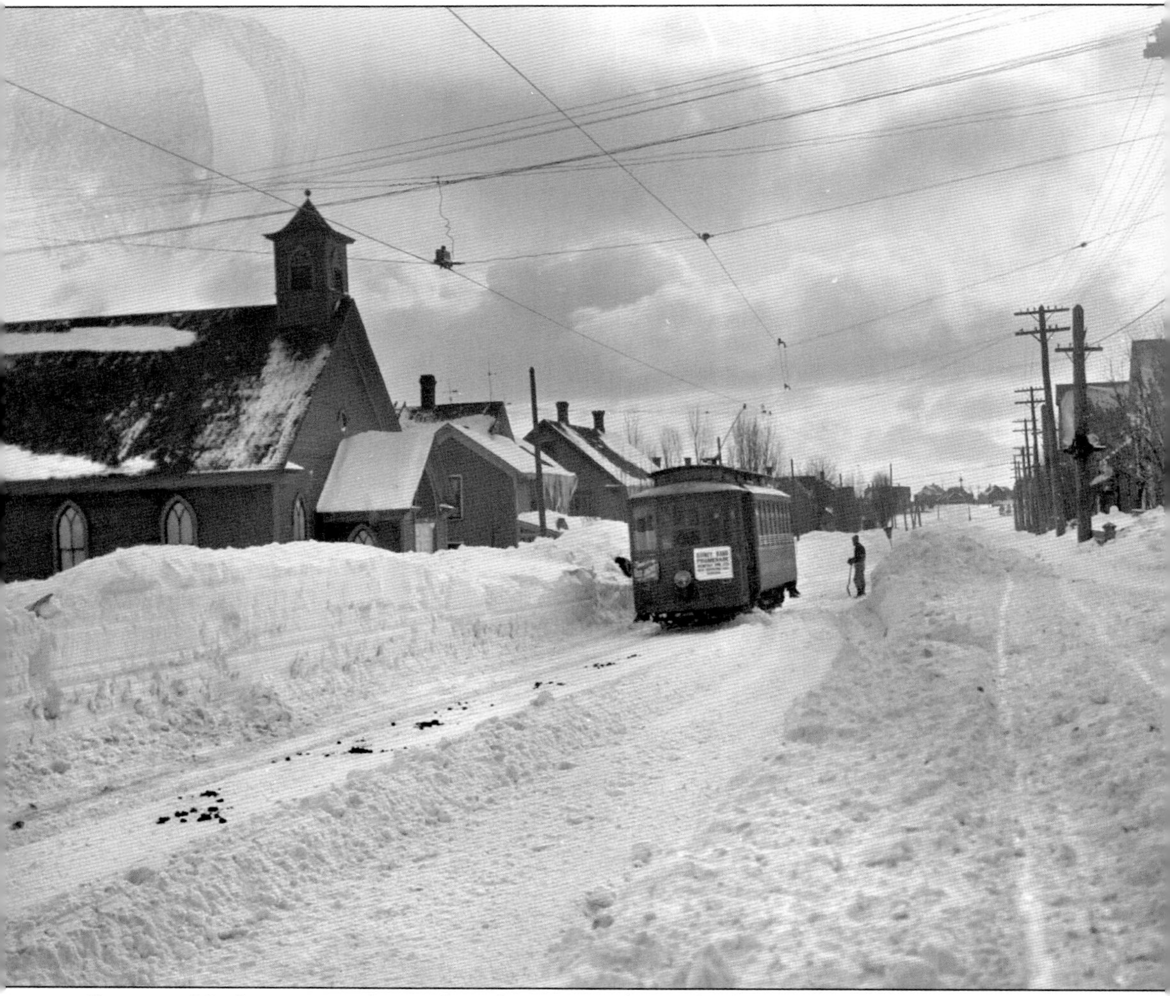

Streetcar No. 3 appears to be stuck in the snow in front of a church on Pine Street in Red Jacket. Men are attempting to dig it out so it can continue to operate. (Michigan Technological University Archives/Copper Country Historical Collection.)

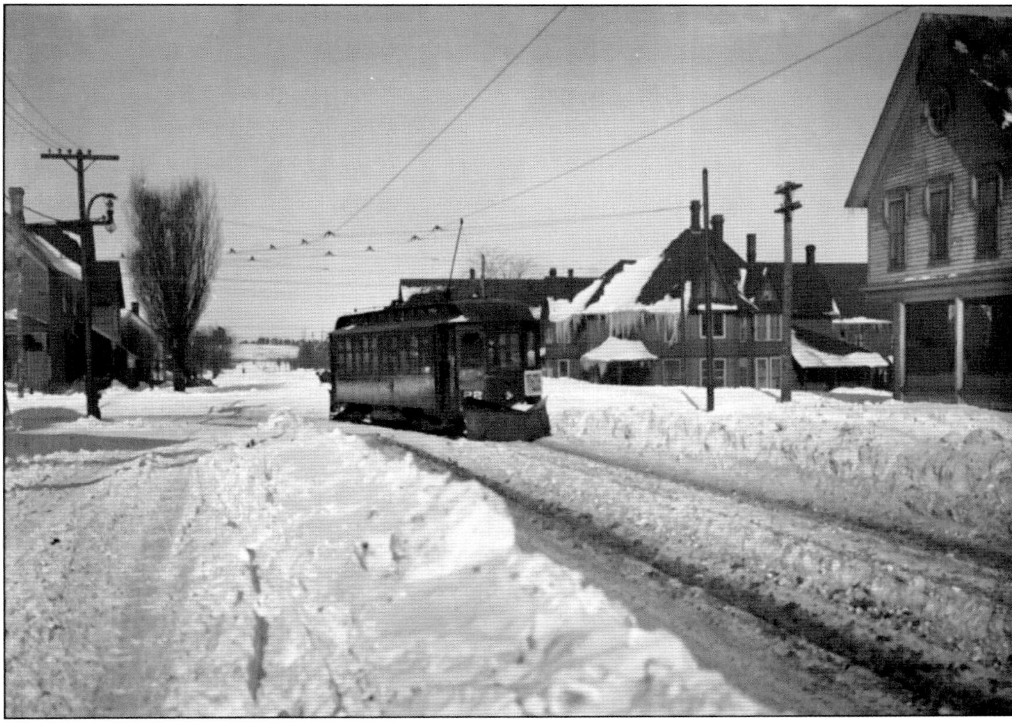

Streetcar No. 22 is turning from Pine Street onto Sixth Street. The route ran through Red Jacket. (Michigan Technological University Archives/Copper Country Historical Collection.)

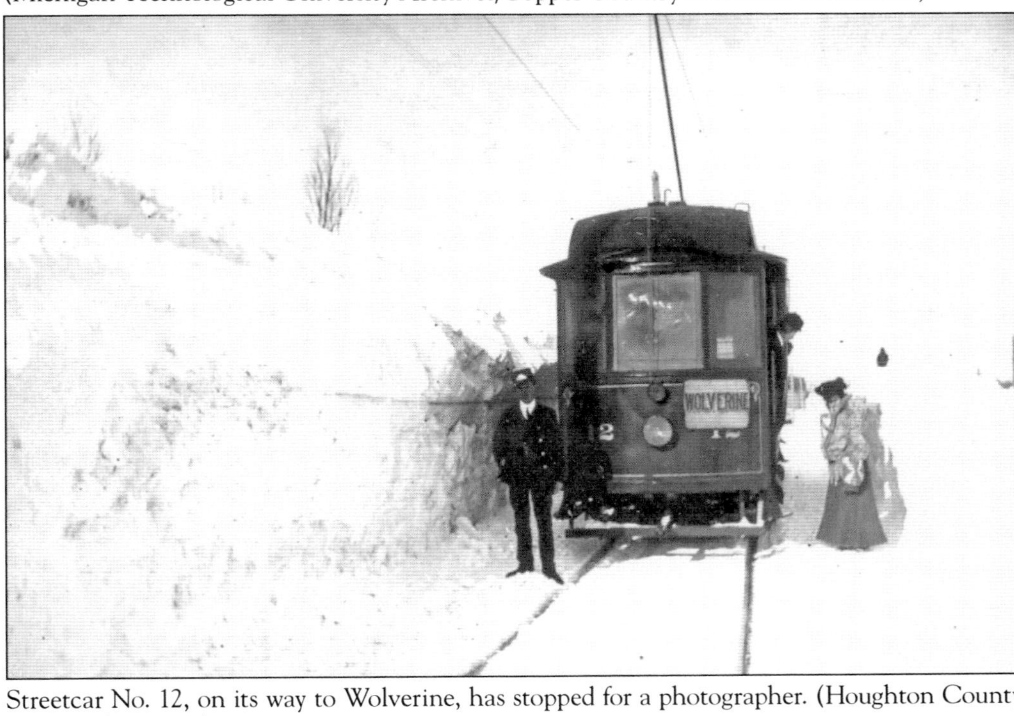

Streetcar No. 12, on its way to Wolverine, has stopped for a photographer. (Houghton County Historical Society.)

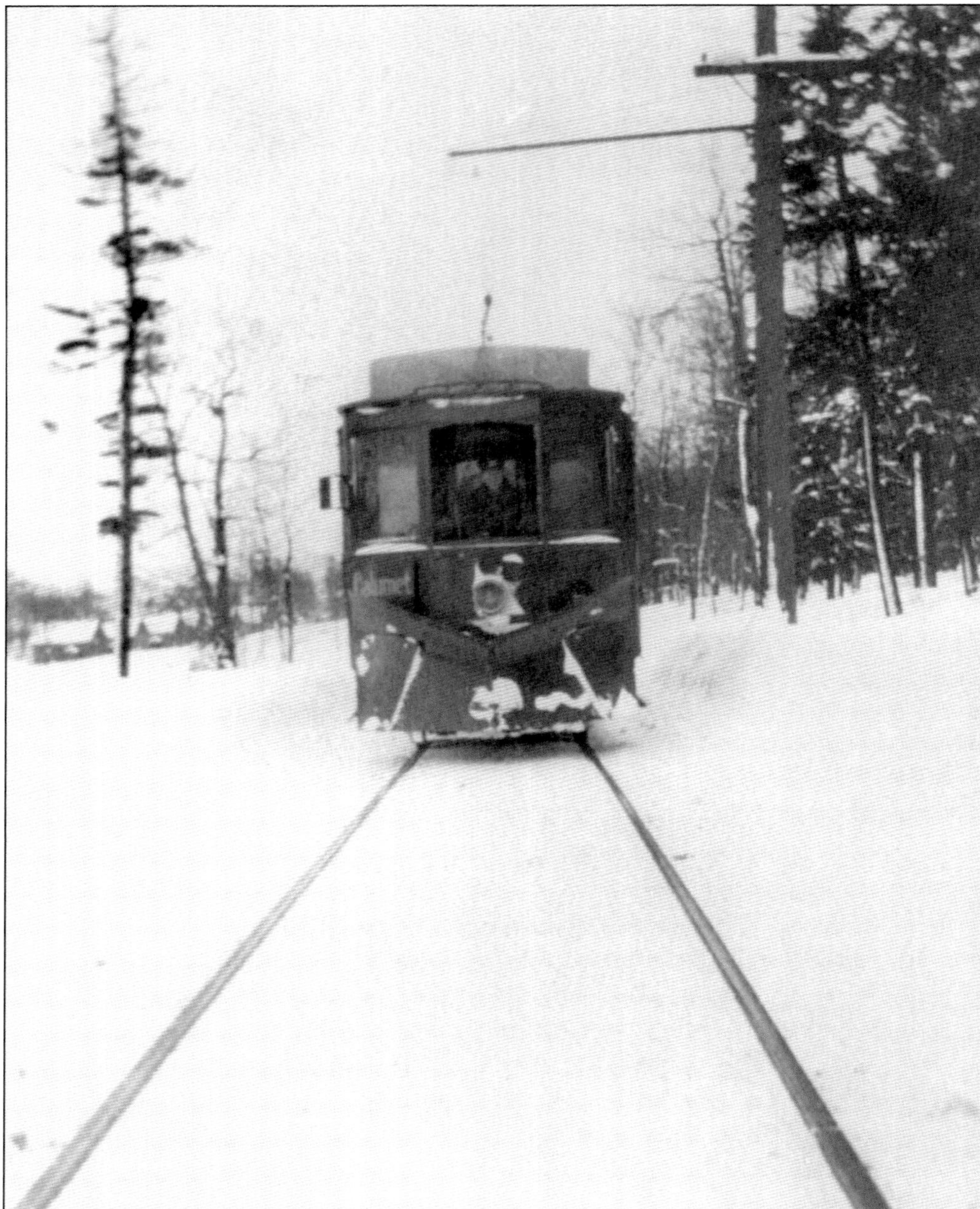

Scraper plows were installed on several Brill cars to keep the track clear after lighter snowfalls. This car with a scraper plow is heading to Calumet. (Houghton County Historical Society.)

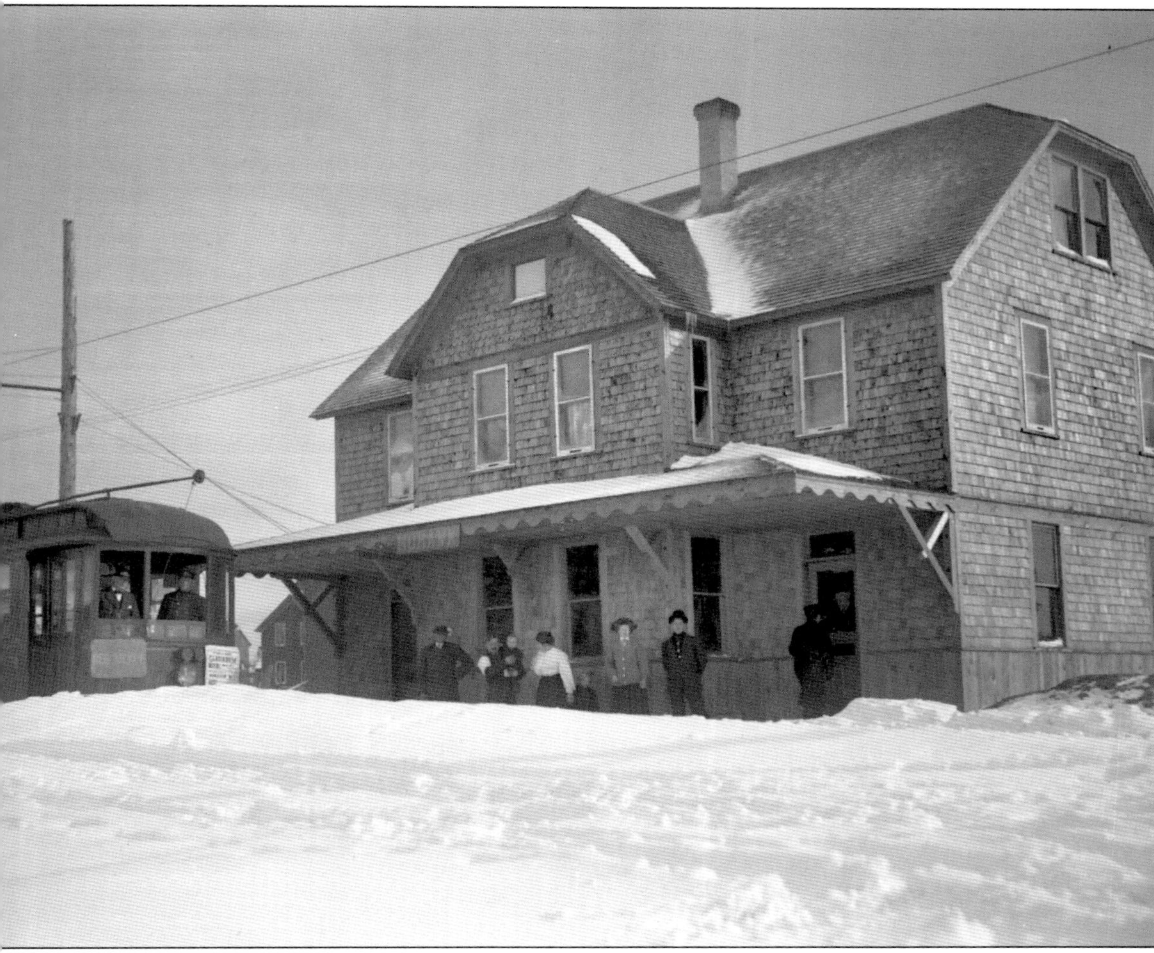

A streetcar is pulling into the Mohawk station. This is the end of the line, so the motorman will switch the trolley pole for the southbound trip to Calumet. (Michigan Technological University Archives/Copper Country Historical Collection.)

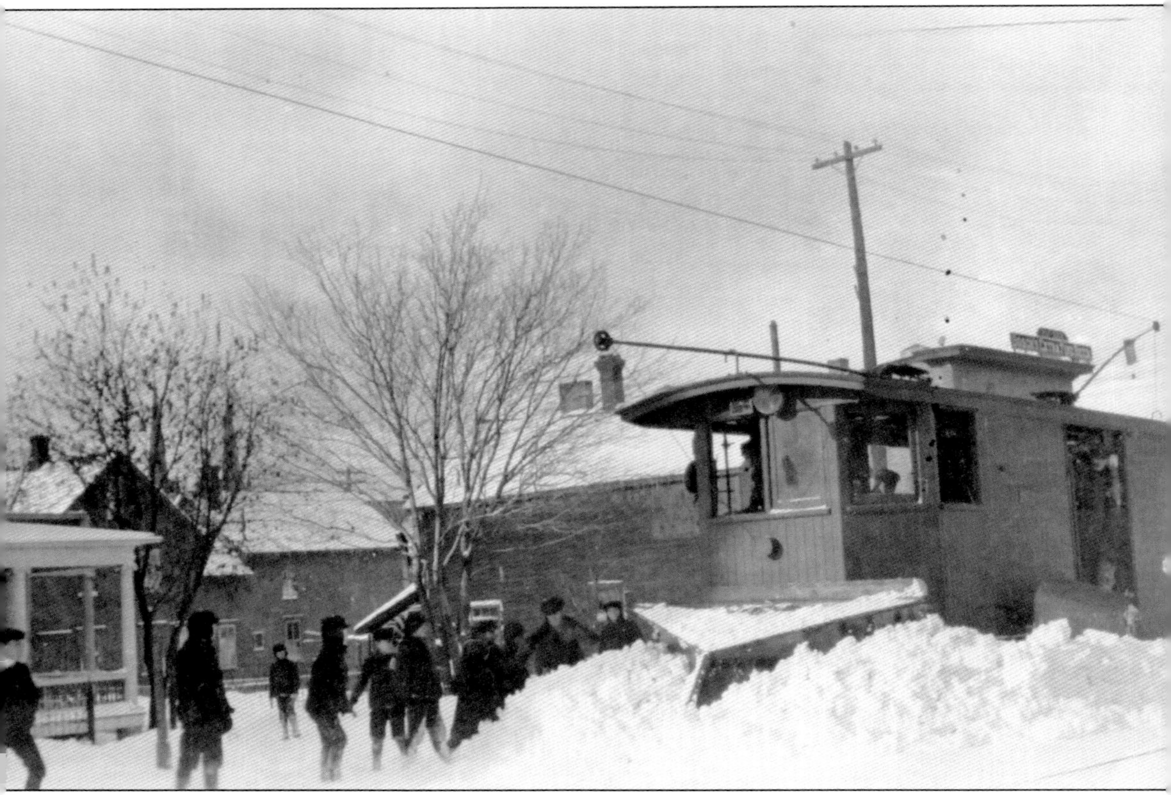

In the event of heavier snowfalls, special streetcar plow vehicles were used. This photograph shows children at play as the streetcar plow passes. (Michigan Technological University Archives/ Copper Country Historical Collection.)

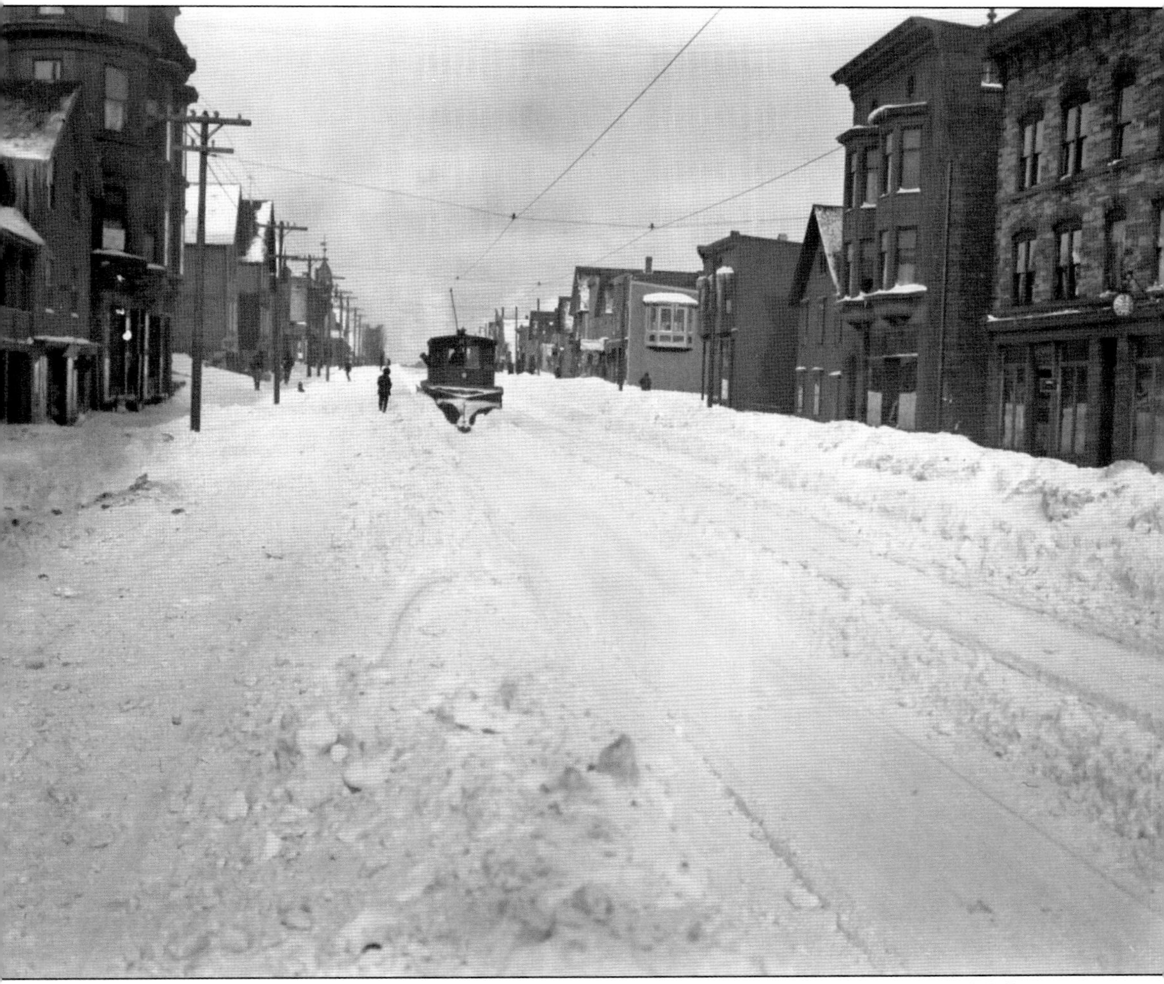

A streetcar plow vehicle clears the tracks in Calumet. Such equipment was crucial following heavier snowfalls in the area. (Houghton County Historical Society.)

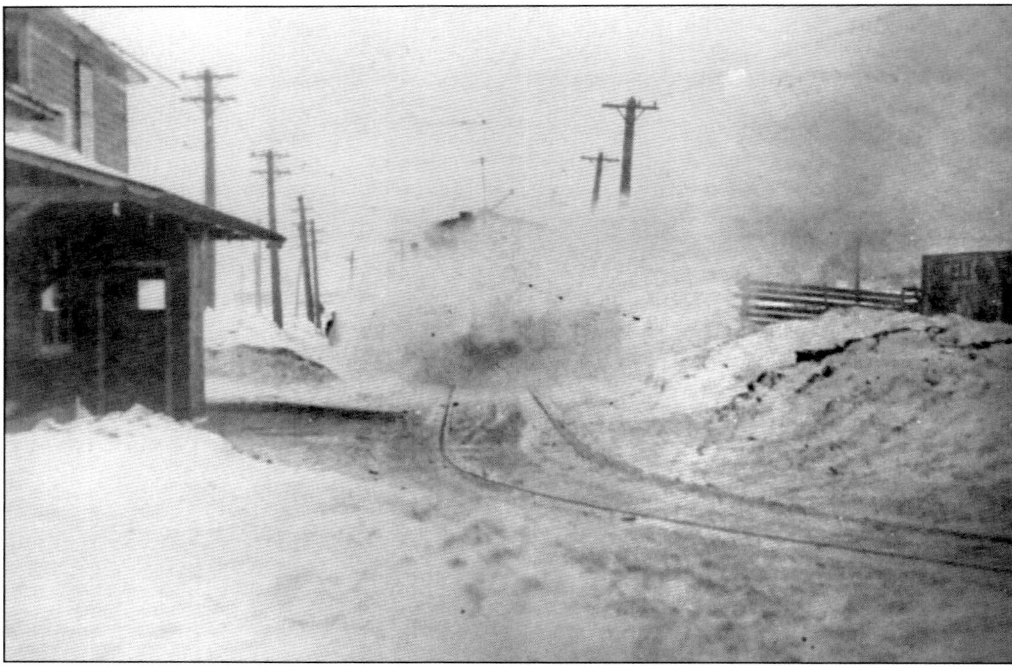

A rotary snowplow approaches the Albion station in near-blizzard conditions. These were used to clear the tracks after heavy snowfalls when drifting was caused by high winds. (Houghton County Historical Society.)

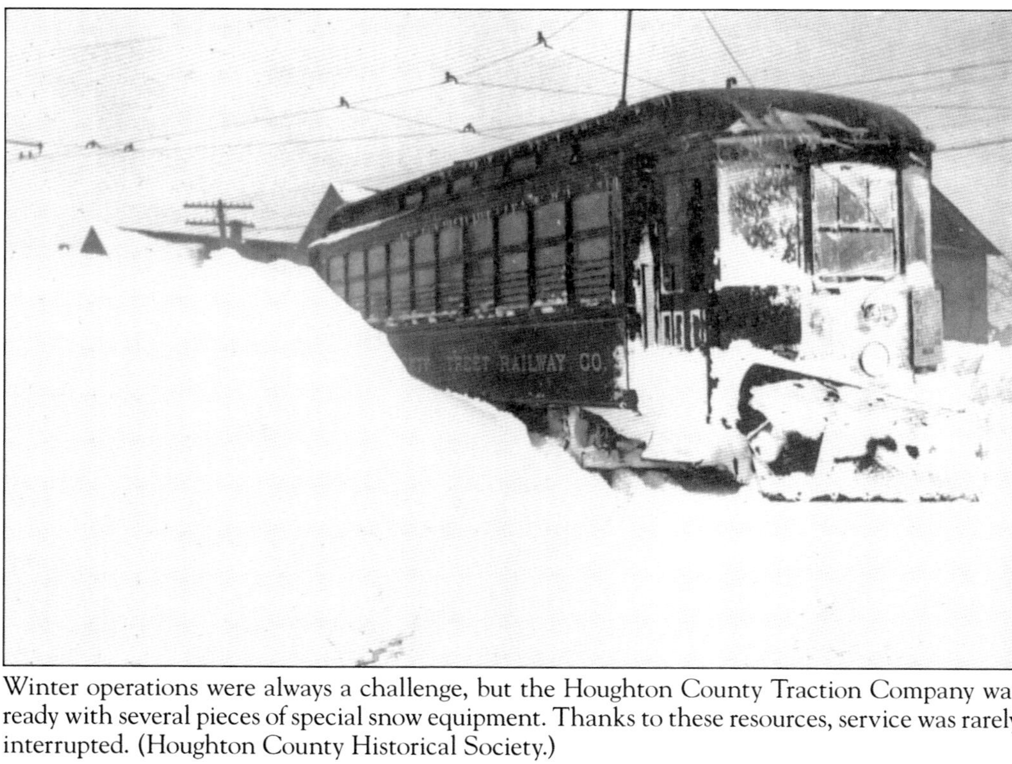

Winter operations were always a challenge, but the Houghton County Traction Company was ready with several pieces of special snow equipment. Thanks to these resources, service was rarely interrupted. (Houghton County Historical Society.)

Five

Electric Park

As a way to increase ridership, many streetcar companies throughout the United States built amusement parks along the line or extended a line and advertised new weekend schedules. The Houghton County Street Railway Company saw this as an exciting opportunity. It leased property south of Calumet from the LaSalle Copper Company (James MacNaughton was its vice president) and constructed an amusement park in the spring of 1902. The park, originally named Anwebida (Chippewa for "here may we rest"), opened on June 15, 1902. Anwebida featured a 5,000-square-foot hall with seating for 800 people, an outdoor bandstand, refreshment booths, and a variety of playground equipment. The park quickly became a popular place for visitors on weeknights and weekends from May to September, as admission was free to all those who paid the streetcar fare. In 1905, the park was renamed Electric Park following the trend of naming these streetcar amusement parks across the United States. With the new name came better lighting and a large sign spelling out the park's name. After the original pavilion burned down in 1906, the company took the opportunity to expand the pavilion and add a baseball diamond. The company also banned the sale or possession of alcohol on the grounds.

Over the years, Electric Park hosted many musical groups at the pavilion on Friday and Saturday evenings, and the popular Calumet & Hecla Band performed at the bandstand on Sunday afternoons and weeknights. The park was also rented to outside groups and organizations for private picnics and events. Annual park attendance averaged 45,000 between 1910 and 1912.

Although the streetcar company went out of business in 1932, Electric Park carried on, and a road was built to connect it to US 41. The buildings were sold in 1935 to the Calumet & Hecla Band, which extended the lease from the LaSalle Copper Company. Events continued for a few more years until 1943, when the band sold the buildings to a local company that dismantled the pavilion and the remaining buildings and used the lumber to build a potato warehouse for the Vitton brothers in nearby Boston. Although Electric Park outlasted its parent company by a decade, little remains of what was once the most popular summer resort in the Copper Country.

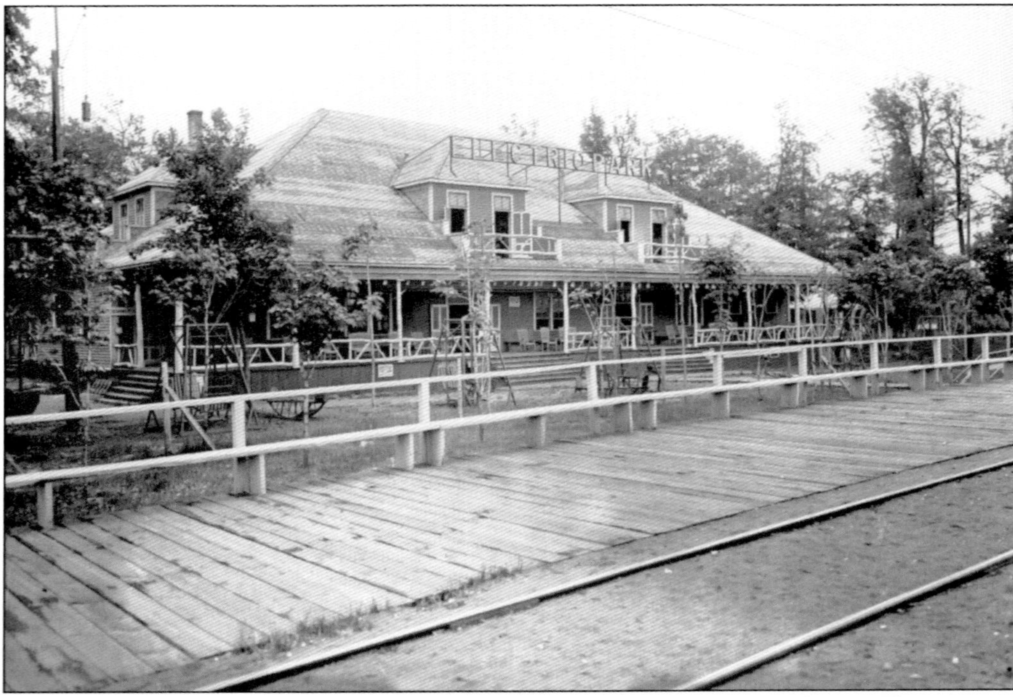

The main pavilion at Electric Park was the showcase building. It was constructed in 1906 to replace an original, smaller pavilion that had burned down. The building was almost 10,000 square feet and had a large dance floor. (Michigan Technological University Archives/Copper Country Historical Collection.)

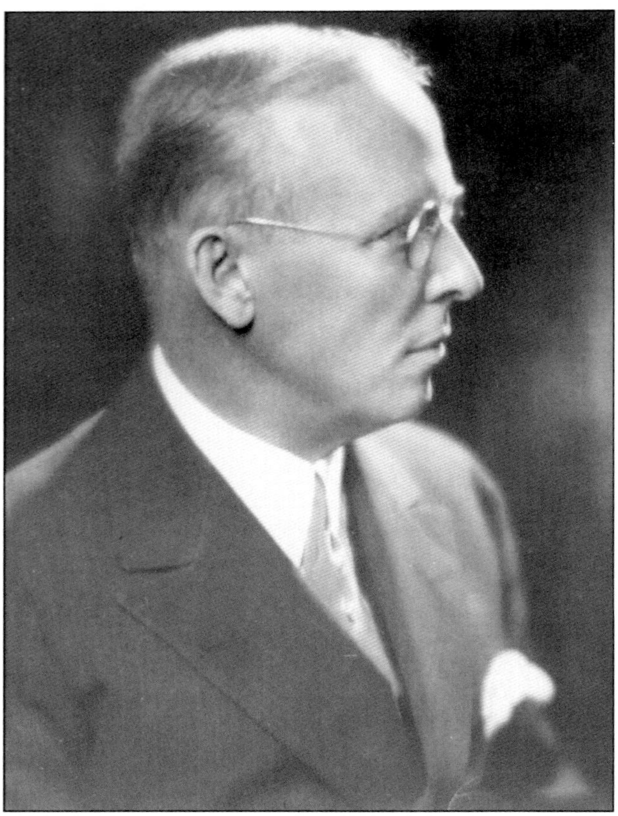

James MacNaughton was the vice president of the LaSalle Copper Company, which leased the land for Electric Park to the Houghton County Street Railway Company. MacNaughton eventually became a powerful community leader and president of the Calumet & Hecla Mining Company. (Michigan Technological University Archives/Copper Country Historical Collection.)

An advertisement for Electric Park was placed by the Houghton County Traction Company in a Calumet & Hecla booklet, published in 1916, to inform readers of the park's amenities. (Michigan Technological University Archives/Copper Country Historical Collection.)

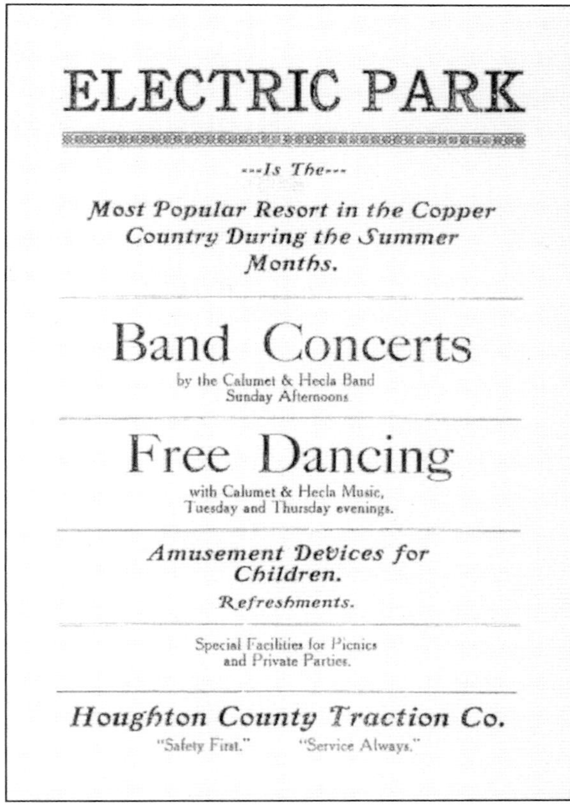

ELECTRIC PARK

---Is The---

Most Popular Resort in the Copper Country During the Summer Months.

Band Concerts

by the Calumet & Hecla Band
Sunday Afternoons

Free Dancing

with Calumet & Hecla Music,
Tuesday and Thursday evenings.

Amusement Devices for Children.

Refreshments.

Special Facilities for Picnics and Private Parties.

Houghton County Traction Co.

"Safety First." "Service Always."

This is a 1911 photograph of Electric Park on a summer Saturday evening. Electric lights were installed throughout the park, and a large, 40-foot-by-3-foot sign spelled out "Electric Park." (Houghton County Historical Society.)

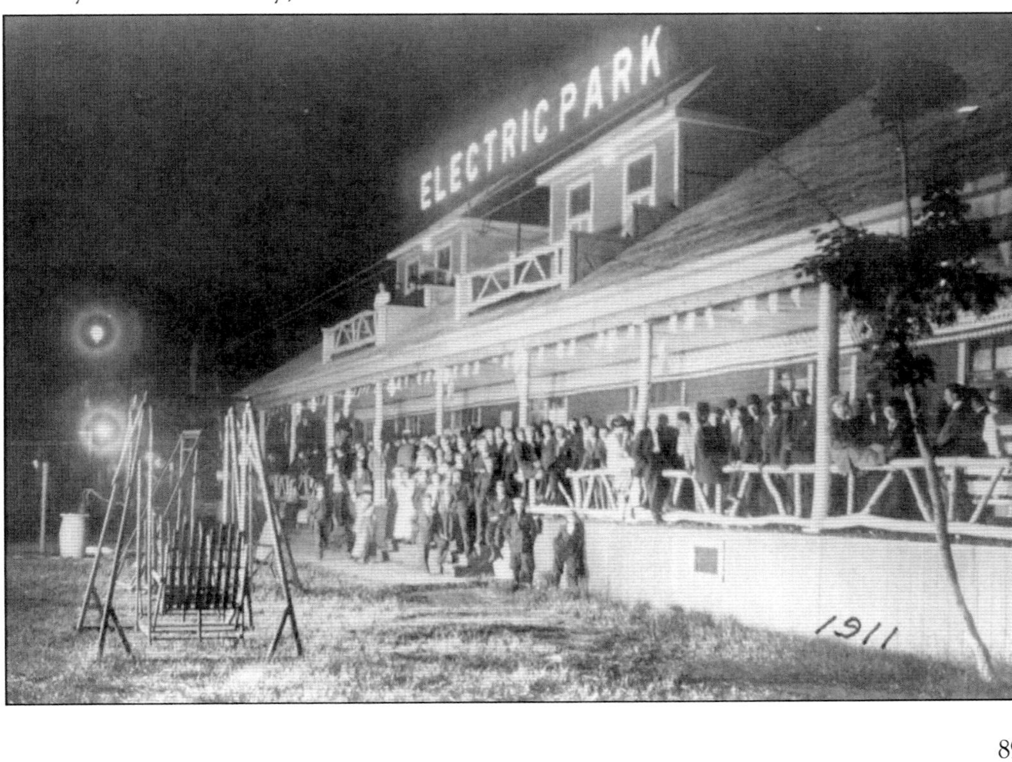

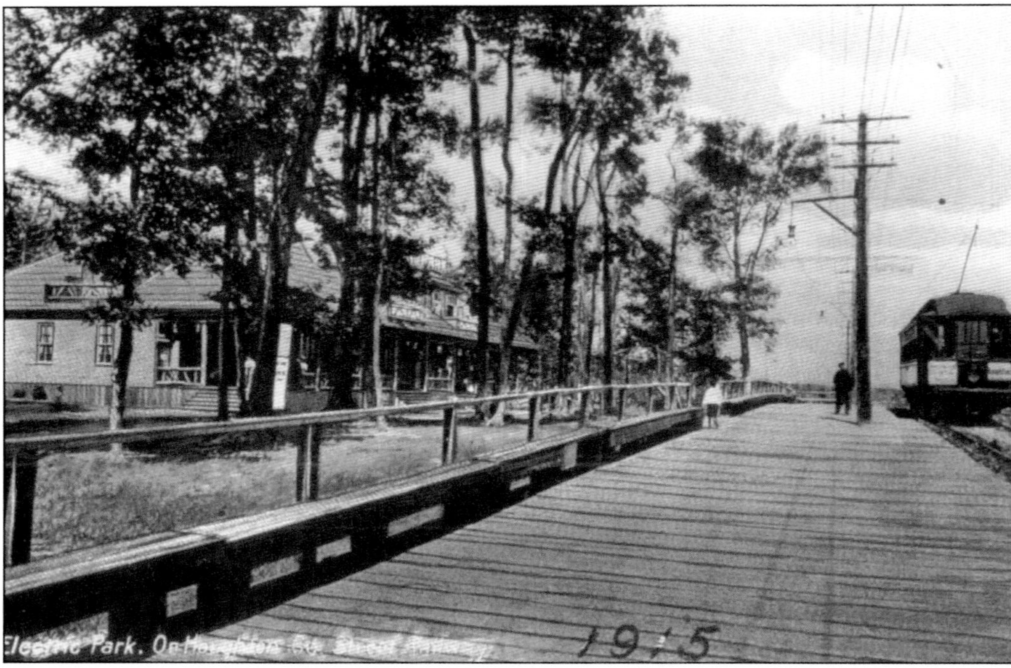

This 1915 postcard shows a streetcar arriving at Electric Park. A wooden platform made for easy waiting for streetcar passengers, and the station was just a short walk from the main pavilion. (Houghton County Historical Society.)

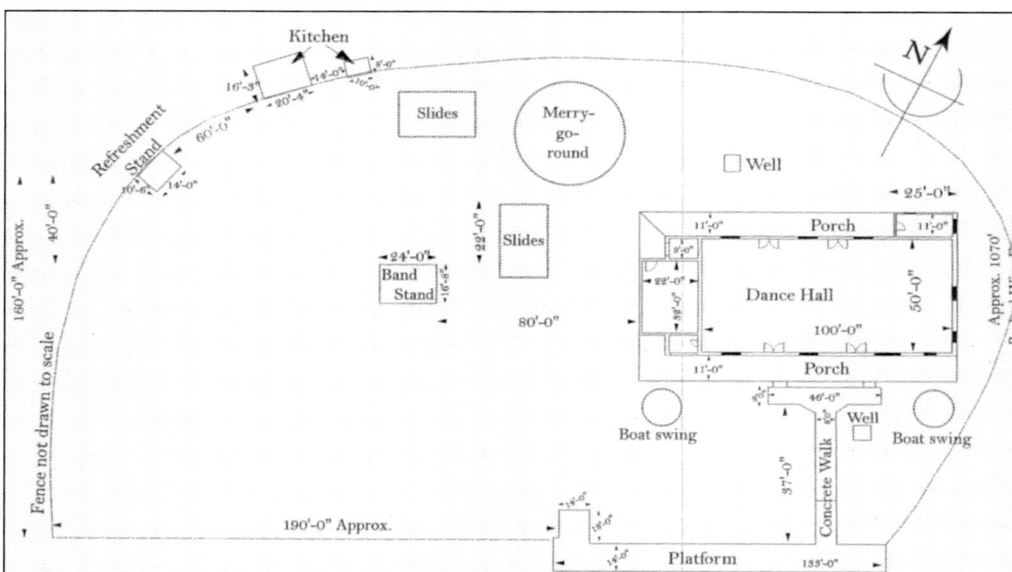

Here is a drawing of the site plan for the original Anwebida amusement park grounds. The original park included a smaller pavilion, picnic areas, and a children's playground. (Keweenaw National Historical Park.)

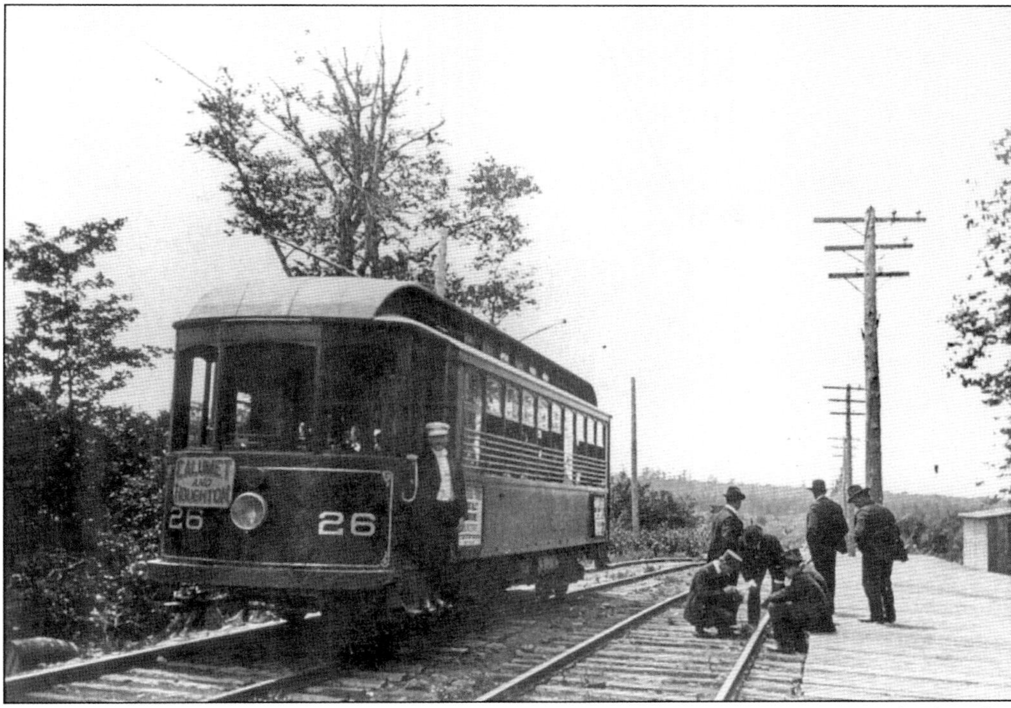

Streetcar No. 26 waits for passengers at the Electric Park station. Posters were often displayed on streetcars to announce coming events at the park. (Michigan Technological University Archives/ Copper Country Historical Collection.)

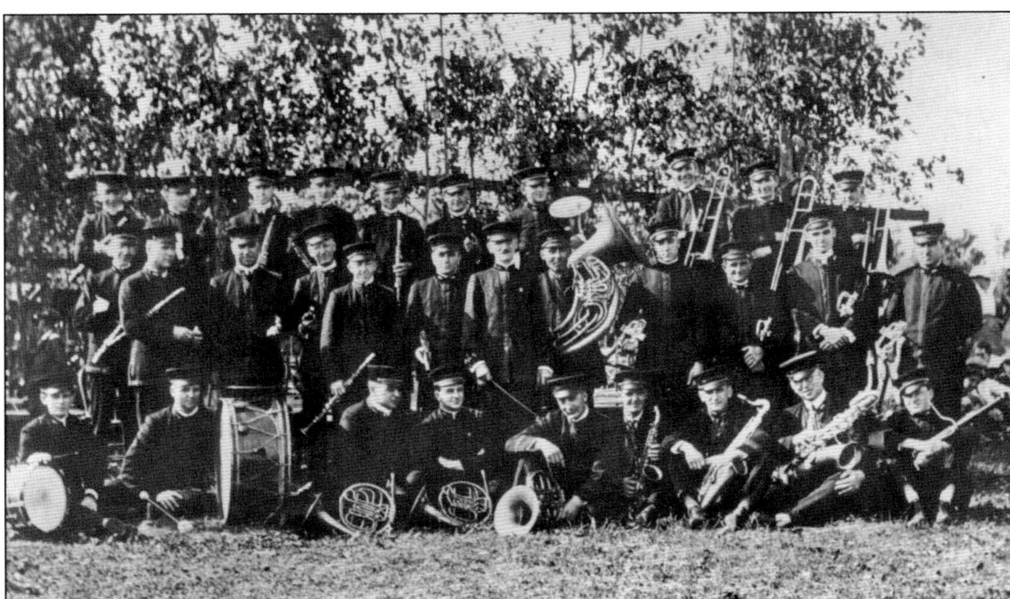

The Calumet & Hecla Band was a frequent performer for events at Electric Park and would often played at the bandstand on Sunday afternoons and weeknights. (Keweenaw National Historical Park.)

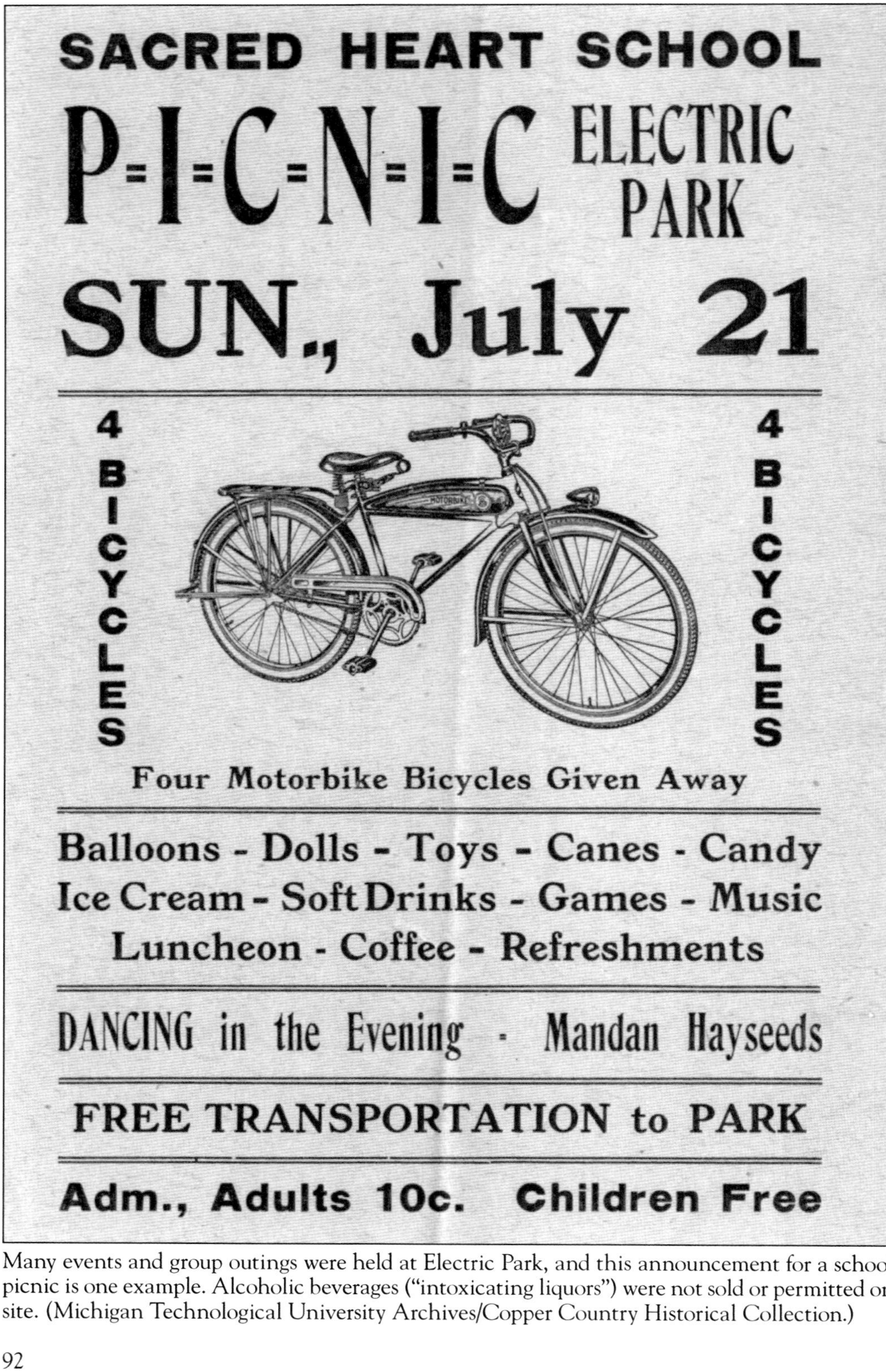

Many events and group outings were held at Electric Park, and this announcement for a school picnic is one example. Alcoholic beverages ("intoxicating liquors") were not sold or permitted on site. (Michigan Technological University Archives/Copper Country Historical Collection.)

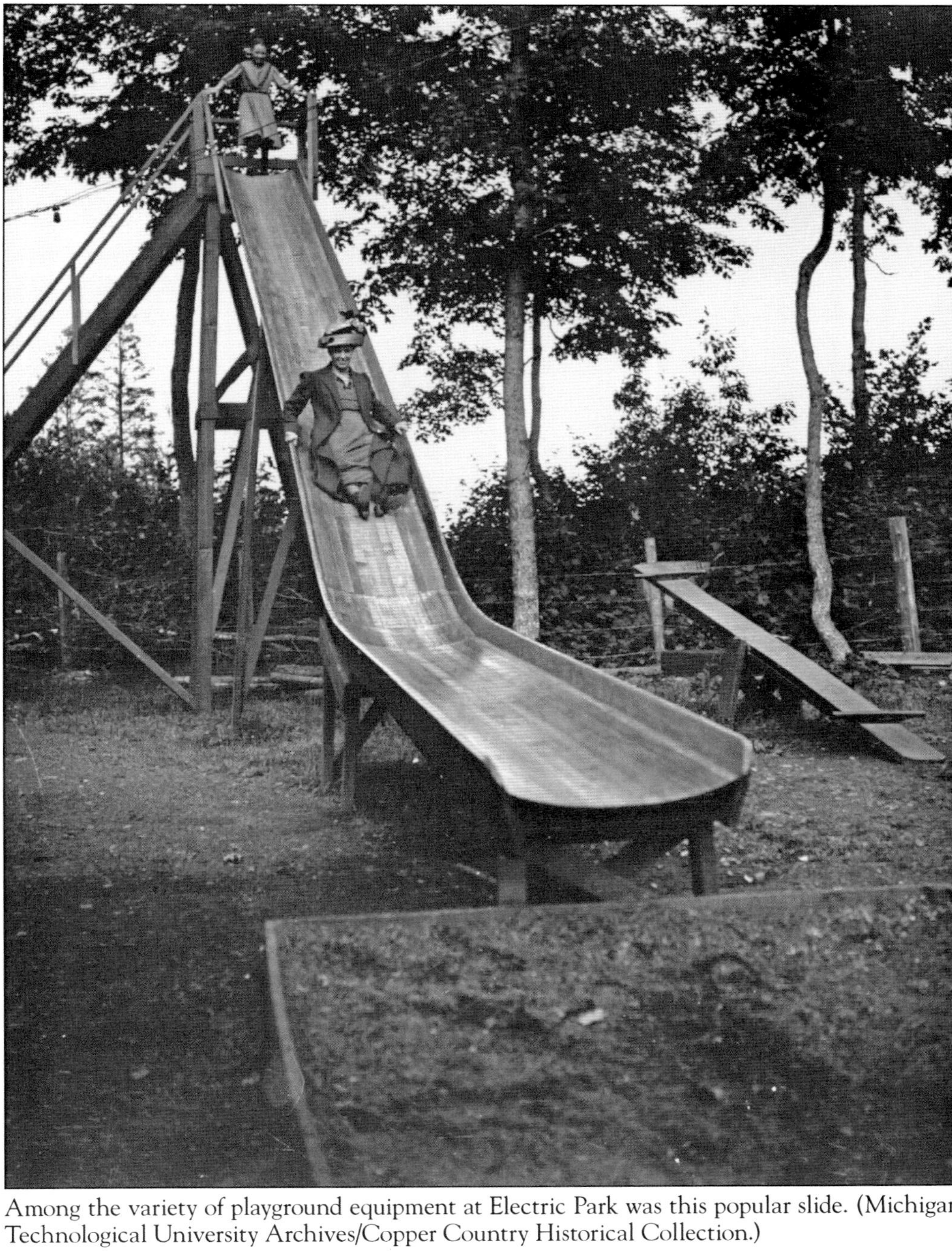

Among the variety of playground equipment at Electric Park was this popular slide. (Michigan Technological University Archives/Copper Country Historical Collection.)

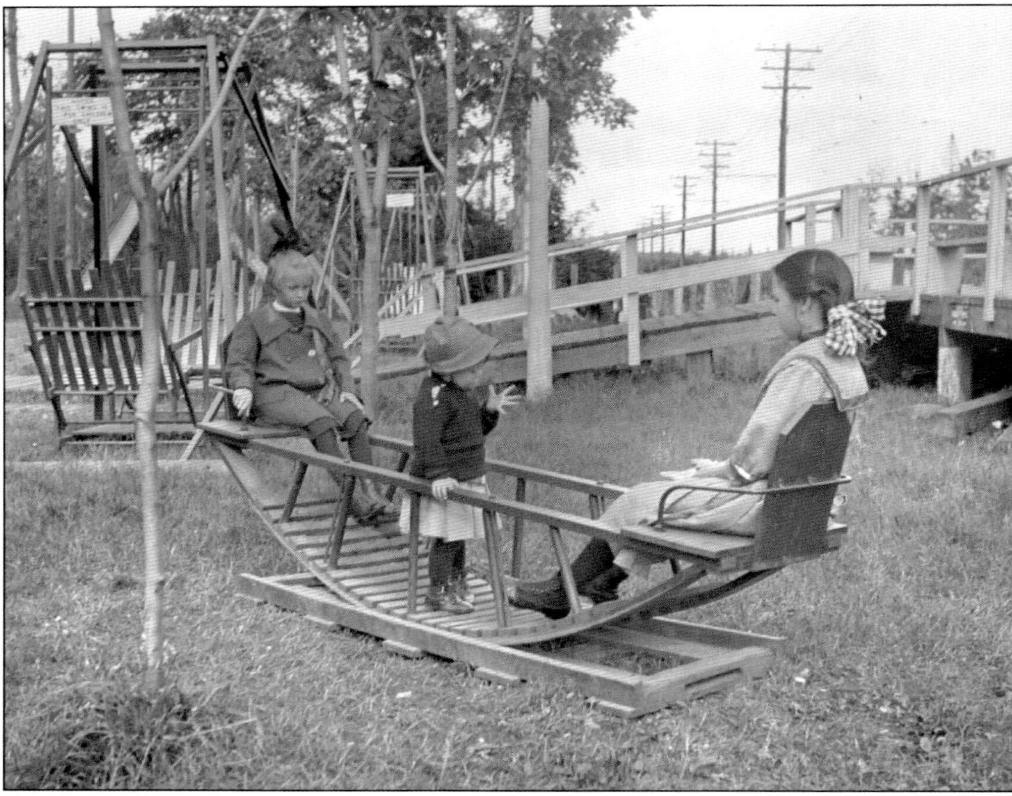

Several pieces of playground equipment were unique to Electric Park. Children in the area were fascinated by the pieces and were eager to try the newest additions. (Michigan Technological University Archives/Copper Country Historical Collection.)

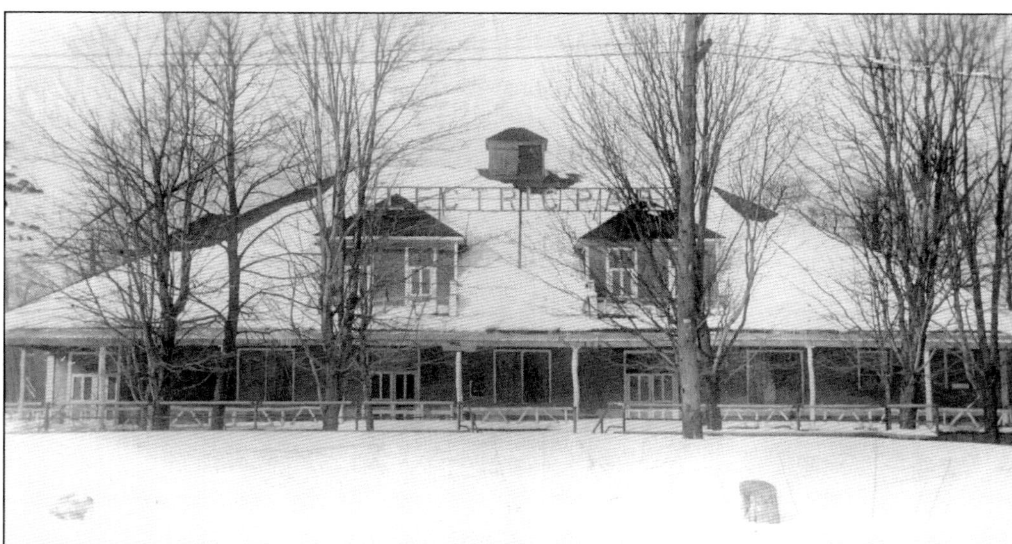

The park was closed in the winter. This photograph shows the main pavilion as it would be seen from a passing streetcar on a sunny winter day. (Houghton County Historical Society.)

Six

Attractions and Events

Streetcars provided opportunities for people to visit other communities and attend numerous attractions and events throughout the Copper Country. When the Kerredge and Calumet Theatres held special attractions, additional streetcars were needed to handle theater patrons. The same happened for hockey games at the Amphidrome in Houghton, as several streetcars would queue on Shelden Avenue to carry spectators home following a game. In the summer and fall of 1913, the Copper Country was faced with a miners' strike that changed the region. The issues involved included work hours, higher pay, the abolishment of the one-man drill, and the right to form a union with a system for hearing workers' grievances. During the strike, many residents rode the streetcars to participate in protest marches and parades in the Calumet area.

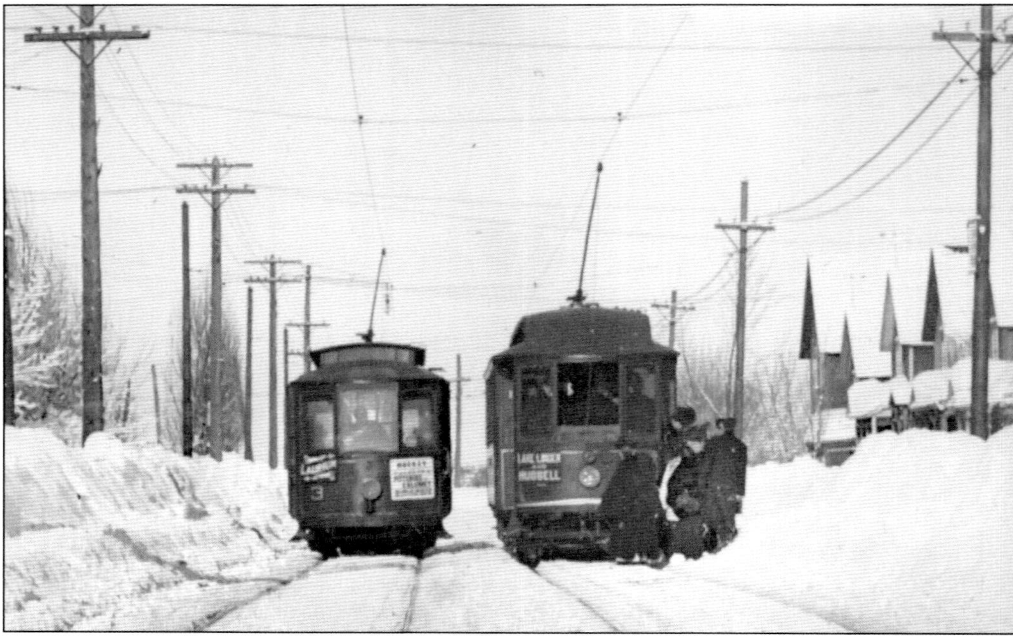

This is a winter photograph of two streetcars passing between Lake Linden and Laurium. The sign on the front of one car advertises a hockey game (similar to what can be seen on pages 73 and 77) between Pittsburgh and Calumet at the Palestra in Laurium. (Michigan Technological University Archives/Copper Country Historical Collection.)

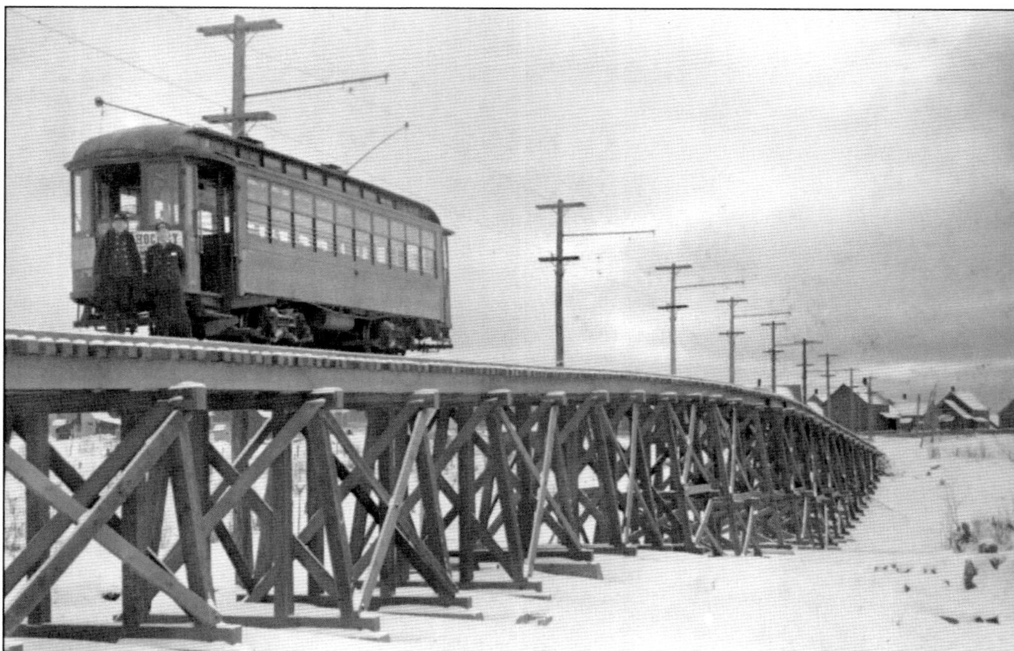

A streetcar has stopped on a trestle for a photographer. Again, note the poster on the front of the car advertising a hockey game. (Michigan Technological University Archives/Copper Country Historical Collection.)

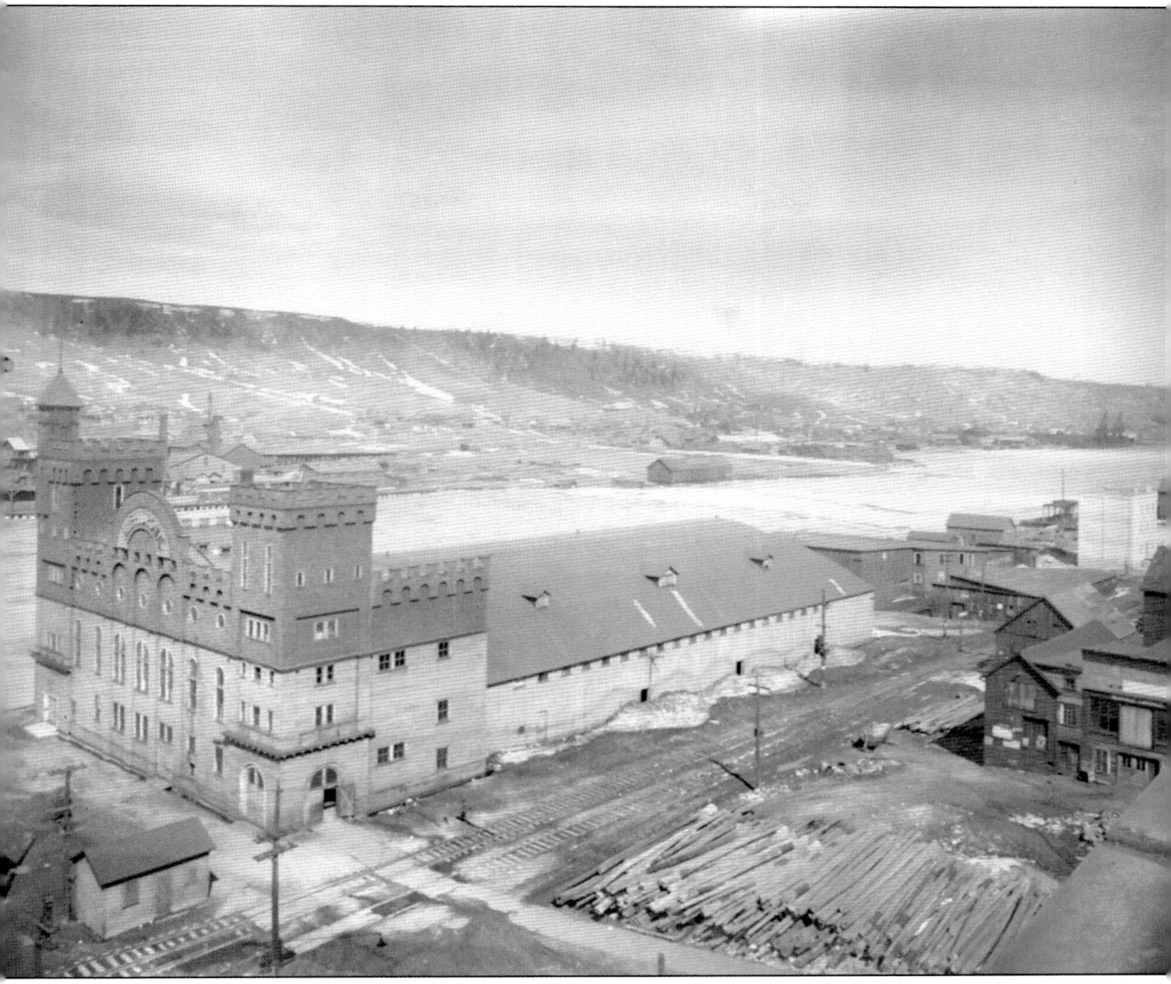

One of the area's largest hockey arenas was the Amphidrome. It was built by James Dee and opened in December 1902. The Amphidrome was located in Houghton on the Portage Lake waterfront, a few blocks from the main Houghton railroad station and the streetcar line downtown. (Michigan Technological University Archives/Copper Country Historical Collection.)

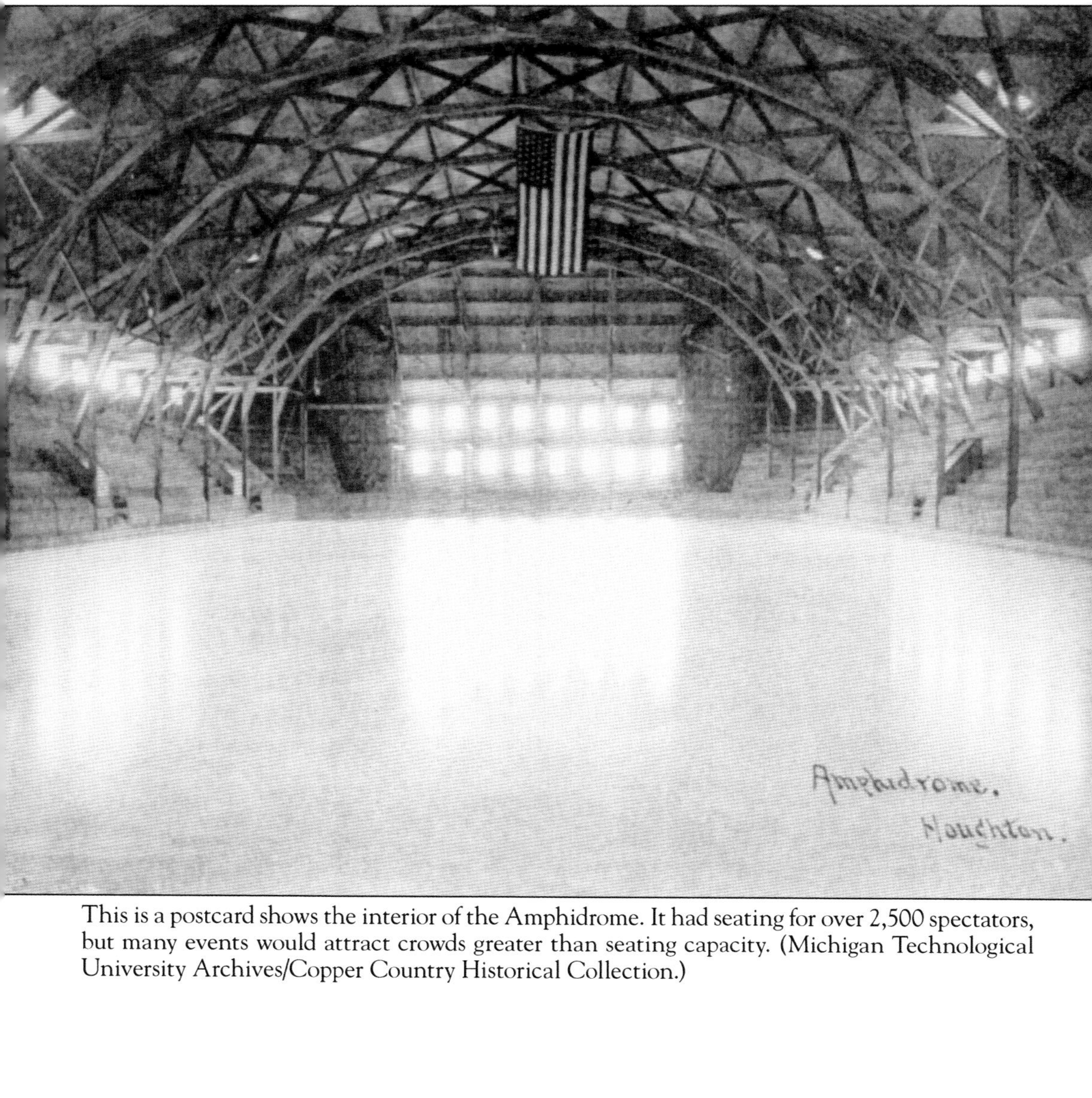

This is a postcard shows the interior of the Amphidrome. It had seating for over 2,500 spectators, but many events would attract crowds greater than seating capacity. (Michigan Technological University Archives/Copper Country Historical Collection.)

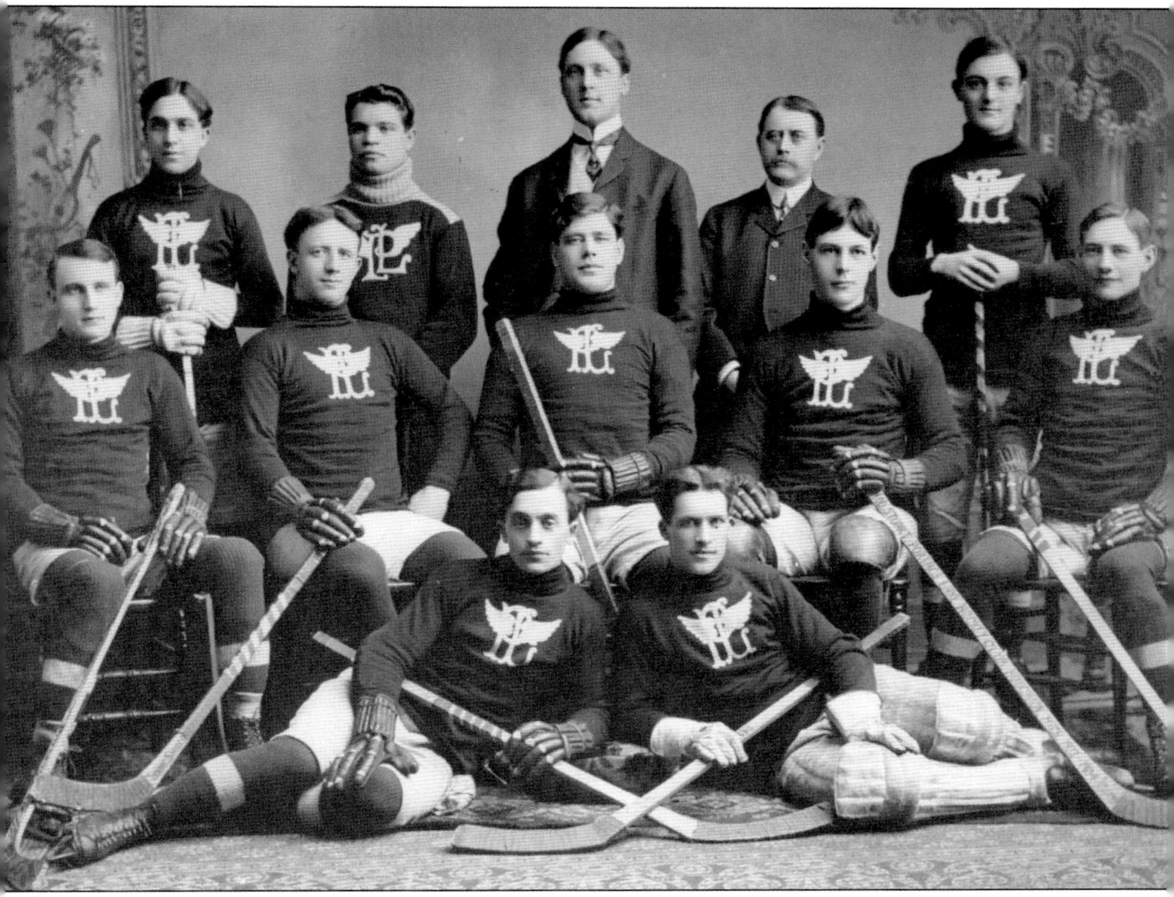

This is the 1903–1904 Portage Lake hockey club, which many believe to be the first professional hockey team. James Dee provided the financial backing for the team, and Jack "Doc" Gibson recruited players from Canada that were paid to play. The team's home arena was the Amphidrome. (Michigan Technological University Archives/Copper Country Historical Collection.)

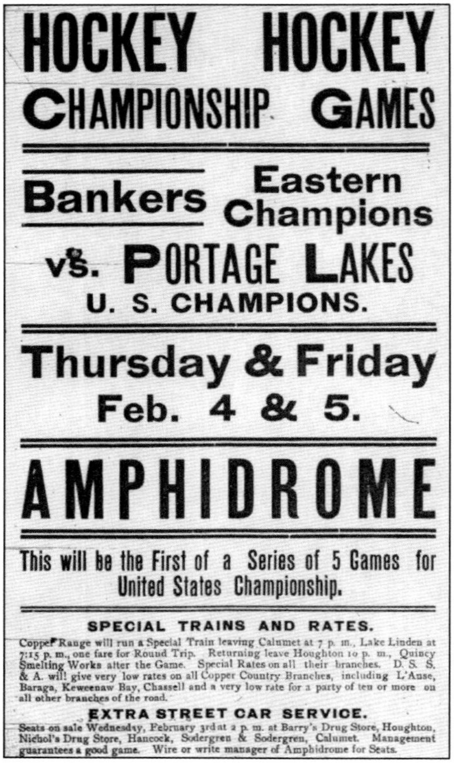

A *Houghton Daily Mining Gazette* advertisement announces the first two games of the United States Championship between the Pittsburgh Bankers and Portage Lakes. The series was to be played in the Amphidrome on February 4 and 5, 1904. Special rates for rail and streetcar users were available. Portage Lakes won the series, and several residents talked about a challenge for the Stanley Cup. (Michigan Technological University Archives/Copper Country Historical Collection.)

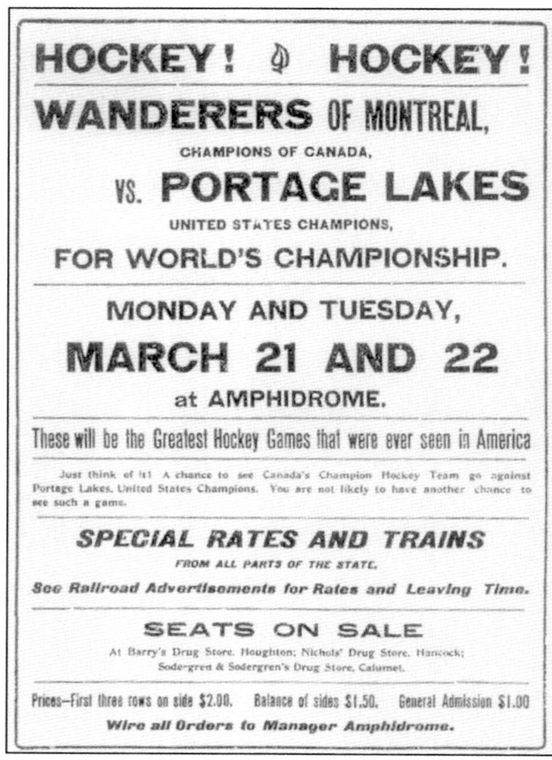

Before one could be made, the Montreal Wanderers had already challenged the Portage Lake team to a two-game series in Houghton. This advertisement in the *Houghton Daily Mining Gazette* announced games between the two teams on March 21 and 22, 1904, for what was billed as the "World's Championship." Portage Lakes won the series. That summer, James Dee and Doc Gibson worked to promote the formation of the first professional hockey league, which began play in the fall. (Michigan Technological University Archives/ Copper Country Historical Collection.)

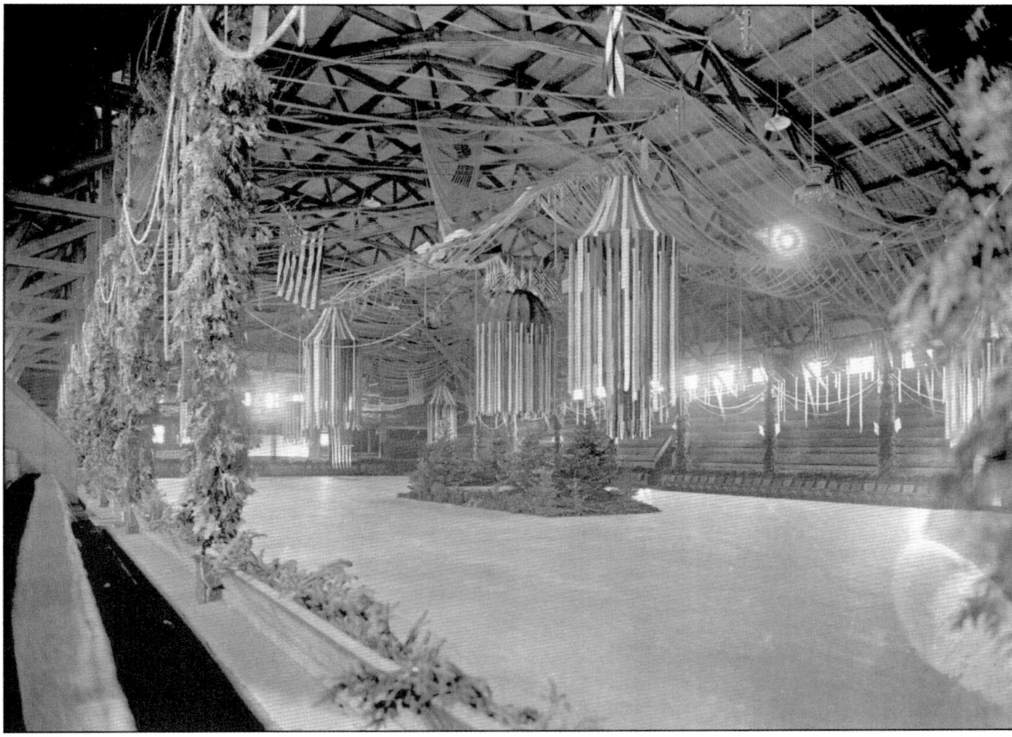

The Amphidrome became the site of many community events outside of hockey games. It developed into a popular location for skating, banquets, parties, weddings, boxing and wrestling matches, and the Houghton County Fair. (Michigan Technological University Archives/Copper Country Historical Collection.)

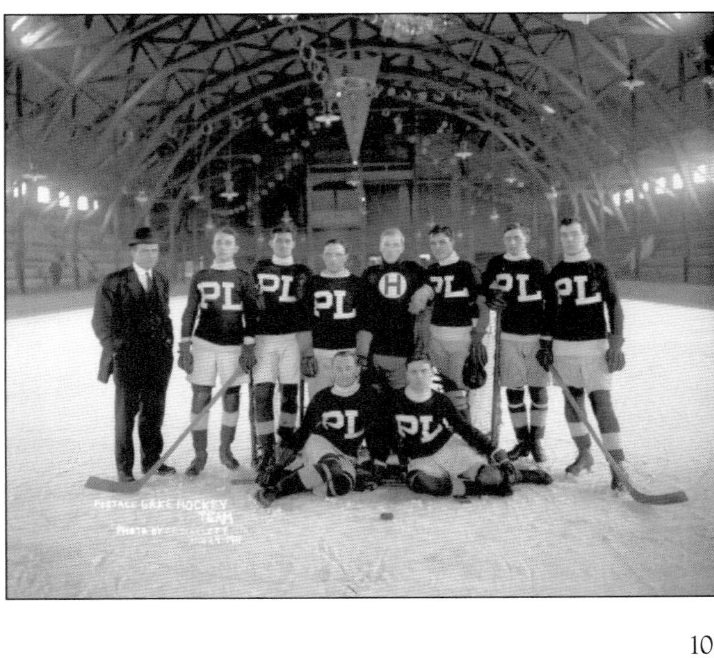

Hockey has remained a popular sport in the Copper Country, and the streetcar was an ideal means for teams and spectators to travel between towns during the winter months. Here, the 1911 Portage Lake hockey team poses in the Amphidrome. (Michigan Technological University Archives/ Copper Country Historical Collection.)

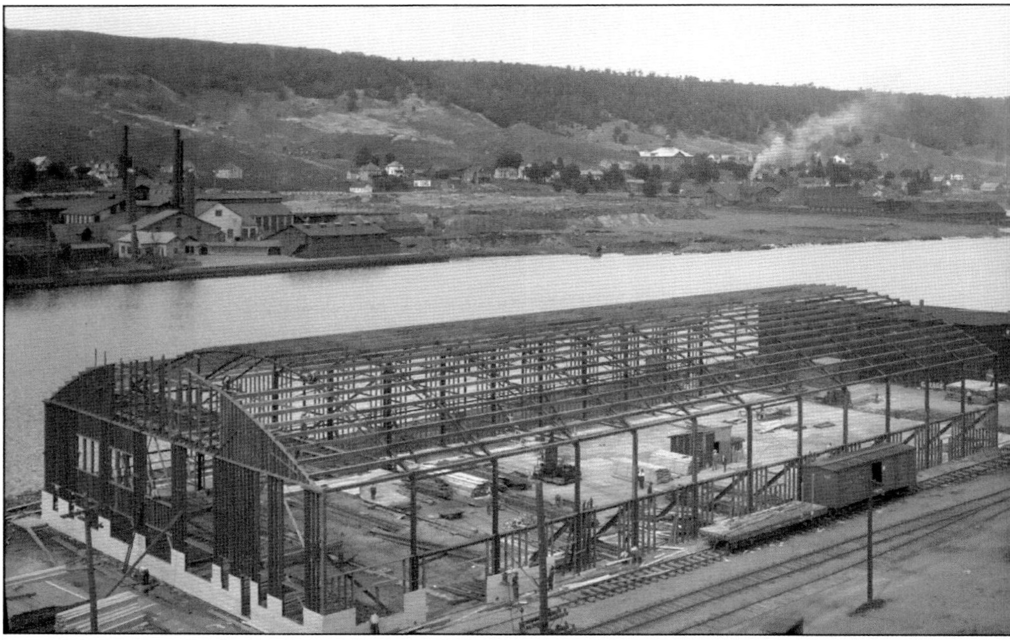

In 1927, the Amphidrome burned down, but it was rebuilt by James Dee and opened as the New Amphidrome the following year. This photograph shows the new arena under construction. (Michigan Technological University Archives/Copper Country Historical Collection.)

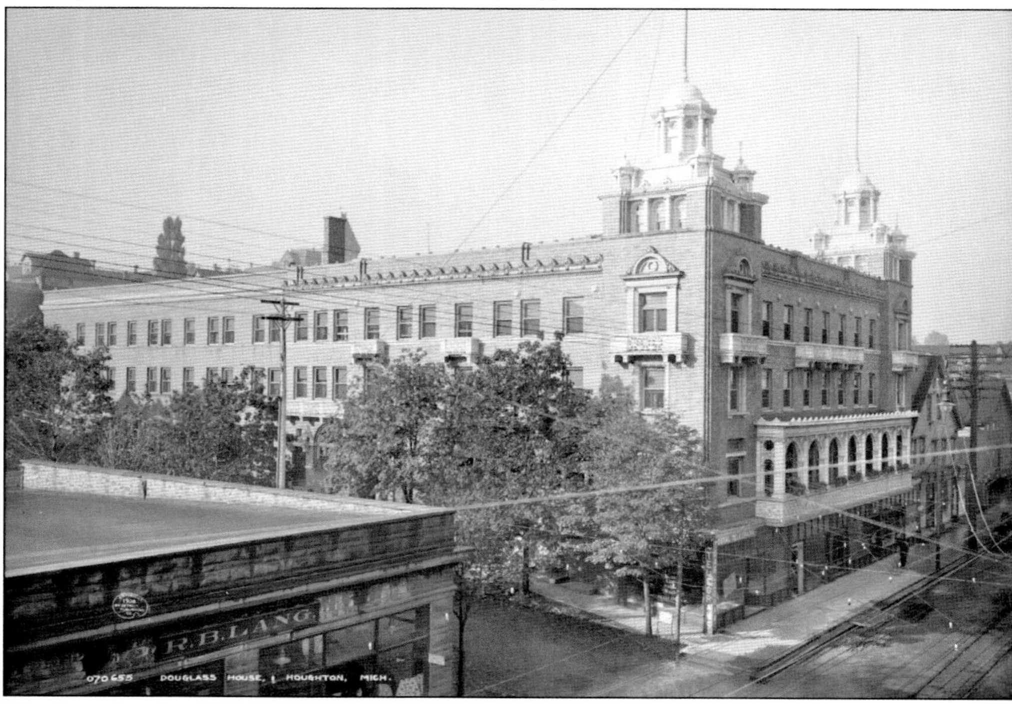

The finest hotel in Houghton was the Douglass House, located on Shelden Avenue on the streetcar line. The original hotel was built in 1860, and an addition was made in 1899 so that it fronted Sheldon Avenue. (Library of Congress.)

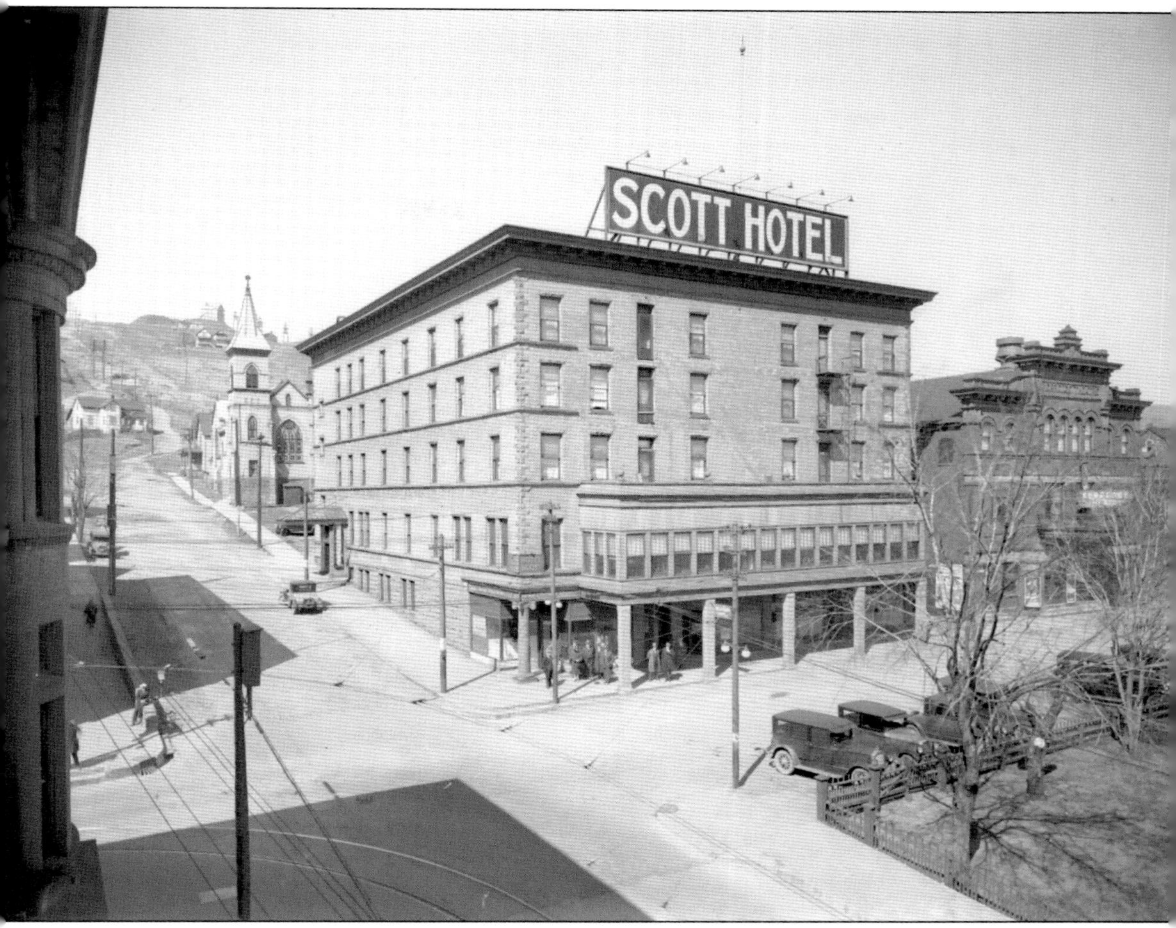

The premier hotel in Hancock was the Scott Hotel, financed by Hancock's first mayor, A.J. Scott. It was located on the northeast corner of Quincy and Reservation Streets. Note that the streetcar line turns at this intersection. Next to the Scott Hotel was the Kerredge Theatre, one of the best stage theatres in the Upper Peninsula. It attracted the top entertainers and vaudeville groups of the era. The Kerredge burned down in 1959. (Michigan Technological University Archives/ Copper Country Historical Collection.)

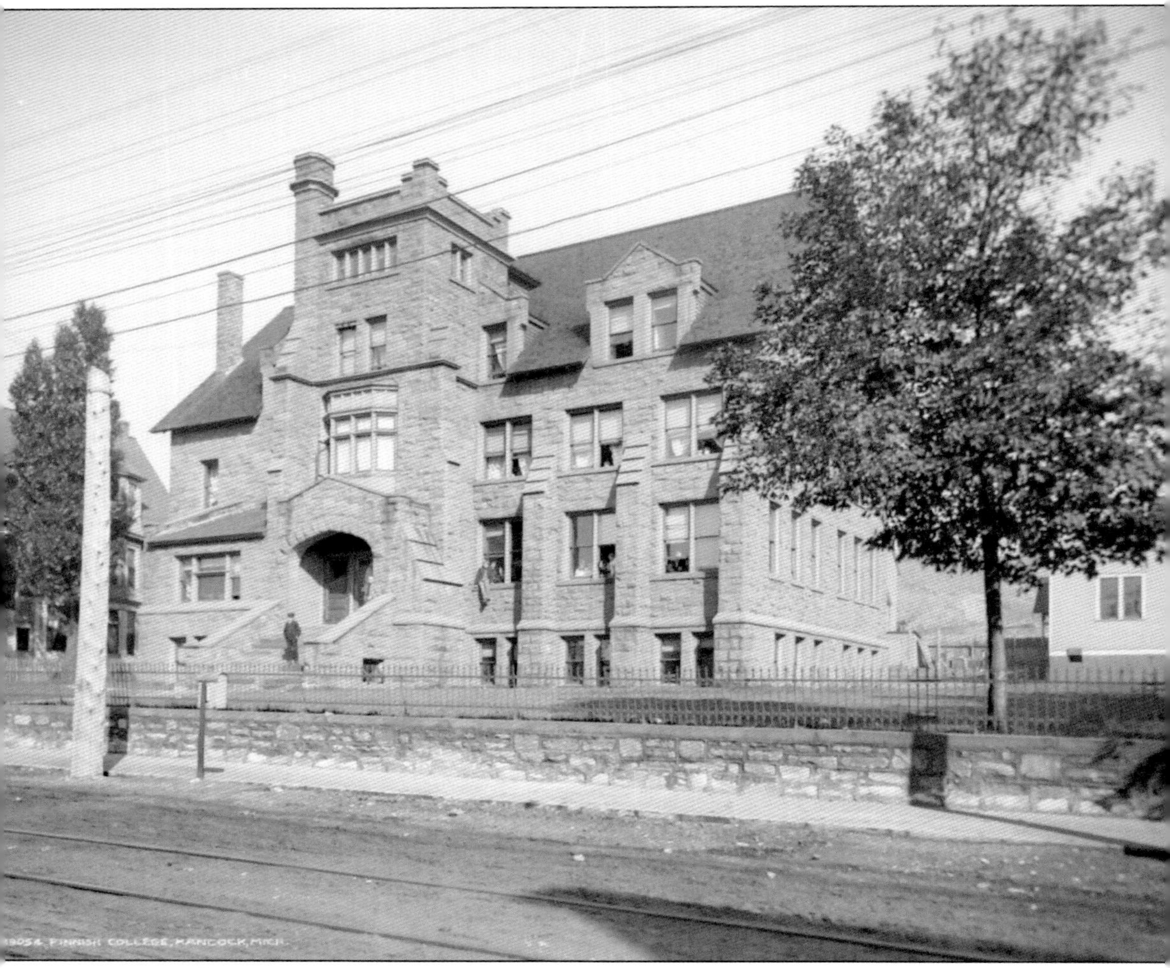

Suomi College was founded in 1896 by Finnish immigrants as a private liberal arts college. The founders wanted a college that would educate their children but retain a cultural heritage. The Old Main Building on Quincy Street, seen here, opened in 1899. It was located on the streetcar line in Hancock. In 2000, Suomi College became Finlandia University. (Library of Congress.)

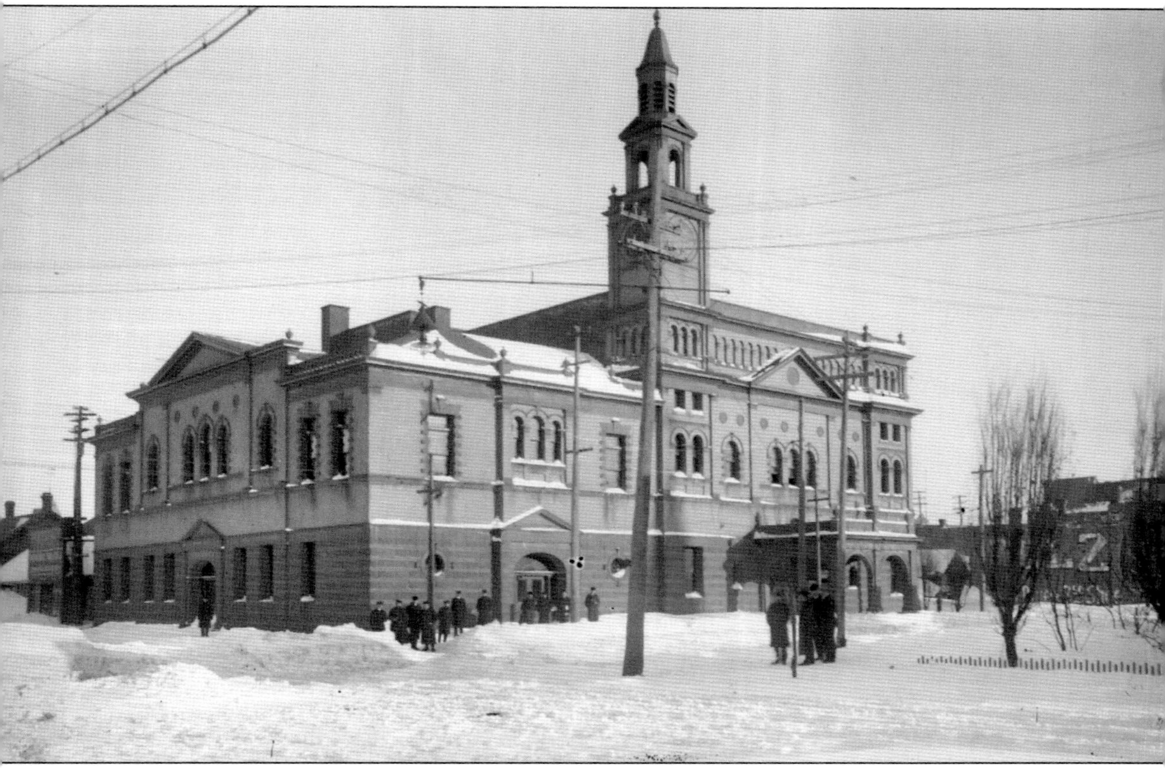

The Calumet Theatre opened in 1900 and was the cultural center in the region. Nationally renowned performers, including John Phillip Sousa, Lillian Russell, and Sarah Bernhardt, made it a stop on their tours. It is located on Sixth Avenue at Elm Street in Red Jacket on the streetcar line. The Calumet Theatre still operates today. (Michigan Technological University Archives/ Copper Country Historical Collection.)

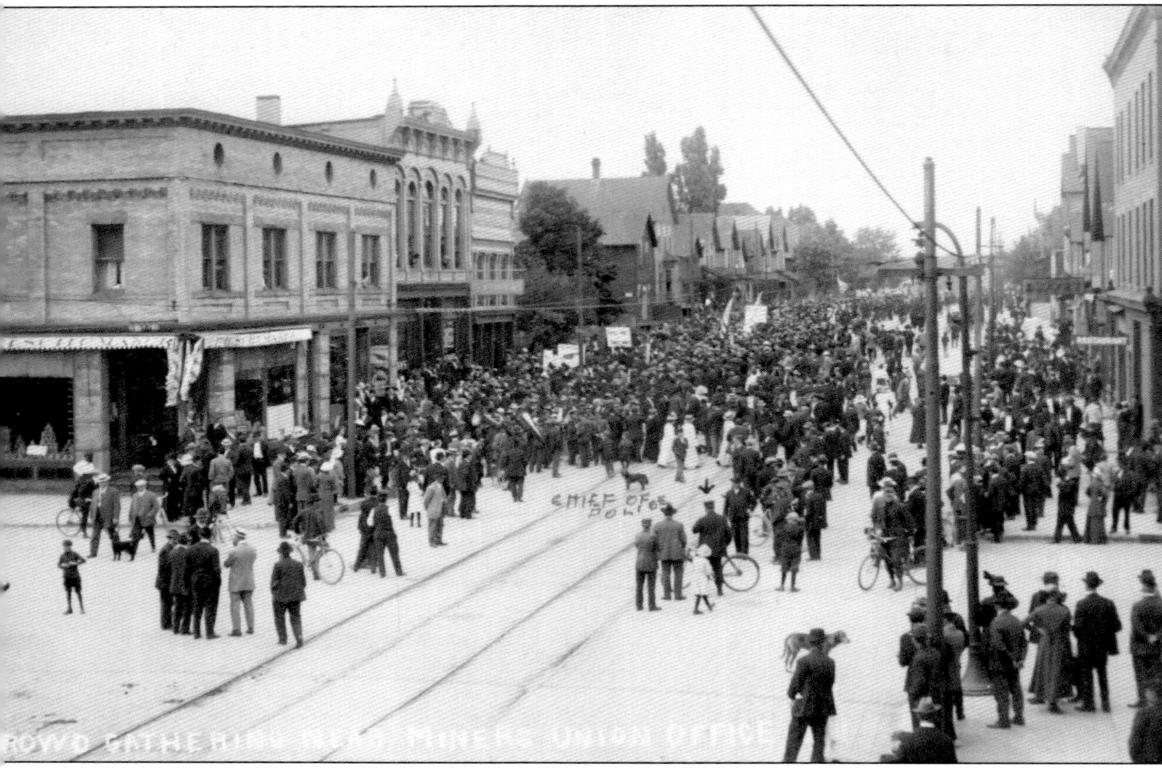

Tensions between mine workers and copper-mining companies came to a head in July 1913, when thousands of workers took to the streets to protest. Strained relations developed between workers and the companies, between neighbors, and even between family members. The Michigan National Guard was dispatched, and there were many instances of violence, including the shootings of both strikers and strikebreakers. This 1913 photograph shows a crowd gathering near the Miners Union office on Sixth Street in Red Jacket. (Michigan Technological University Archives/Copper Country Historical Collection.)

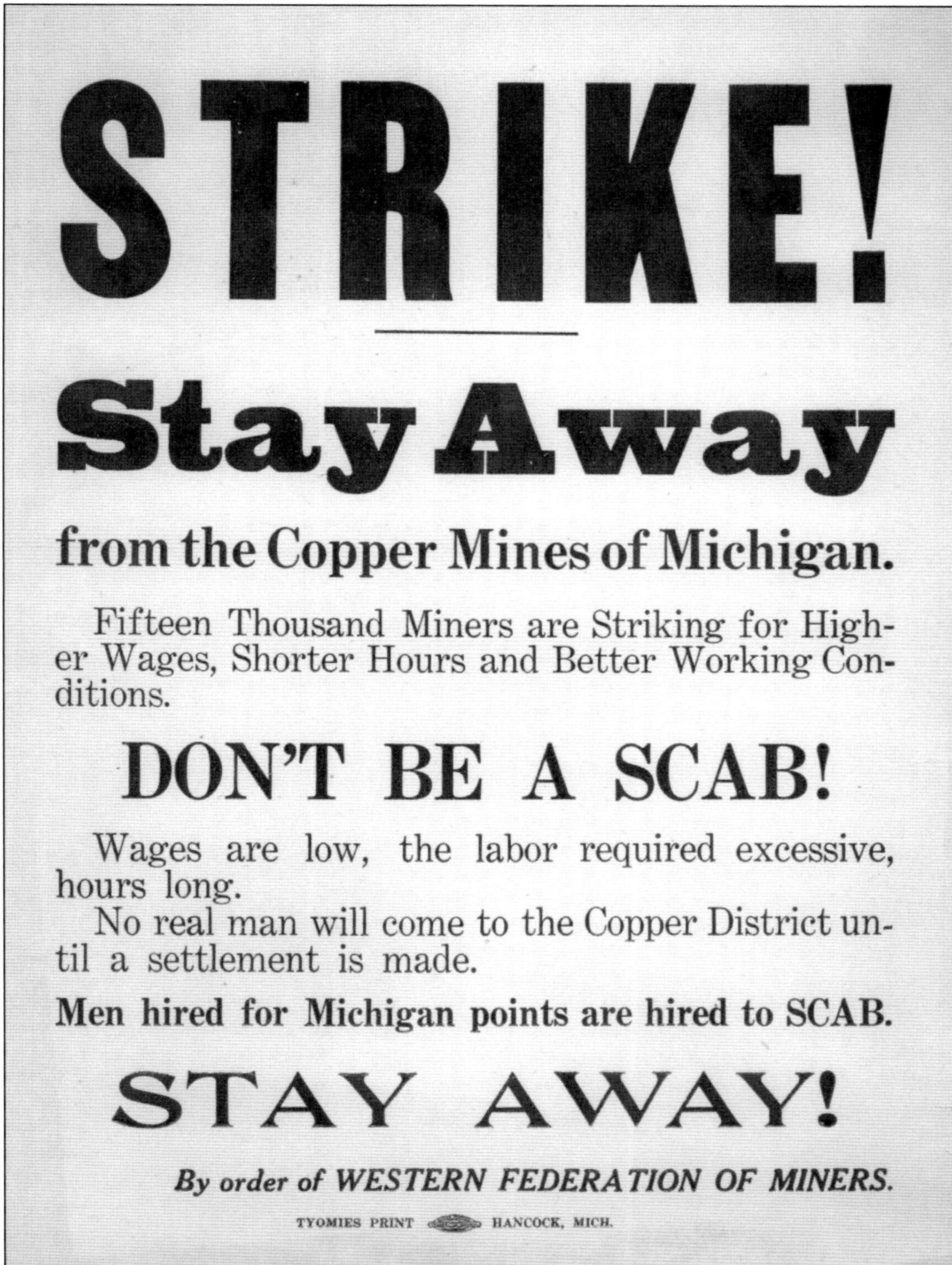

Immediately after the strike was called, companies put out a call for workers to replace striking miners and surface workers. This flyer was distributed by the Western Federation of Miners during the 1913 strike to discourage workers from coming to the Copper Country. (Michigan Technological University Archives/Copper Country Historical Collection.)

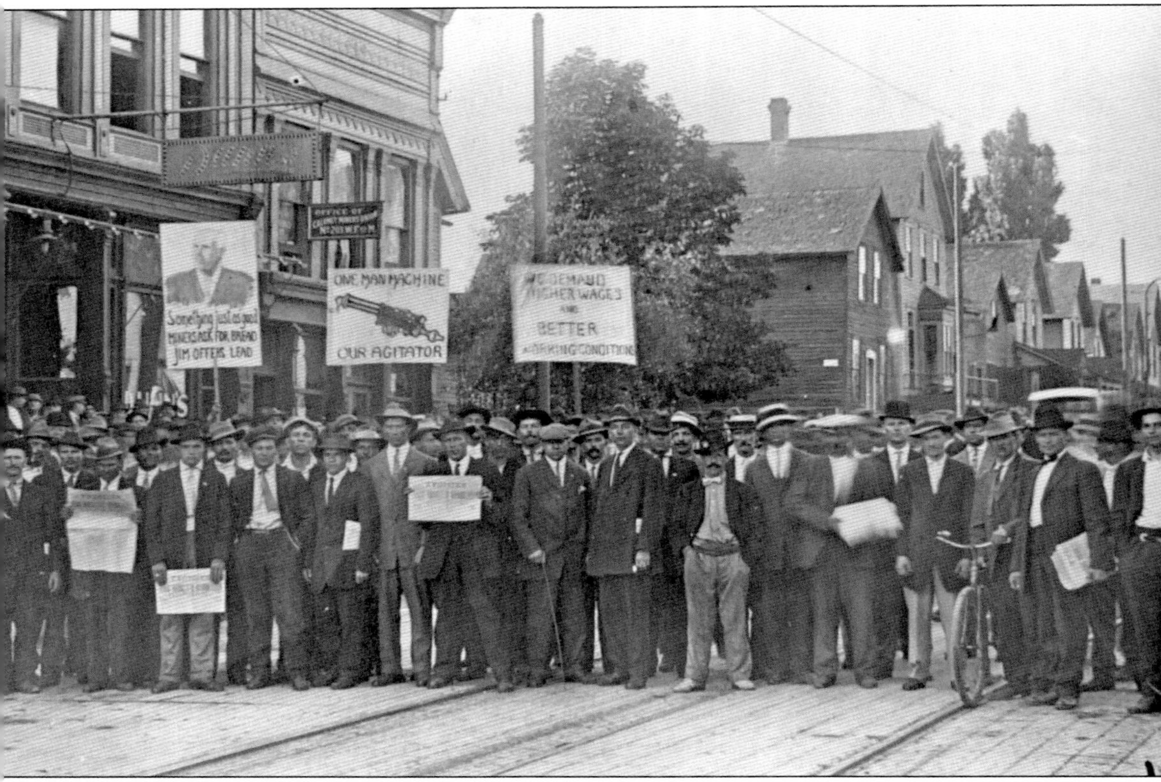

Demonstrations and rallies were common during this time. Here, a demonstration is taking place in front of the union office on Sixth Street. Miners protested, carried signs, and marched in parades during the strike. Times were difficult for men and their families without a paycheck. (Michigan Technological University Archives/Copper Country Historical Collection.)

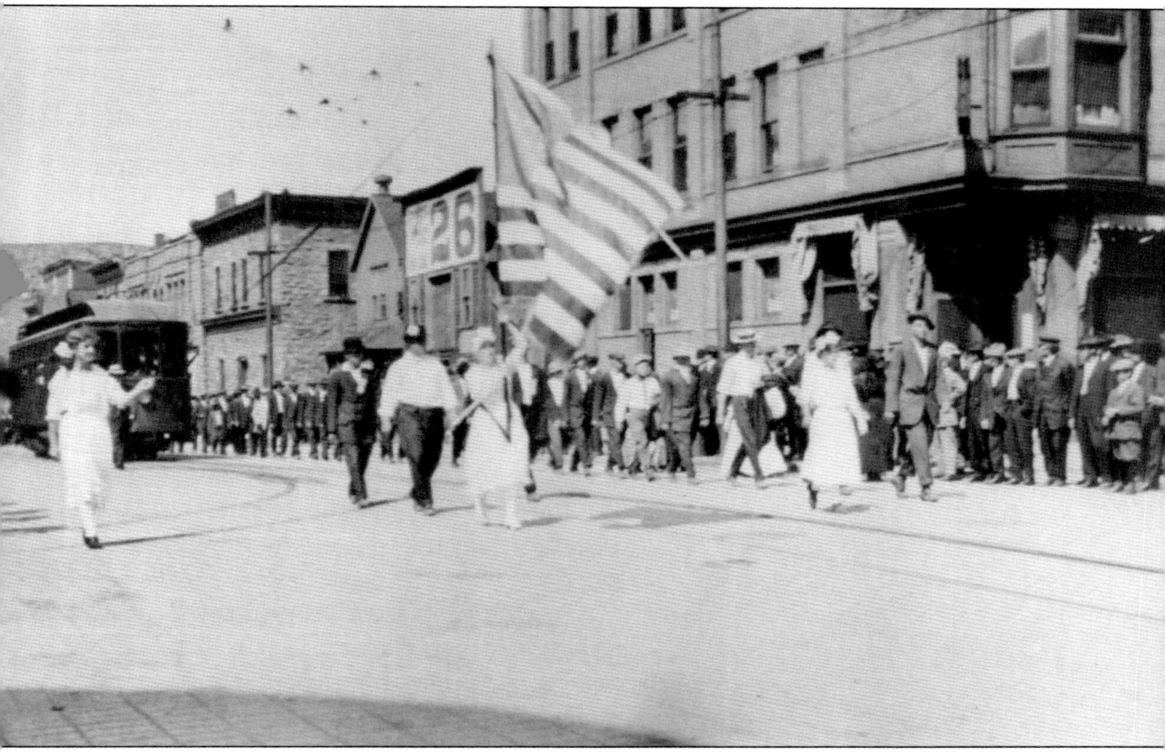

A 1913 rally parade on Sixth Avenue at Oak Street in Red Jacket passes the Michigan House. Note the streetcar following behind the marchers. (Michigan Technological University Archives/ Copper Country Historical Collection.)

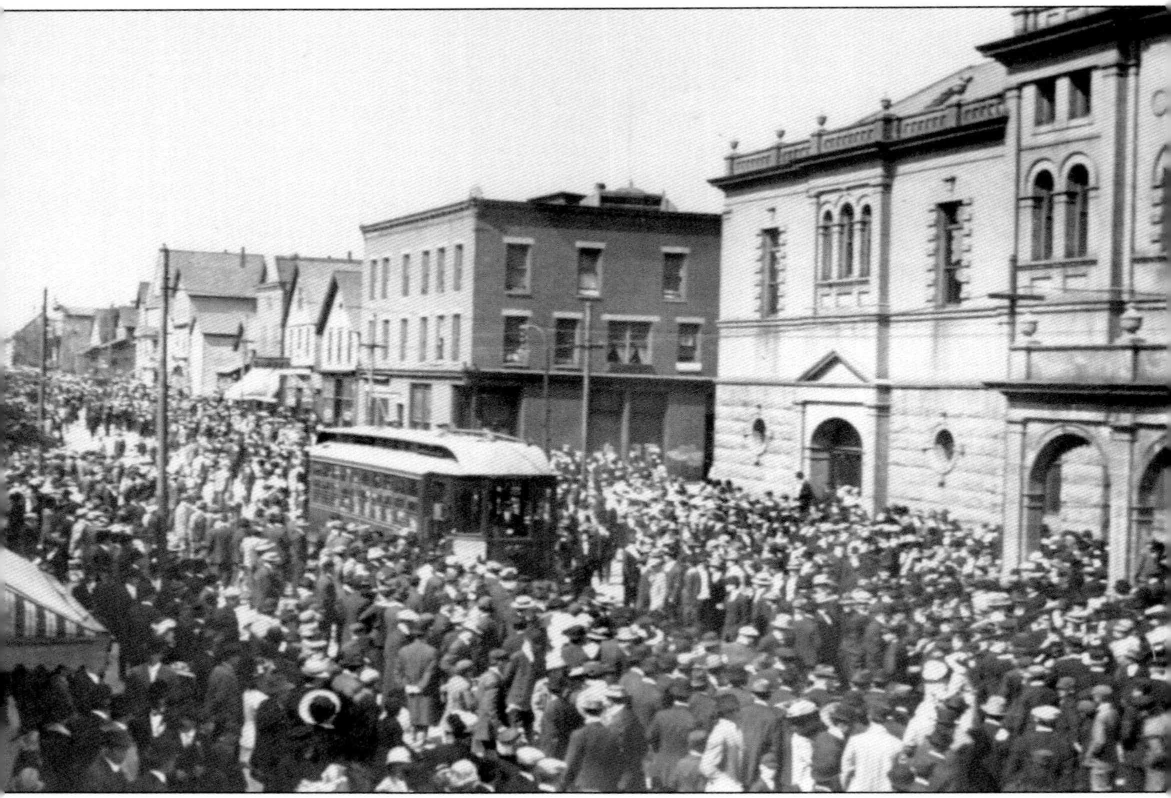

Here, a union rally event and meeting is under way at the Calumet Theatre. It took place before the strike on June 8, 1913. (Michigan Technological University Archives/Copper Country Historical Collection.)

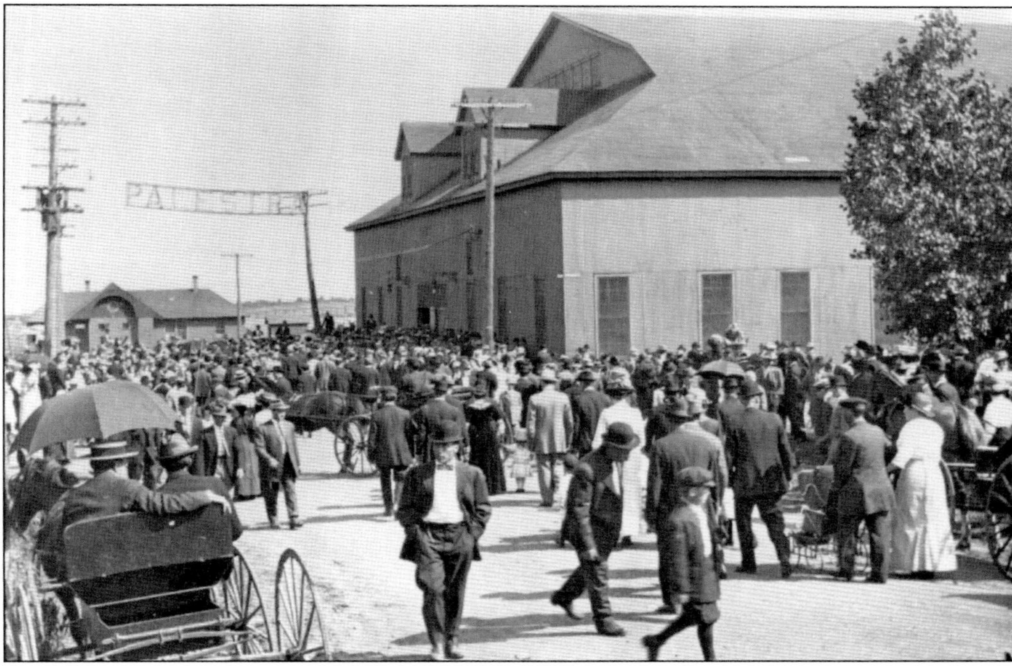

Strikers parade to a rally at the Palestra in Laurium. The Palestra was located on the corner of Third and Isle Royale Streets, a few blocks east of the streetcar line. In the winter, hockey was played there. (Michigan Technological University Archives/Copper Country Historical Collection.)

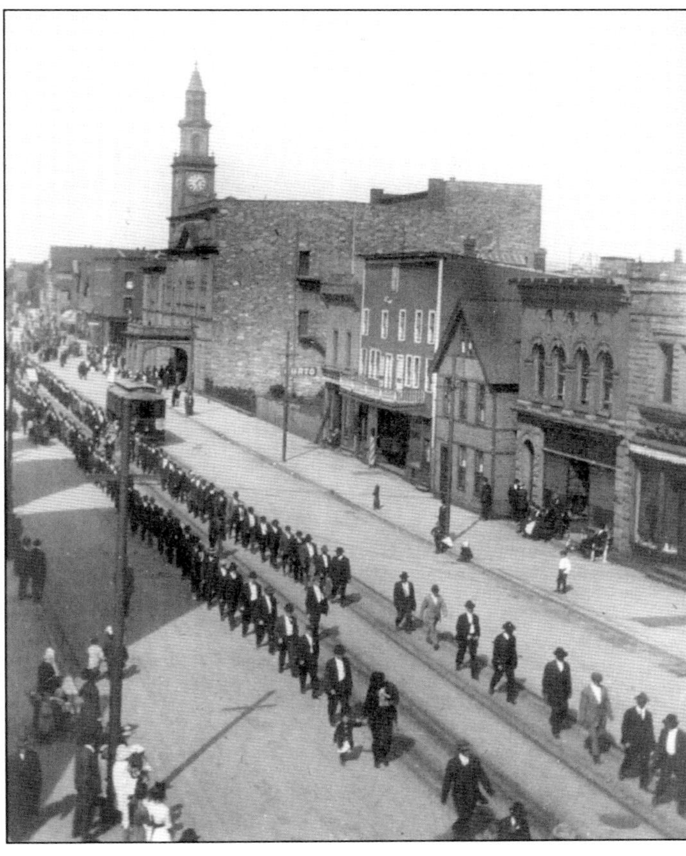

This photograph shows another rally march on Sixth Avenue in Red Jacket. Again, note the streetcar. (Houghton County Historical Society.)

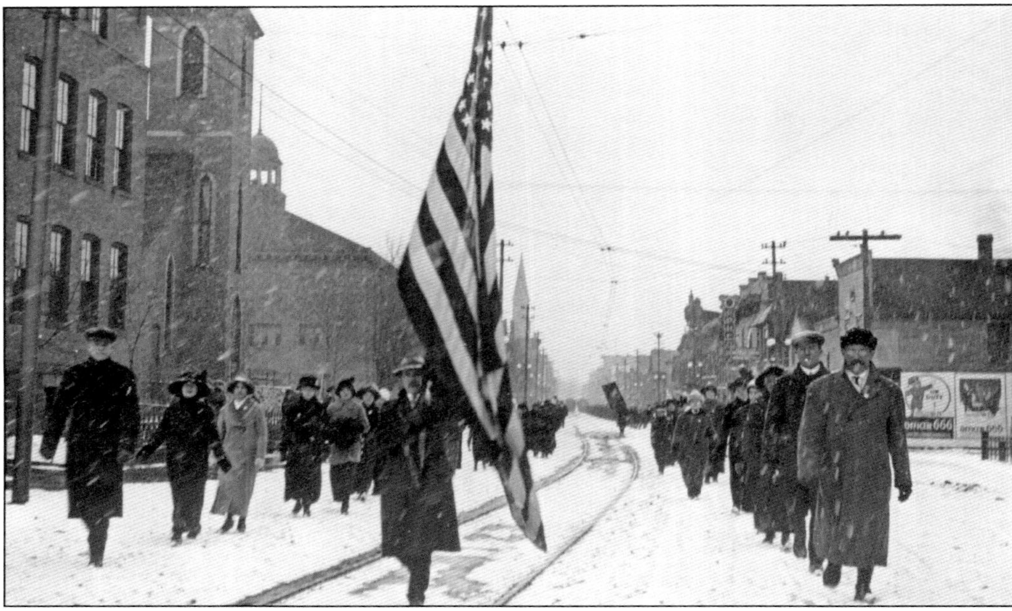

The demonstrations went beyond the Calumet area. This photograph shows a rally march on Quincy Street in Hancock in support of the miners' strike. (City of Hancock.)

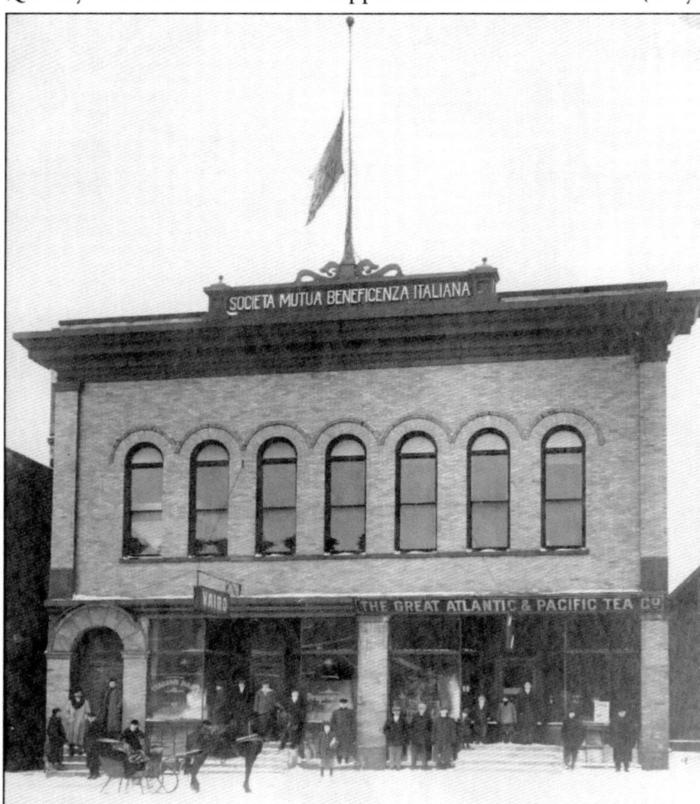

The Italian Hall in Red Jacket was the site of one of the most tragic events during the strike. More than 70 people, mostly children, died during a Christmas Eve party at the hall when they were trampled in a rush to escape the building when someone yelled, "Fire!" (Michigan Technological University Archives/Copper Country Historical Collection.)

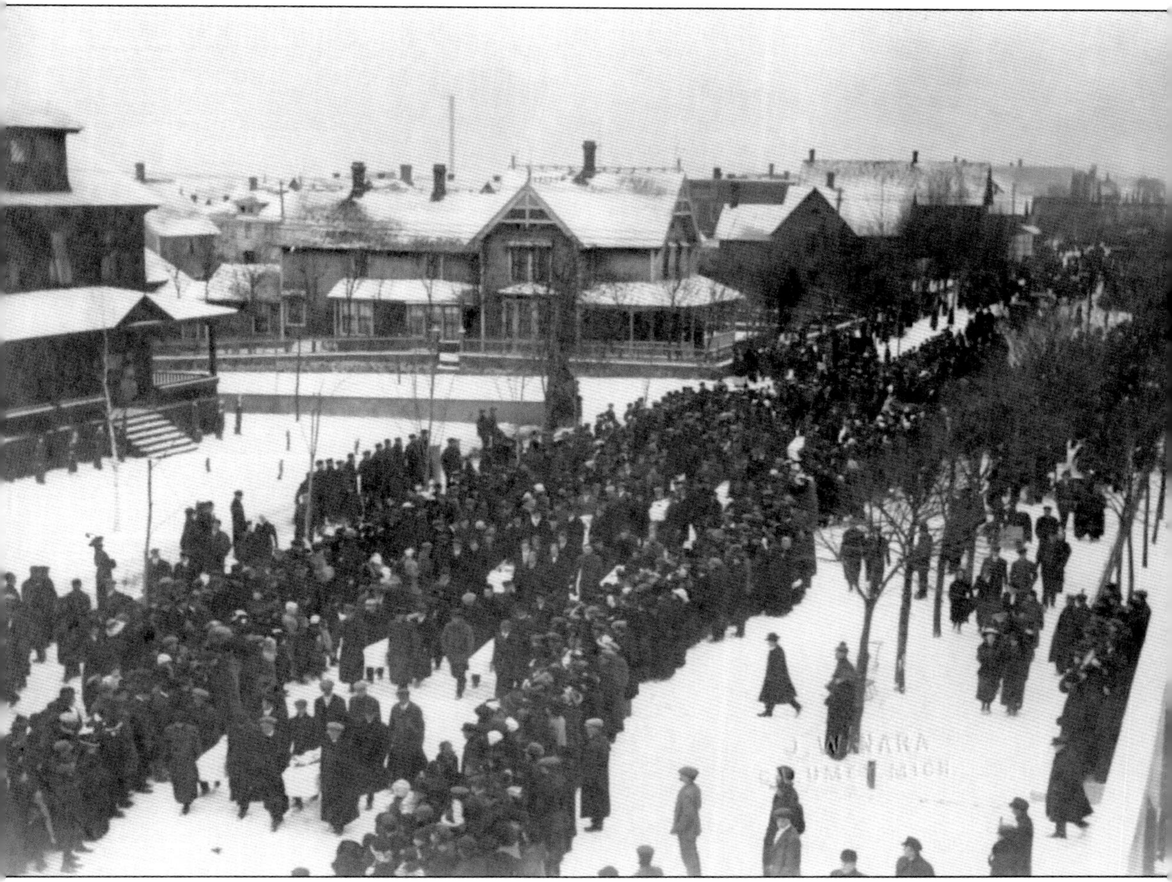

Shown here is the funeral parade for those who died in the Italian Hall tragedy. Following the funerals, the mood in the Copper Country became more somber, and by the end of January 1914 the strike was essentially broken. Mine managers refused to recognize the Western Federation of Miners, and the local union finally voted to end the strike on April 12, 1914. (Michigan Technological University Archives/Copper Country Historical Collection.)

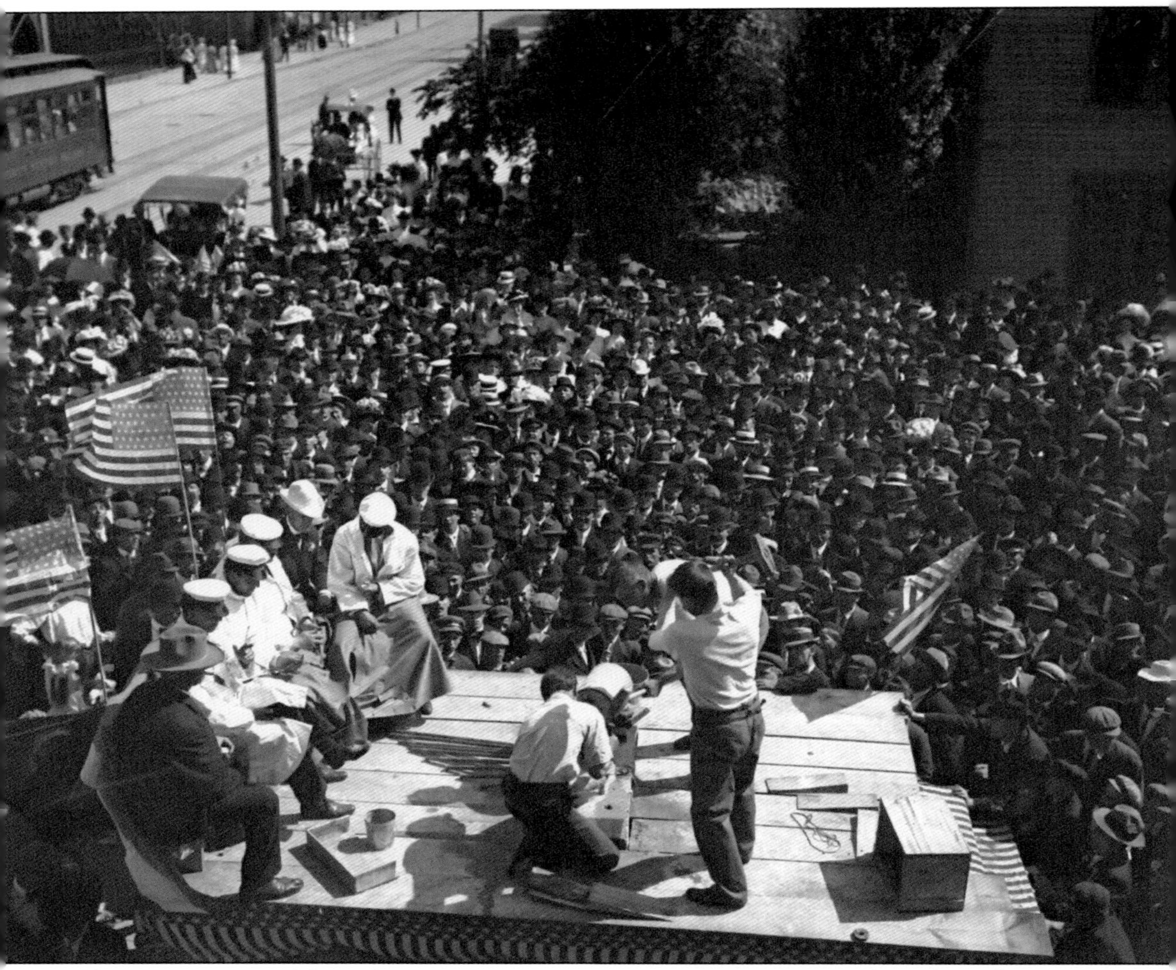

Street activities and festivals were a common occurrence in communities throughout the Copper Country. This 1909 photograph shows a hammer and drill contest at the corner of Sixth and Elm Streets in Red Jacket. Note the streetcar in the background. (Michigan Technological University Archives/Copper Country Historical Collection.)

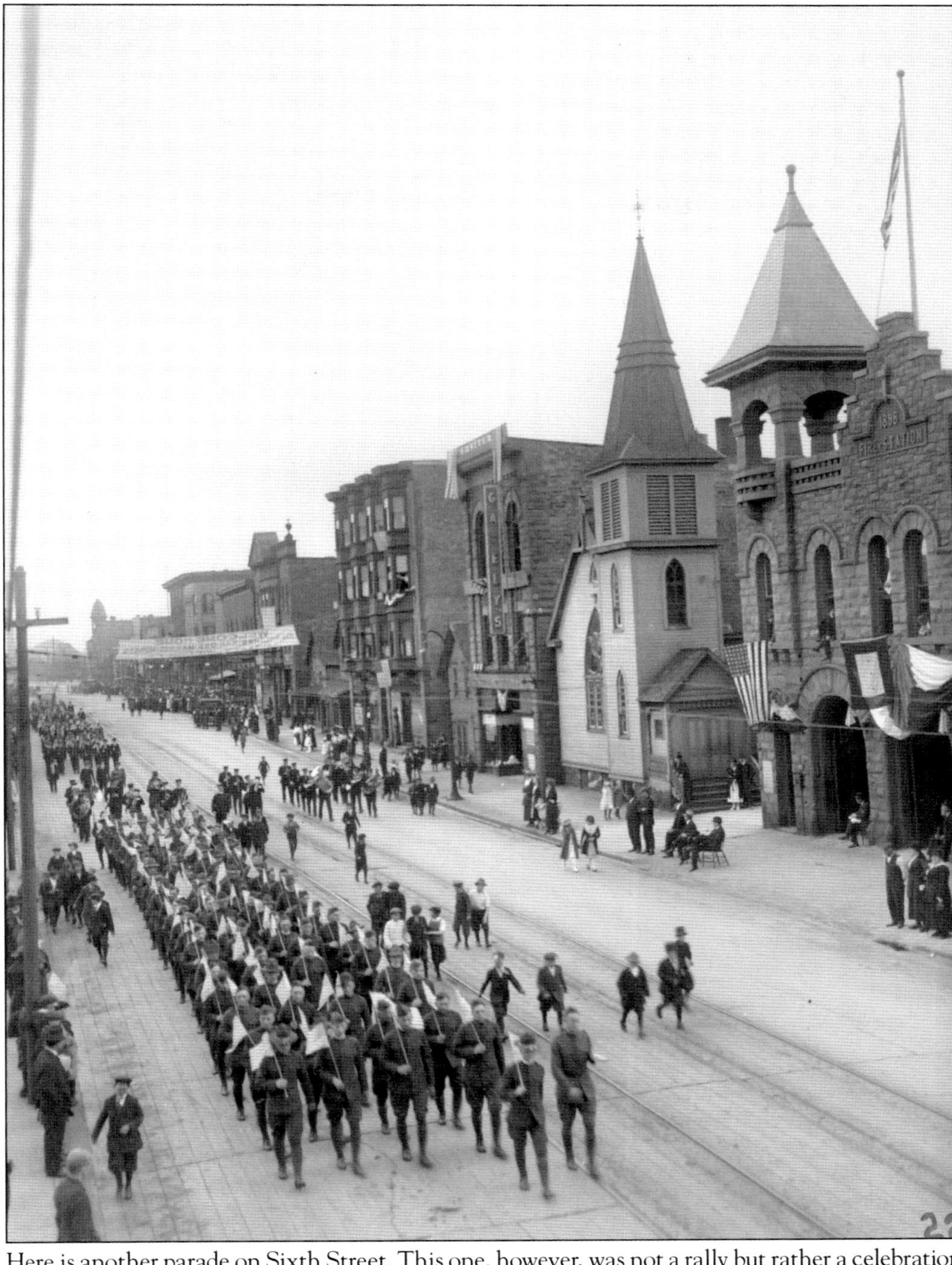

Here is another parade on Sixth Street. This one, however, was not a rally but rather a celebration honoring the return of World War I troops. (Michigan Technological University Archives/Copper Country Historical Collection.)

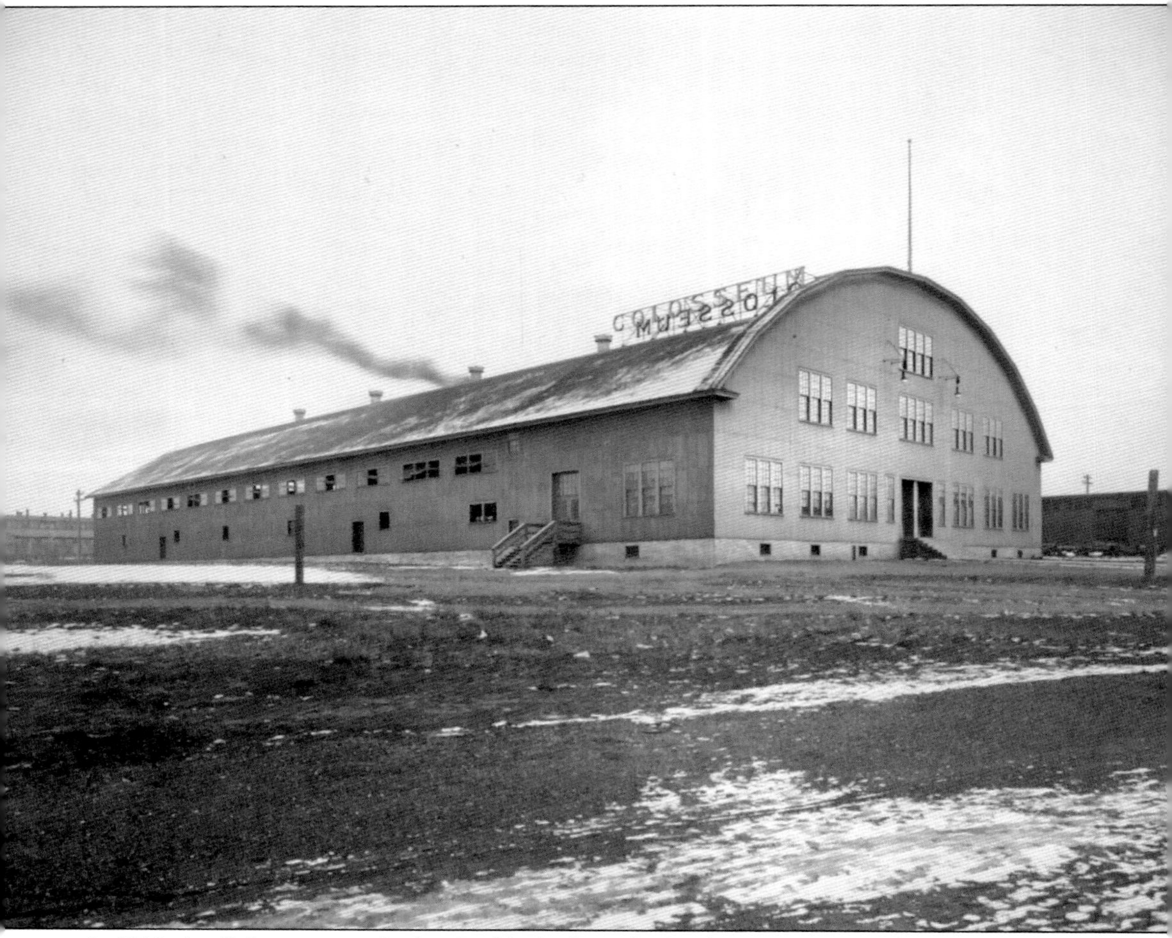

In 1913, the Colosseum was built a few blocks from the Sixth Street streetcar line in Red Jacket. It is still open today and is believed to be the oldest continuously operating indoor ice arena in the world. (Michigan Technological University Archives/Copper Country Historical Collection.)

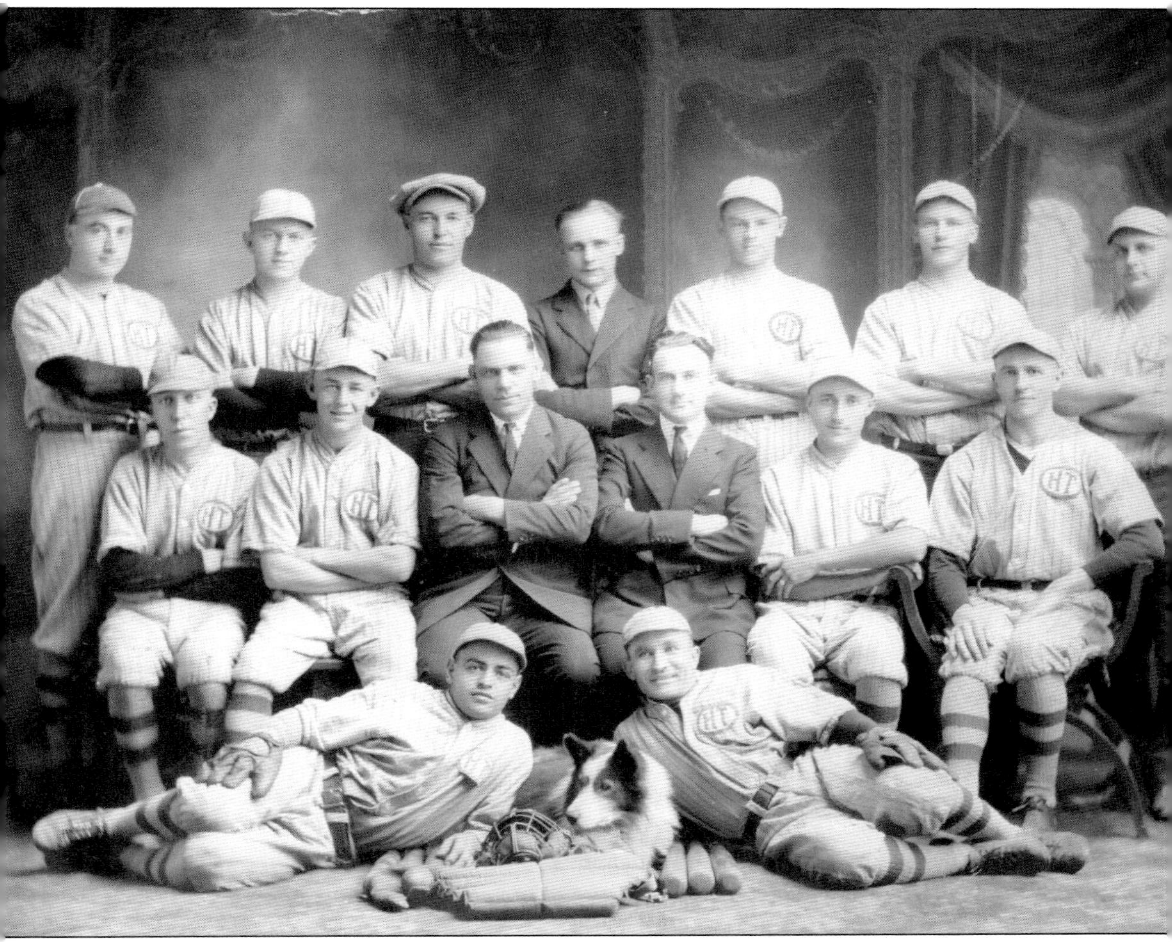

Baseball was always a popular summer sport in the Copper Country, and community teams competed in several leagues. Baseball fields were located in virtually every community in the region. Here, members of the 1922 Hancock baseball team, the champion of the Copper Country Twilight League, pose for a photograph. Their home field was located just west of the carbarn in West Hancock. (Michigan Technological University Archives/Copper Country Historical Collection.)

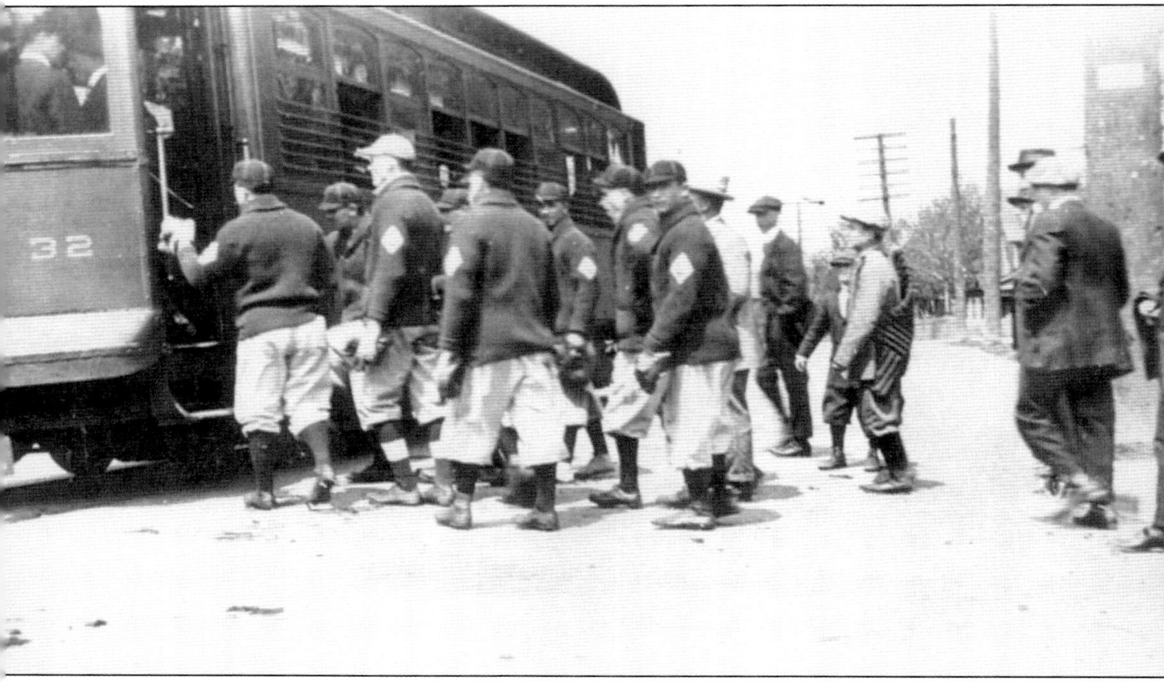

Baseball squads and other sports teams would ride the streetcar to games throughout the Copper Country. Here, a team boards a streetcar in Calumet. (Michigan Technological University Archives/Copper Country Historical Collection.)

Seven

Famous Passengers

Annual ridership on the line reached a peak of almost 6.5 million passengers in 1909, but near the end of operations yearly ridership had fallen to less than 2 million. Streetcars were an extremely popular means of transportation in the Copper Country, and during the peak years average daily ridership would range from 10,000 passengers during the winter to 16,000 passengers in the summer. Over the years, several famous passengers rode the Copper Country streetcars.

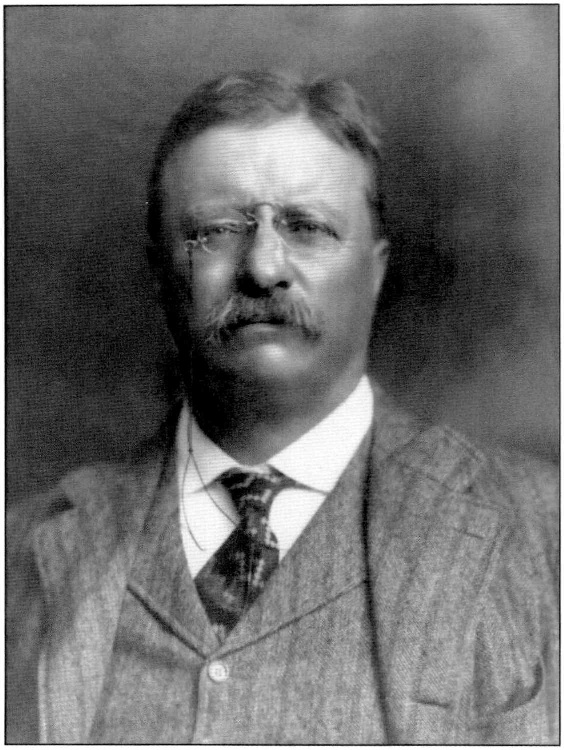

Theodore "Teddy" Roosevelt became the 26th president of the United States when he was sworn in following the assassination of Pres. William McKinley in 1901. He came to the Copper Country in October 1912 on a campaign tour as the leader of a third party that was popularly known as the Bull Moose Party. Although Roosevelt did not actually ride the streetcar, his campaign appearances at the Amphidrome and Palestra drew thousands of streetcar users. A few days after his Copper Country visit, an assassination attempt was made on the former president during a Milwaukee campaign stop. (Library of Congress.)

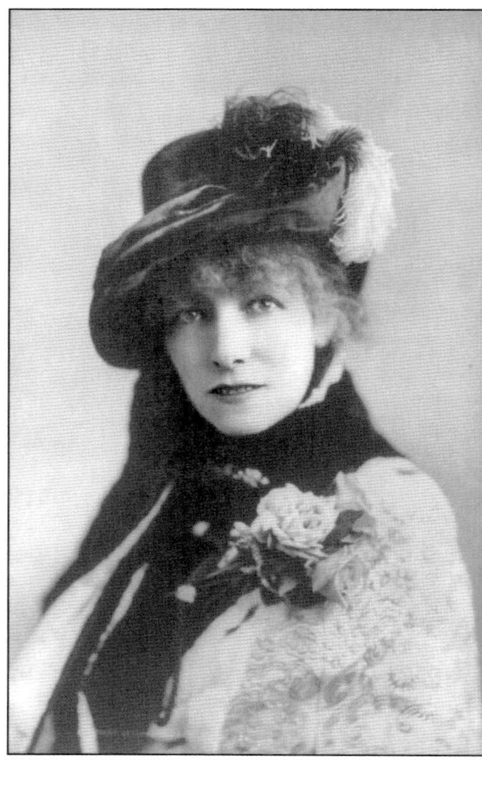

Sarah Bernhardt was a French stage and early film actress in the late 1800s. She performed at the Calumet Theatre and Hancock's Kerredge Theatre in 1911, often riding the streetcar during her stay. Bernhardt was once referred to as "the most famous actress the world has ever known." (Library of Congress.)

Annie Clemenc, known as "Big Annie," was a young miner's wife who led many of the protest marches and parades during the 1913–1914 strike. She was very active in the community and was in charge of the 1913 Christmas Eve party at the Italian Hall. (Michigan Technological University Archives/ Copper Country Historical Collection.)

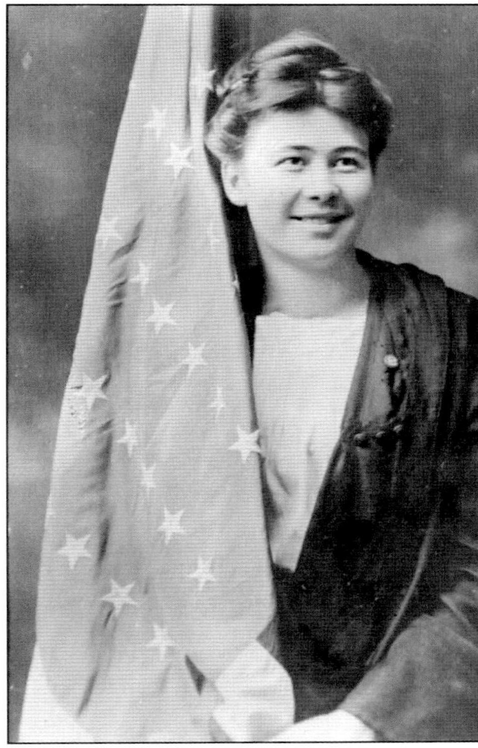

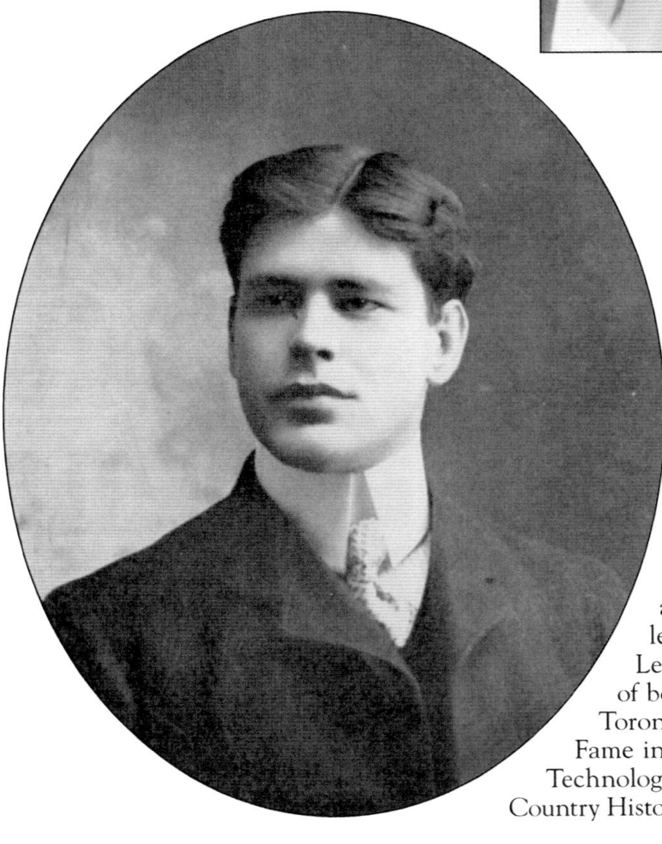

Jack "Doc" Gibson was an outstanding athlete from Canada who came to Houghton to begin a dental practice in 1900. He also became involved in local hockey and helped form its first professional league, the International Hockey League, in 1904. Gibson is a member of both the Hockey Hall of Fame, in Toronto, and the US Hockey Hall of Fame in Eveleth, Minnesota. (Michigan Technological University Archives/Copper Country Historical Collection.)

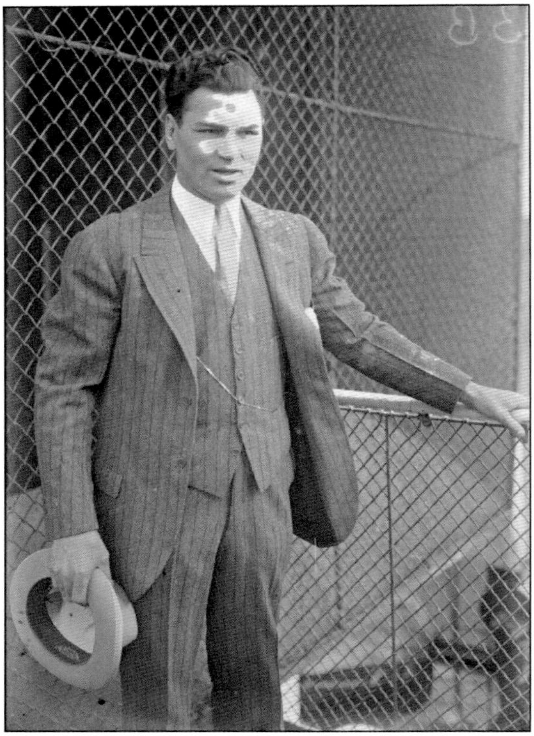

Jack Dempsey rose to sports stardom in the 1920s when he became the world heavyweight boxing champion. Early in his career, he fought in mining communities and often attended boxing matches throughout the country. In the early 1920s, he attended a boxing event at the Amphidrome and rode the local streetcar. (Library of Congress.)

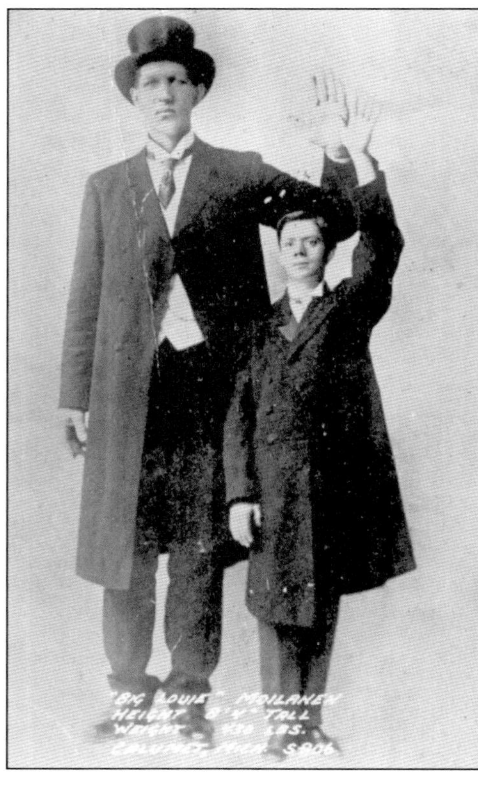

Louie Moilanen was born in Finland in 1886 and, at a young age, settled on a small farm near Boston. At 18, "Big Louie" became famous when he gained recognition as the world's tallest man, standing over eight feet tall. For a couple of years, he toured with the Ringling Brothers circus as a sideshow attraction but returned to the Copper Country, where he frequently rode the streetcar from home to work in Hancock until his death in 1913. (Michigan Technological University Archives/Copper Country Historical Collection.)

Eight

End of Service

Several factors contributed to the ultimate demise of the Houghton County Traction Company. Falling ridership numbers, increased competition from the automobile, a decline in the local population, a faltering economy, and rising operating costs resulted in a growing debt for the company. It was really never able to rebound after falling into receivership in 1921, and it eventually ceased operations on May 17, 1932. The Copper Country Motor Bus Company was granted a franchise to provide service between Houghton, Hancock, and Calumet, and it began operations on May 30, 1932. The bus company added routes to outlying areas that had not been served by the streetcars. Unfortunately, the bus service became a losing proposition, and the last route was abandoned in 1955.

Unlike many streetcar and interurban systems at that time, the Houghton County Traction Company refused to cut service on sections of the system and ended operations across the entire system all at once. Reducing the number of daily cars along lines and reductions in crew sizes helped to reduce operating costs, but it was not enough to continue. When compared to the streetcar industry in the United States, the Houghton County system was typical. It was born at the start of the 1900s and disappeared 30 years later. It was a time when both local and state governments were funding the expansion and upgrading of roads throughout the area as the automobile became a popular means of transportation that provided users with greater freedom and flexibility.

After the closing of the system, the cars and several snowplows were dismantled and sold. Much of the equipment was purchased by a Chicago firm, but some cars ended up at different local sites as clubhouses, residences, or hunting camps. A few residents remember the system and have special memories of riding the cars and visiting Electric Park. Some, however, also recall the sadness they felt when the service ended and the lines removed. It was the end of a truly exciting era in Copper Country history.

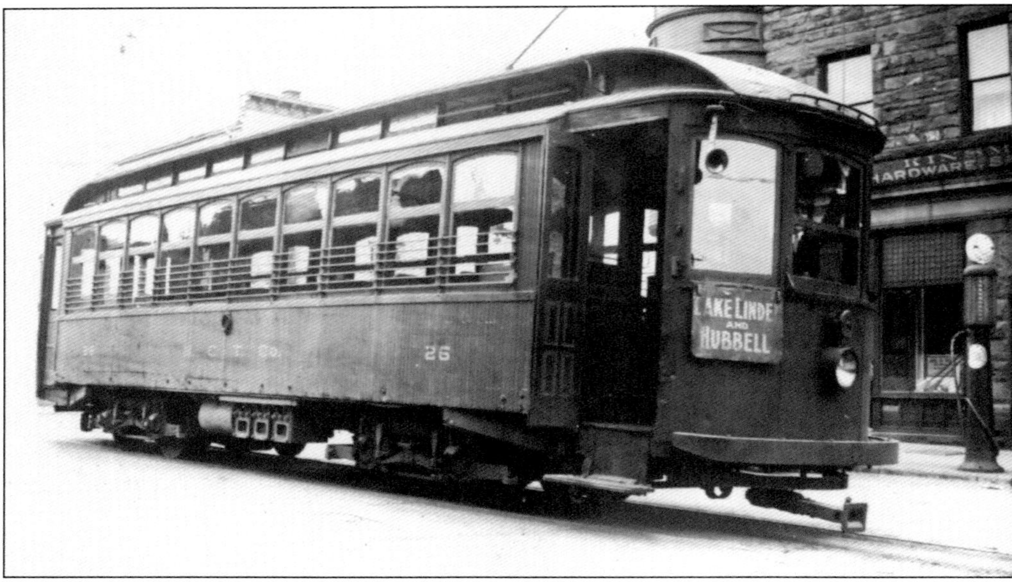

Streetcar service ended on May 17, 1932. This is a photograph of streetcar No. 26 on its final run. (Keweenaw National Historical Park Collection.)

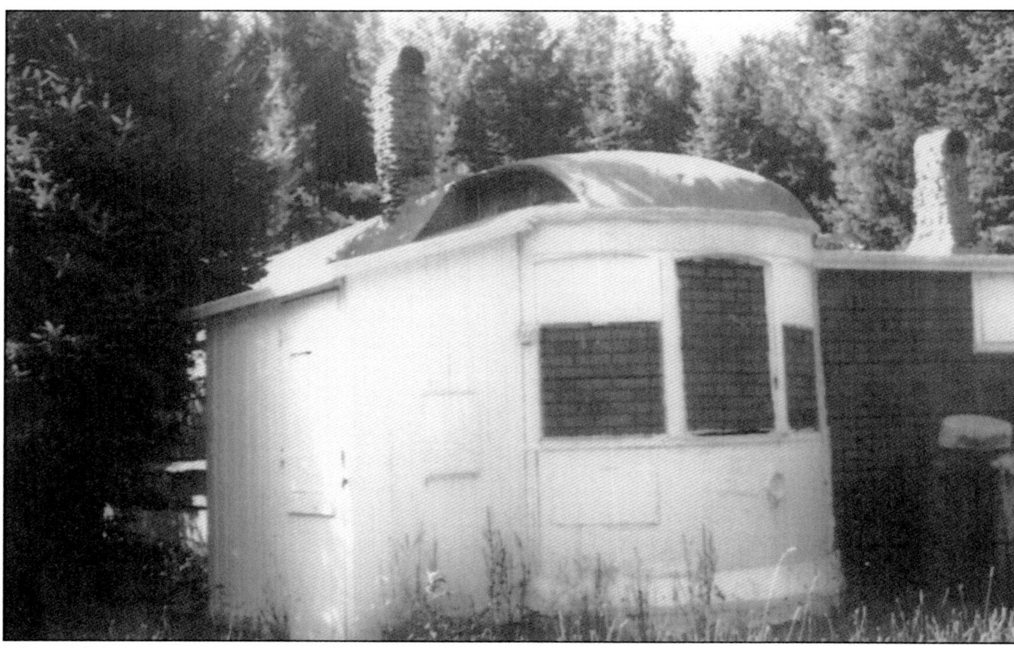

Most of the equipment was either transported from the area for scrap or destroyed; however, a few cars were sold and ended up in local fields or became homes or hunting camps. (Houghton County Historical Society.)

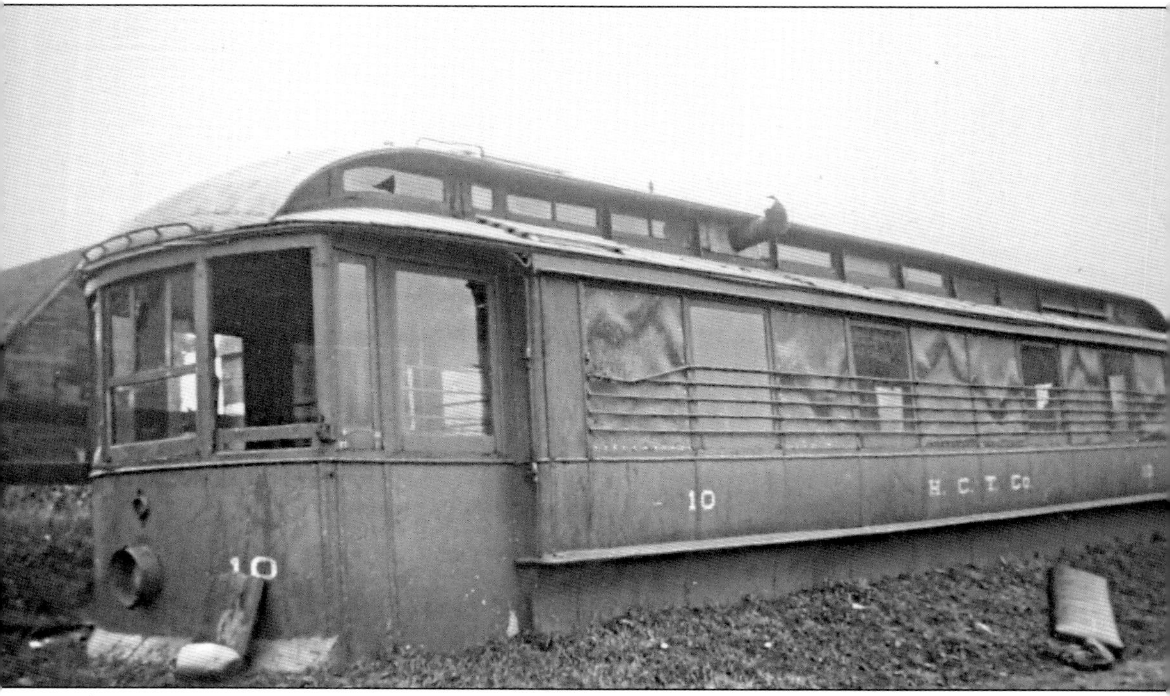

Like No. 26, streetcar No. 10 made its final run and ceased carrying passengers. Here, it is apparent that No. 10 assumed a new role as a residence. (Houghton County Historical Society.)

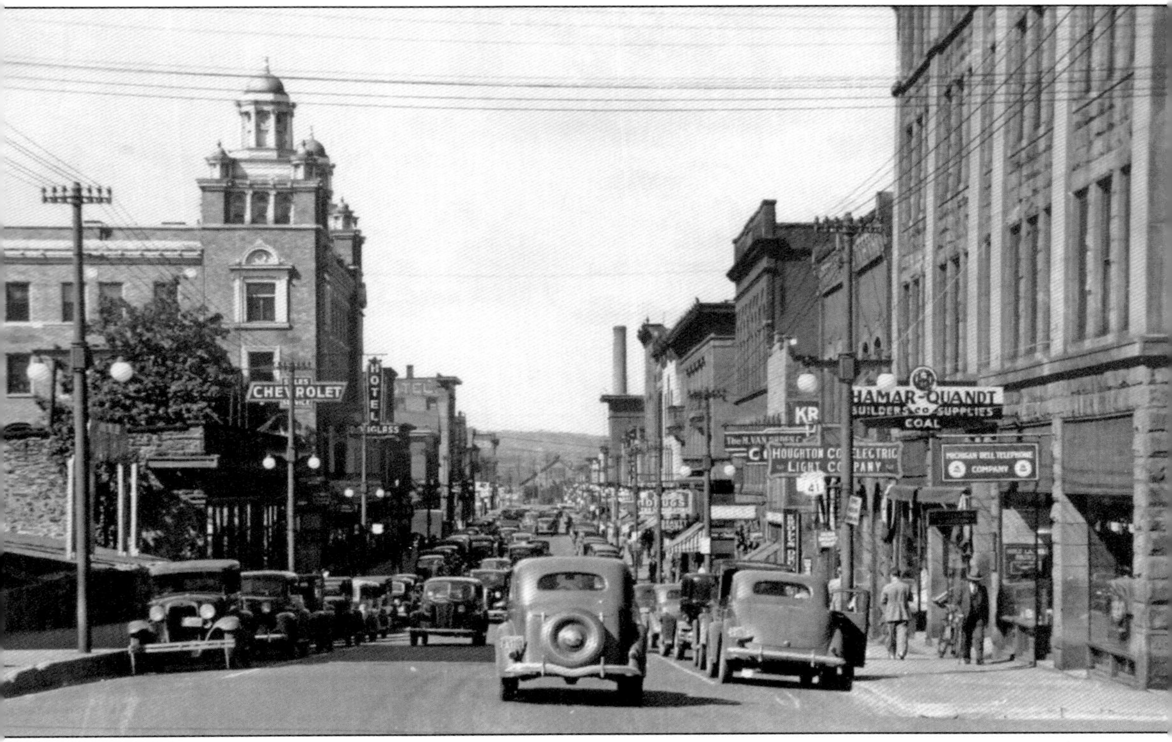

As the Michigan College of Mines grew, it became the Michigan College of Mining and Technology in 1927 and then Michigan Technological University in 1963. Houghton became the commercial center of the region. This is a view of downtown Houghton looking west on Shelden Avenue in 1936, a few years after streetcar service ended. (Michigan Technological University Archives/ Copper Country Historical Collection.)

SUGGESTED READINGS

Alain, James. "The Houghton County Traction Co." *Headlights*: vol. 39, no. 5–6, May-June (1977): 2–10.

Anderson, George E. and Richard E. Taylor. *Copper Country Rail*. Charleston, SC: Arcadia Publishing, 2008.

Hoagland, Alison K. *Mine Towns: Buildings for Workers in Michigan's Copper Country*. Minneapolis: University of Minnesota Press, 2010.

Lankton, Larry. *Cradle to Grave: Life, Work, and Death at the Lake Superior Copper Mines*. New York: Oxford University Press, 1991.

———. *Hollowed Ground: Copper Mining and Community Building on Lake Superior, 1840s–1990s*. Detroit: Wayne State University Press, 2010.

Molloy, Lawrence J. *A Guide to Michigan's Historic Keweenaw Copper District*. Hubbell, MI: Great Lakes GeoScience, 2008.

Monette, Clarence J. *Houghton County's Streetcars and Electric Park*. Calumet, MI: self-published, 2001.

Taylor, Richard E. *Houghton County, 1870–1920*. Charleston, SC: Arcadia Publishing, 2006.

Thurner, Arthur W. *Calumet Copper and People: History of a Michigan Mining Community, 1864–1970*. Hancock, MI: self-published, 1974.

———. *Strangers and Sojourners: A History of Michigan Keweenaw Peninsula*. Detroit: Wayne State University Press, 1994.

Discover Thousands of Local History Books Featuring Millions of Vintage Images

Arcadia Publishing, the leading local history publisher in the United States, is committed to making history accessible and meaningful through publishing books that celebrate and preserve the heritage of America's people and places.

Find more books like this at
www.arcadiapublishing.com

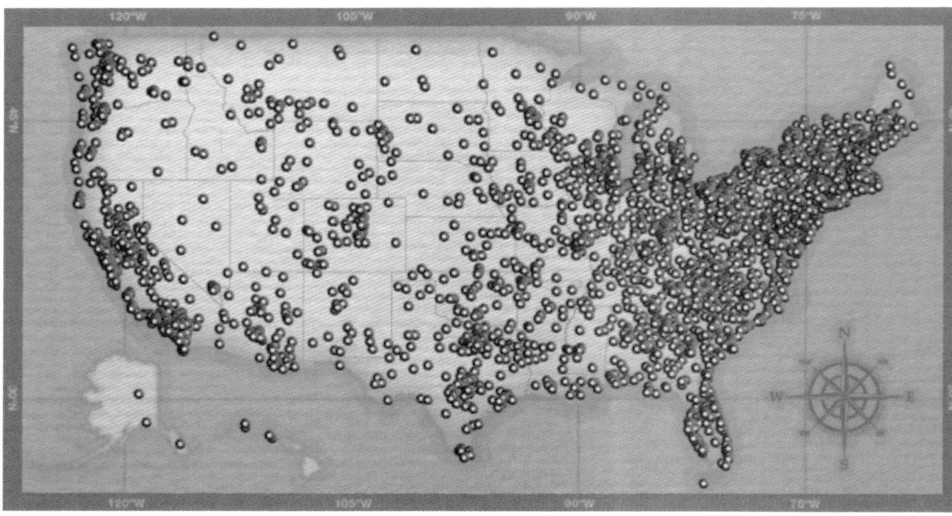

Search for your hometown history, your old stomping grounds, and even your favorite sports team.

Consistent with our mission to preserve history on a local level, this book was printed in South Carolina on American-made paper and manufactured entirely in the United States. Products carrying the accredited Forest Stewardship Council (FSC) label are printed on 100 percent FSC-certified paper.

MADE IN THE USA